The Economics of Collusion

The Economics of Collusion

Cartels and Bidding Rings

Robert C. Marshall and Leslie M. Marx

The MIT Press
Cambridge, Massachusetts
London, England

BUSINESS
HF
5417
.M37
2012

MIT Press books may be purchased at special quantity discounts for business or sales promotional use. For information, please email special_sales@mitpress.mit.edu or write to Special Sales Department, The MIT Press, 55 Hayward Street, Cambridge, MA 02142.

This book was set in Palatino by Toppan Best-set Premedia Limited. Printed and bound in the United States of America.

Library of Congress Cataloging-in-Publication Data

Marshall, Robert C.
The economics of collusion : cartels and bidding rings / Robert C. Marshall and Leslie M. Marx.
    p. cm.
Includes bibliographical references and index.
ISBN 978-0-262-01732-9 (hardcover : alk. paper)
1. Price fixing.   2. Cartels.   3. Competition.   I. Marx, Leslie M.   II. Title.
HF5417.M37   2012
338.8′2—dc23
2011044177

10   9   8   7   6   5   4   3   2

We dedicate this book to our spouses, Anne Marshall and Jeffrey Wilcox

Contents

Preface

This book is about explicit collusion. By *explicit* collusion we mean an agreement among competitors that relies on interfirm communication and/or transfers to suppress rivalry.[1] In general, rivalry between competitors erodes profits. The suppression of rivalry increases profits.

Some scholars have the view that explicit collusion is rare and that firms generally exhibit something like tribalism in the ferocity of their competition. Others have the opposite view, quoting Adam Smith, the father of Economics, who noted in the *Wealth of Nations*: "People of the same trade seldom meet together, even for merriment and diversion, but the conversation ends in a conspiracy against the publick, or in some contrivance to raise prices."[2]

We do not have either view. Our view is that firms pursue profits, accounting for risks associated with their decisions. If some action has a higher expected rate of return, considering risks, for a given amount of resource investment than another activity, then a firm will pursue the former over the latter. It might be that explicit collusion is the former, or it might be that it is the latter.

This being said, we admit to a fascination with collusive conduct. The successful suppression of competition is a thing of economic beauty. Each of us would rather read European Commission decisions for cartel cases than best-selling nonfiction literature. However, it is a tragedy to read about firms that were fined huge amounts for engaging in nominally anti-competitive actions that had no chance of being successful. We have read of managers of competing firms, meeting at fast-food restaurants or coffee shops, discussing bids or prices, and

1. In the text, whenever we use the word "collusion" we mean explicit collusion unless otherwise specified.
2. Smith 1981 reprint, ch. 10, para. 27, p. 145.

then meeting again the following week to complain that their discussions failed to yield results. How could a competent manager believe that substantial gains in profits are available for the price of a lunch and one hour of conversation? Successful explicit collusion requires planning, investments in administration, clear thinking, and hard work.

This book comes from over two decades of thinking about collusion. Much of that research concerns collusion by bidders at auctions, but in the last decade that work has broadened to cartels, largely because of our involvement in major cartel cases as testifying and consulting experts.

The level and scope of the book has been a challenge. We wanted it to be accessible to advanced undergraduates, and we wanted the audience to include antitrust practitioners and law students, as well as applied economists with an interest in antitrust. We have strived to keep the mathematical requirements of the book to a minimum because some of our target audience is uncomfortable with mathematical arguments and presentations. Our reader is expected to understand basic economic reasoning. More mathematical material in the book is contained in sections flagged with asterisks.

This book does not do everything that one might envision regarding the economics of collusion. As examples, we have virtually no discussion of enforcement policy. Also, our discussions of cartels focus on those that produce an intermediate good to be sold to other firms rather than cartels that sell consumer goods or services directly to individuals. We refer to the former as industrial cartels. Much of our discussion of collusion at auctions and procurements[3] is rooted in a particular informational framework.[4] Our main goal in writing the book is to provide readers with simple ways to understand collusive behavior—what it is, why it is profitable, how it is implemented, and how it might be detected.

Many of the statements in the book are offered starkly, without extensive qualifications or caveats. In part, this is a natural consequence of moving away from the precision of mathematical models in order to cover comprehensively the central issues of collusion for our target audience while enhancing readability. Also, although many statements

3. When we use the words auction or procurement, we mean the simultaneous consideration of offers to buy or sell, respectively.
4. The informational framework is referred to in the economics literature as the "independent private values" model. See, for example, Krishna (2009).

are conditional on a product/market/industry, it is just too tedious for a reader to frequently forebear that qualification.

We gratefully acknowledge the support of many. The firm of Bates White, LLC, in which we are both partners, and Matt Raiff as leader of the cartel practice at Bates White, LLC, have provided us with a remarkable window to understand and study cartels.

We have benefitted from financial support provided to Penn State's Center for the Study of Auctions, Procurements, and Competition Policy (CAPCP) by the Human Capital Foundation, and especially Andrey Vavilov, who has demonstrated an inspiring dedication to the advancement of economic research at Penn State. Funding from the Human Capital Foundation has allowed CAPCP to post data and software that are available for all to use, including the Russian oil and gas auction data that are discussed, in part, in the appendix to chapter 12.

We received substantial comments on various parts of this book from Dave Barth, Lee Greenfield, Joe Harrington, Jeff Howard, Paul Johnson, Chip Miller, Mark Schechter, Terry Vaughn, and especially Steve Schulenberg. Workshop participants at Wilmer Hale and the Federal Trade Commission provided insightful comments as well. We are grateful to George Bittlingmayer for discussions about the Addyston case and for providing us with the Transcript of Record for the case proceedings. Discussions over the years with Jim Anton, John Asker, Susan Athey, Pat Bajari, Laura Baldwin, Charley Bates, Doug Bernheim, Kalyan Chatterjee, Bobby Filipi, Eric Gaier, John Geweke, Dan Graham, Ed Green, Randy Heeb, Ken Hendricks, Keith Hylton, Barry Ickes, Jim Jordan, Ehud Kalai, Brett Katzman, Evan Kwerel, Vladimir Kreyndel, Vijay Krishna, Bernard Lebrun, Scott Lobel, Pino Lopomo, David McAdams, Mike Meurer, Roger Myerson, Rob Porter, Jean-Francois Richard, George Rozanski, Joel Sobel, Martha Stancill, Jeroen Swinkels, Bob Weber, and Hal White have substantially contributed to our depth of understanding of key issues relevant to collusion. A special thanks is owed to Bill Kovacic, who recently completed his term as a Commissioner of the Federal Trade Commission, for numerous enlightening discussions. It is enormously reassuring that government service can still attract people of such intellectual depth and dedication as Bill.

Michele Moslak provided excellent support for all aspects of the work. We benefited from the presentation insights of Lucy Pless. Research assistance was provided by John Dougherty, Yuriy Horokhivskyy, Andrei Karavaev, Pradeep Kumar, Vikram Kumar, Chris Lengerich, Lily Samkharadze, and Dane Wilburne. We were lucky to have as our editor John Covell, who provided insightful comments and help throughout the process. In addition we are grateful to the very able staff at the MIT Press, especially Dana Andrus and Katie Hope.

Finally, our families have suffered so that our readers may benefit. Hopefully, we have produced something worthy of the sacrifice.

Bob Marshall and Leslie Marx

1 Introduction

1.1 Motivating Example

Figure 1.1 shows a plot of the price for vitamin A acetate 650 feed grade, which is a vitamin product used to supplement the feed of livestock.[1]

Perhaps the most noticeable feature of the price plot in figure 1.1 is the increase in the price from 1990 through 1994. There could be numerous explanations for the price of a product changing through time. What accounts for this dramatic increase?

The primary manufacturers of vitamins pled guilty to participation in a worldwide price-fixing conspiracy for much of the 1990s. The conspiracy went far beyond vitamin A. It included vitamins A, B_1, B_2, B_5, B_6, C, D, E, beta-carotene, biotin, carotenoids, choline chloride, and others. During the 1990s, the world's leading manufacturer of vitamins was Hoffman la Roche. Roche's criminal fine in the United States was $500 million.[3] BASF, another leading vitamin manufacturer during the 1990s, paid a criminal fine in the United States of $225 million.[4]

1. The figure is obtained from the Expert Report of B. Douglas Bernheim, MDL No. 1285, In Re: Vitamins Antitrust Litigation, Misc. No. 99–0197 (TFH), May 24, 2002. This report was submitted as exhibit number 243 in *In re: Vitamins Antitrust Litigation*, case No. 99–0197 (TFH) filed in the District Court of the District of Columbia. We obtained the document through a request to the law clerk to Chief Judge Thomas F. Hogan. The document was made available based on DC Local Civil Rule 79.2 and the United States District Court for the District of Columbia's policy of not retaining exhibits that are admitted into evidence at trial in civil cases.
2. As described in the caption of the figure, the price shown is the seven-month centered moving average for United States "tel quel" price from the Roche ROVIS data. The qualifier "tel quel" means that these are prices for vitamin sold in their straight form rather than as part of a blend of different vitamin products.
3. Marshall, Marx, and Raiff (2008, tab. A.4).
4. Marshall, Marx, and Raiff (2008, tab. A.4).

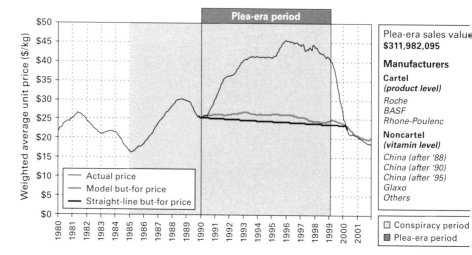

Figure 1.1
Data on vitamin A acetate 650 feed grade. Seven-month centered moving average for U.S. "tel quel" feed price from Roche ROVIS data. Source: Bernheim (2002, fig. 12.6).

Purchasers of vitamins, who were charged higher prices during the 1990s as a consequence of the conspiracy, recovered billions of dollars in damages from the major vitamin manufacturers through civil litigation.[5] In addition, several executives of the major vitamin manufacturers served time in prison for their roles in the criminal endeavor.[6]

Examples of price-fixing cartels are not difficult to find. Over the last century, many cartels have been prosecuted by enforcement authorities,[7] and it is reasonable to believe that the list of cartels that have been

---

5. Figure 1.1 shows the "but-for price," which is the price that would have prevailed in the absence of the conspiracy. We discuss the econometrics underlying the construction of a but-for price in chapter 11.

6. See Conner (2008, p. 466). See also the U.S. Department of Justice press release of April 6, 2000, titled "Four Foreign Executives of Leading European Vitamin Firms Agree to Plead Guilty to Participating in International Vitamin Cartel: Executives to Plead Guilty, Serve Time in U.S. Prisons, and Pay Substantial Fines," available at http://www.justice .gov/opa/pr/2000/April/179at.htm (accessed April 7, 2011).

7. See, for example, Stocking and Watkins (1991) and the reference list of EC decisions cited in this book. Enforcement authorities typically acquire their information through leniency programs, discovery, subpoena, and investigatory probes. According to Hammond (2005, slide 2), "Since its revision in 1993, the [U.S. Department of Justice] Antitrust Division's Corporate Leniency Program has been the Division's <u>most</u> effective investigative tool." On the impact of leniency and whistleblowing programs on cartels, see Aubert, Kovacic, and Rey (2006). On leniency, see also Motta and Polo (2003), Spagnolo (2004), and Miller (2009).

apprehended by enforcement authorities is small relative to the total number of cartels that have functioned over that time.

Because collusive agreements are illegal,[8] the members of a cartel cannot enter into legally binding collusive contracts with one another. There is no external judicial authority to enforce the agreements. Compliance comes from within the cartel's inner workings and from each member's willingness to comply. This creates many difficulties and precludes certain kinds of agreements. Economists often note that repeated interaction can sometimes solve these problems. There are many theoretical constructs that speak directly to the veracity of this. However, it appears that repeated interaction is not enough in practice, at least not for many firms in many industries. Even for duopolies, such as methylglucamine, vitamin A500 USP, and beta-carotene,[9] explicit collusion was required to substantially elevate prices and profits.

1.2 Collusion within Porter's Five Forces

1.2.1 Market Structure

Ideally, firms want to maximize the expected discounted value of the flow of profits, accounting for risks associated with their actions. For publicly traded companies, this is often stated as maximizing the price of a common share of stock.

By definition, the firms in an industry produce products or services that are, at a minimum, reasonably good substitutes for one another. At one extreme, when no reasonable substitutes exist for the product of a firm, then that firm is a monopoly. At the other extreme, we have perfect competition when (1) there is a large number of firms in an industry, (2) the product made by any firm is a perfect substitute for what any other firm in the industry makes, and (3) information about the product price is publicly available. The competition between the firms will be such that they take the price in the market as given and recognize that they cannot individually affect the market price in a meaningful way.

At one extreme, we have a monopoly firm that is only constrained by the demand curve in choosing price, and at the other extreme, we have perfect competition, where no individual firm has influence over price and each firm takes price as given.

8. See Turner (1962).
9. See the European Commission (EC) decisions in *Methylglucamine* and *Vitamins*. See the references for the complete citations for EC decisions referenced in this book.

Intermediate between the extremes of monopoly and perfect competition are industries with more than one firm, where each firm has some degree of market power. Such industries are referred to as oligopolies. In an oligopoly, the bulk of production is typically done by a few firms, and these firms recognize that their actions will be taken into account by other firms in the industry. The other firms may react to those actions with actions of their own. For example, if a major car manufacturer increases the warranty on its cars, other manufacturers may do so as well. Firms in an oligopoly recognize their mutual interdependence in the market.

There is no single characterization of competition among oligopolistic firms. In some industries, the firms may be aggressive competitors; in other industries, the competition may be less fierce.

1.2.2   Forces Affecting Profits

A variety of factors affect the profitability of an oligopolistic industry. As just mentioned, the extent of interfirm rivalry is one factor, but there are others as well. If there are substantial barriers to entry in the industry, then this will be a positive contributor to industry profits. If the firms have substantial leverage against suppliers of inputs, then this will contribute positively to industry profits. If there are few good substitutes for the products made by the firms in the industry, then this will contribute positively to industry profits. If the producers have substantial leverage in their dealings with purchasers, then this will contribute positively to industry profits. There can also exist government regulations that improve industry profitability.

The forces that affect industry profitability have been enumerated by Michael Porter in his book *Competitive Strategy*. These "Five Forces" are depicted in figure 1.2.

Within the Five Forces diagram, collusion acts on the center force, suppressing interfirm rivalry. Actions that suppress rivalry increase industry profits and the profits of individual firms. Not depicted in the diagram are actions an individual firm can take to improve its own profits, such as reducing production costs or introducing new successful products. An individual firm allocates scarce resources to those activities that yield the greatest expected returns in terms of profitability. In contrast to many investments that individual firms can make to increase their profits, the successful suppression of interfirm rivalry can produce relatively quick improvements in profits.

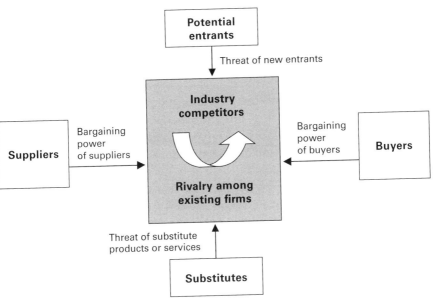

Figure 1.2
Five Forces diagram. Source: Porter (1980, fig. 1.1). Adapted and modified with the permission of Free Press, a Division of Simon and Schuster, Inc., from *Competitive Strategy: Techniques for Analyzing Industries and Competitors* by Michael E. Porter. Copyright © 1980, 1998 by the Free Press. All rights reserved.

If the suppression of interfirm rivalry has such an immediate positive impact on profits, why do not all firms in an industry do it to the maximal extent and essentially function as a single firm, thus earning monopoly profits?[10] In answer to this, first, there are many circumstances in which collusion is illegal, and second, collusion is often difficult work for the firms involved. Part of the difficulty comes from the fact that colluding firms are not a single corporate entity. Each firm is responsible to its owners to seek its own profits.

Firms can potentially overcome the difficulty associated with not being a single corporate entity by merging; however, there are legal and administrative issues related to mergers as well as potentially increasing costs of control as firm size increases.[11] Although we do not consider mergers in detail, it is useful to understand why firms that are

10. This is a fundamental motivating query in the economics field of Industrial Organization.
11. See, for example, Coase (1937) and Williamson (1985).

willing to take actions to suppress interfirm rivalry might choose collusion over merger. We address this in chapter 1.3.3.

1.3 Difficulties of Collusion

We now return to the question of what, other than legal issues, makes collusion difficult.

1.3.1 Communication and Transfers

As we mentioned in the preface, we use the term *explicit* collusion to mean an agreement among competitors that relies on interfirm communication and/or transfers to suppress rivalry.[12] Thus, communication and transfers are key features of the cartels and bidding rings considered in this book.

Communication that directly supports the implementation of collusive agreements and collusive structures (see chapter 6 on collusive structures) are conveyances of information that could be unilateral, bilateral, or multilateral.[13] In addition, the communication could be public or private in the sense that the conveyed information may or may not be observable to those not directly involved in the communication.

Firms may also engage in information exchanges that could be conducive to collusion but are not directly part of the implementation of a cartel agreement or collusive structure. These conveyances may be pro-collusive or pro-competitive. As examples, communication related to patent licensing, arranging product swaps, or organizing lobbying efforts may serve a dual purpose, potentially providing consumer benefits as well as potentially supporting collusion.[14]

Transfers may involve direct cash payments between firms or, alternatively, some other kind of interfirm transaction that results in the movement of resources between firms. For example, product transac-

---

12. For a discussion of explicit collusion and agreement from a legal perspective, see Kovacic et al. (2011).
13. In the economics literature, the role of communication in supporting collusion is highlighted in, for example, Kandori and Matsushima (1998), Athey and Bagwell (2001), and Harrington and Skrzypacz (2010), where ongoing communication is part of equilibrium behavior, and in Green and Porter (1984), where it is natural to think that communication would be required to establish agreement on which equilibrium would be played (see Green and Porter 1984, p. 89, n. 5).
14. See Priest (1977).

tions made between firms at nonmarket prices are transfers between the firms.

1.3.2 Secret Deviations

A key difference between producers in a monopolistic versus a competitive industry is that a monopolist chooses to produce less than what would have been produced by competitive firms. By restricting output, the monopolist is able to increase its profits. Similarly, if the firms in an oligopolistic industry collude, they can restrict output and thereby earn higher profits. Holding all else constant, an output restriction causes prices to increase.

A monopolist internalizes the consequences of decreased output and so achieves enhanced profits. In contrast, when prices increase as a consequence of collusion, each colluding firm has a strong profit incentive not to restrict its own output. Each firm wants to sell more, not less, at higher prices. If the other colluding firms cannot observe that a fellow conspirator has breached the agreement to restrict output, then the deviant firm may be able to get away with cheating on the agreement, at least partially and at least for a while.

In the same light, even if all firms are initially complying with the agreement to restrict output, it may be the case that one firm finds the temptation irresistible to obtain a large customer account by reducing price and increasing output. Other colluding firms may find it difficult to observe the identity of the firm who landed the big customer account, and even if they do discover it, they may not be able to learn the terms.

The central difficulty of collusion is that it is often profitable for firms to secretly deviate from the collusive agreement. Cartels recognize this issue and create structures to limit or avoid this problem. In general, firms in an oligopolistic industry that successfully collude create: (1) pricing structures that enable them to implement price increases, (2) allocation structures that allow them to divide the collusive gain and reallocate resources among one another when things do not go as expected, and (3) enforcement structures that facilitate monitoring and establish the threat of punishment for noncontrite deviant behavior.[15]

In some environments, these tasks can be accomplished without communication and without transfer payments between firms, but

---

15. A typical "punishment" is the abandonment of the attempt to collude.

in many environments they cannot. We explore this distinction in chapter 1.4.

1.3.3 Advantage of Collusion over Merger

The current-day environment of laws, administrative processes, and litigation associated with collusion and mergers obviously affects firms' choices regarding each. However, looking back at the history of U.S. industrial organization, we see examples of firms choosing collusion over merger when there was no meaningful legal encumbrance to either.[16] In other words, although collusion is difficult, it is chosen when a seemingly good alternative is available.

Prior to 1895, firms were essentially unencumbered in choosing between merger and collusion,[17] yet many firms chose collusion.[18] For a more recent example, prestressing steel manufacturers in Europe, including the large firms Arcelor and Mittal, were found to have participated in a cartel from at least 1984 to 2002, and then in 2006 the two firms merged.[19] This suggests that a cartel was chosen for the suppression of interfirm rivalry instead of a merger for at least eighteen years.

Although it would seem that a merged entity could do anything a cartel could do, plus many other things, a cartel has the key advantage over a merged entity in that a merger is common knowledge to all market participants, but a cartel is a clandestine operation. Suppliers and buyers know that the divisions of a merged entity are not actively competing against each other and, therefore, that competitive processes are not providing the same benefits that they provided pre-merger. In contrast, given the secretive nature of a cartel, buyers and suppliers

16. Efficiency grounds are often offered as a justifications for mergers. Putting that aside, we focus on the suppression of interfirm rivalry associated with a merger.

17. From 1890 to 1910, while federal antitrust laws were only in their infancy and their meaning only clarified as cases worked through the system, there was no meaningful encumbrance to mergers. (Bittlingmayer 1985)

18. This began to change with the "first great merger wave" in U.S. economic history, which took place from 1895 to 1904. During that period, almost half of U.S. industrial activity was consolidated through mergers. (Bittlingmayer 1985) The fact that many colluding firms chose to merge during this time shows that merger was a feasible alternative for those firms. Industries where this occurred include gun powder, wire nails, tin cans, tin plates, newsprint, strawboard, wallpaper, petroleum refining, agricultural machinery, cotton oil, and cordage. (Kumar et al. 2011)

19. For the 2006 merger decision, see Case No. COMP/M.4137—Mittal/Arcelor Decision 2/6/2006. For a summary of the cartel decision, see the October 6, 2010, EC press release "CORRECTED Antitrust: Commission fines prestressing steel producers € 458 million for two-decades long price-fixing and market-sharing cartel," IP/10/1297.

may still believe that the firms are acting noncollusively and that competitive processes are still functioning in a meaningful way to police market transactions. This provides a cartel with a distinct advantage over a merged entity.[20]

1.4 Environments Requiring Explicit Collusion

Economists label collusive equilibria that do not require direct interaction between the firms, such as communication or transfers, as *tacit* rather than *explicit* collusion.[21]

There is a famous result in Economics (known as the "Folk Theorem") characterizing what outcomes firms can achieve through their recognized mutual interdependence.[22] This result can be interpreted as saying that if firms can observe each other's actions and interact with one another sufficiently frequently, then the firms can maximize their joint payoffs (i.e., achieve the monopoly outcome) without communication or transfers.[23]

This result unravels if the underlying assumptions are relaxed. Nevertheless, a fundamental question remains—what do communication and/or transfers allow firms to accomplish in terms of increased profitability that they could not accomplish otherwise? The converse question may be easier to link to the case histories of cartels—if one

20. See Kumar et al. (2011) for a formal treatment.
21. "The communication among colluding sellers needed to ensure successful price reporting may be indirect, in that it all proceeds through a trade association or statistical service, but it is none the less explicit." (Kaysen 1951, p. 266) On this point, Kaysen (1951) cites the Maple Flooring Manufacturers Association discussed in 268 U.S. 563 (1925).
22. See Friedman (1971) and Fudenberg and Maskin (1986). The economics literature that considers "collusive" equilibria that can be supported as noncooperative equilibria of a repeated game includes Porter (1983), Deneckere (1983), Green and Porter (1984), Abreu (1986), Abreu, Pearce, and Stachetti (1986, 1990), Brock and Scheinkman (1985), Abreu (1986), Rotemberg and Saloner (1986, 1989), Benoit and Krishna (1987), Lambson (1987, 1994), Tirole (1988), Wernerfelt (1989), Harrington (1989), Chang (1991), Kandori (1991), Haltiwanger and Harrington (1991), Stenbacka (1994), Friedman and Thisse (1994), Bagwell and Staiger (1997), Bagwell and Wolinsky (2002), Compte (2002), Compte, Jenny, and Rey (2002), Knittel and Stango (2003), Feuerstein and Gersbach (2003), Schultz (2005), Vasconcelos (2005), Liski and Montero (2006), Horner and Jamison (2007), Chakrabarti (2010), and Knittel and Lepore (2010).
23. More formally, a standard Folk Theorem characterizes the set of equilibria of a repeated oligopoly game and shows that for sufficiently patient firms (or for sufficiently short delay between repetitions of the game), the set of equilibria includes strategy profiles that generate the monopoly outcome. The Folk Theorem itself does not address whether firms would choose to play the strategies that generate the monopoly outcome nor how firms might coordinate on those strategies.

removes communication and transfers from interfirm interaction, does firm conduct become more competitive and do profits fall?

In what follows, we describe the distinction between static competition, tacit collusion, and explicit collusion using a series of examples.

1.4.1 Example 1: Observable Posted Prices

Consider a small town where, on opposing street corners, there are two vendors who sell the same product.[24] These vendors are the only two vendors that sell this product in the town. Other vendors who sell products exactly like this are at least 150 miles away from this town.

The vendors can post a price at their location for everyone to see. Each vendor can post a price exactly at the time their business opens in the morning, which is 6 AM for each, but cannot change that posted price until the following morning. Consumers buy from the vendor with the lowest price. Nothing else influences a consumer's purchasing decision. If the two vendors post the same price, then they each get half of market demand.

Scenario 1: Gas Stations, Static Environment
We begin by assuming the vendors are two gas stations, and we label them as A and B. Suppose that each one of these gas stations buys its gasoline for $2 per gallon and that each knows that a price of $3 per gallon maximizes their combined profits.

First, consider what happens in a static environment, where today's profits are all that matters. Each gas station owner decides what price to post before it opens, where prices are posted in one-cent increments. Gas station A considers a number of different possibilities for the price that B might post. If gas station B were to post $3, then gas station A can split the monopoly profit by also posting $3, but this is clearly not the best response by gas station A to B's price of $3. Gas station A can instead post a price of $2.99 and dramatically increase its profit compared to a price of $3 because $2.99 captures all consumer demand for gas while $3 results in only half of consumer demand. So, each firm posting $3 cannot be an equilibrium. Clearly, one firm posting $2.99 while the other posts $3 cannot be an equilibrium because $3 is not a best response to $2.99—$2.98 is a best response to $2.99.

The price that we would expect to observe in equilibrium is $2.01 per gallon. Neither gas station A nor B would have an incentive to change that price. A unilateral increase in price by either would gener-

---

24. This example is based on Carlton, Gertner, and Rosenfield (1997).

ate no sales and any lower price would generate zero profit or negative profit.[25] The pricing is within one cent of the marginal cost of acquiring gas. This is a static competition outcome.

Scenario 2: Gas Stations, Dynamic Environment

Now change this environment to allow more dynamic interaction. Suppose that the future matters almost as much as the present to each of the gas station owners. Each station has to consider not just how today's pricing affects today's profits, but also how pricing today affects profits in future periods. Specifically, if gas station B prices today at $3, and gas station A prices at $2.99, what will happen tomorrow, and thereafter, with regard to the pricing of the two gas stations? Gas station B would know that the zero profit it earned today was due to gas station A's undercutting its price by one cent. What does gas station A expect to be the consequence of its pricing conduct? Perhaps gas station A believes that gas station B will try to price at $3 again tomorrow. And gas station B may in fact try to do so. But, if gas station B continues to experience zero profits from being undercut by gas station A, then gas station B will give up its attempts to maintain high prices. But giving up has to end somewhere, and a natural place to end up is at the price of $2.01.

Gas station A may want to try to move prices above $2.01 once they get to that point, but if gas station B has truly given up all hope of maintaining high prices, then the efforts by gas station A will be futile. With this thought process in mind, it would be reasonable to expect each gas station to price at $3 each day and split the market, knowing that any undercut by either will result in a substantial probability that the other station will abandon hope of maintaining any price above $2.01.

The price of $3 by each gas station in this context is a tacitly collusive outcome. The outcome is no different than what the two firms could have accomplished with explicit private communication and coordination about pricing, but they accomplished this without any private communication. Thus, the outcome is tacit. It emerges from the recognition by each gas station of their mutual interdependence, the ability of firms to observe one another's pricing with certainty, consumers being simple price takers and buying at the posted price from the station with

25. If the gas stations price in tenths of a cent or hundredths of a cent, then the price would get closer to exactly $2 per gallon, which is the marginal cost of acquiring gasoline.

lowest price, and the fact that future periods are valuable to each gas station owner.[26]

1.4.2 Example 2: Unobservable Bid Prices

We now change things again. Suppose that the two vendors are not gas stations but instead are box plants making corrugated or cardboard boxes.

If you think about a typical cardboard box, like that used to mail packages, each side has flat smooth material on front and back with wavy material in between that is glued to each of the flat sides. There may be printing on the outer flat side. Any firm that packages and ships its product, or is engaged in the business of shipping, buys boxes. There are standard boxes constructed of standard materials with no printing on the exterior. An example might be an $18 \times 12 \times 12$ inch corrugated box made from 42 pound linerboard (flat material on front and back) and 23 pound medium (wavy material between the two flat sheets). However, these kinds of standard boxes are typically a small percentage of sales for a box plant. Rather, most sales are to manufacturers or shipping companies that buy large numbers of boxes of specific sizes, where the material used in the box construction, the gluing of the boxes, and the printing on the boxes are specified by the buyer.

Almost all of the purchases of such boxes will be done by procurement. Specifically, a buyer will invite box plants to submit bids, where the details of the box size, construction, and printing will be part of the bid solicitation. The box plants may post a price for the aforementioned $18 \times 12 \times 12$ inch standard box and may offer such boxes at the posted price in small volumes at each firm's office location, but the bulk of sales for each box plant will be through procurements. The posted price for a standard box has no effect on the bid submitted by any box plant in a procurement, and the buyers know that.

Each box plant has a reasonably good idea of the costs of its rival. Also, unlike the gas station example, where no consumer is going to drive 150 miles each way to buy gas from a cheaper nonlocal gas vendor, it is economically viable to buy boxes from a box plant that is 150 miles away, although such a box plant has additional transport costs. The bid by any box plant in any procurement is not revealed by the buyer to the competing firm—a box plant only knows if it won or lost any given procurement. For this example, we assume that each box plant values the future highly.

---

26. For empirical evidence of tacit collusion in retail gasoline, see Borenstein and Shepard (1996). See also Slade (1992).

Scenario 3: Box Plants with Many Buyers

In this setting, suppose that there are a large number of small manufacturers of various products in the area around the town and that these firms frequently conduct procurements for their box needs, some each month and others each quarter. Assume that over the course of a quarter, each box plant expects to receive 500 bid solicitations and that this number is quite stable from quarter to quarter. Suppose that the cost to make a box for a given manufacturer by each of the local vendors is $2 per box. Also, given the outside option of using the box plant 150 miles away, each local box plant knows that it cannot set a price above $3 per box for this local manufacturer. Each of the local box plants can make calculations like this for each bid solicitation it receives each quarter.

How will the firms bid in the procurements? They will not price close to their marginal cost of production; they will instead each price close to the joint-profit-maximizing price (in light of the outside option). Each will expect to receive close to 250 contract awards each quarter. The rationale for such an equilibrium outcome is akin to our last gas station scenario.

As each box plant prices close to the joint-profit-maximizing price, one box plant may consider undercutting the other. However, each box plant knows that even if its rival does not respond to its undercutting immediately, eventually the other firm will undercut as well. Prices will start to decline and each firm will abandon hopes of maintaining high prices. Once such capitulation occurs, it is difficult to resurrect higher pricing, especially in this environment where there is no knowledge of how the other firm has bid, but only knowledge as to whether or not one's own bid won or lost. The fear of triggering this type of price decline will be sufficient to sustain collusive pricing in this environment, in which case the firms can obtain the fully collusive outcome with no communication. This is a tacit outcome.

Examples in which firms achieve the joint-profit-maximizing outcome without explicit agreement lead to a natural question: Why is there ever any need for explicit collusion?

Scenario 4: Box Plants with Few, Large Buyers

To answer the question as to why explicit collusion might be required above and beyond tacit collusion, we alter box plant scenario 3 by supposing that the buyers are not large in number and small in size but, instead, are small in number and large in size. Suppose that the aggregate volume of purchases on a yearly basis from the two box plants is approximately the same between the scenarios. Furthermore, suppose that the large buyers conduct procurements infrequently and at irregular intervals. Suppose that each box plant expects to receive, in total, one bid solicitation each quarter (as opposed to 500 bid solicitations each quarter). Furthermore, suppose that these large buyers may choose to extend their current box contract terms for a year or more without reconducting a procurement.

As opposed to the previous scenario, in this scenario losing a contract has a large marginal impact on profits for a box plant. There are not many contract awards each year—on average, only 4 per year. If one box plant receives only one or even none of the awards, then it will be in dire straits.

For a given procurement, suppose that a box plant submits a bid that is close to the joint monopoly price and observes that it loses the award. This could be random bad luck or it could be that its competitor undercut it in the bidding. Suppose this happens a second time. Now the box plant that has not won a contract in 6 months is really feeling the financial pinch. In the previous scenario, a run of bad luck within a quarter, where a box plant did not win 5 or more consecutive procurements, may not even be a source of mild concern. In this scenario, not winning 5 or more consecutive procurements is a financial disaster. With this reality in mind, as each box plant considers how to bid, it is natural that the bids will move toward marginal cost and away from the joint monopoly price.

The lumpiness and infrequency of the awards makes it much more difficult for the box plants to maintain high prices. Tacit collusion does not let the box plants accomplish a joint monopoly outcome.

Scenario 5: Box Plants with Many Buyers and Uncertain Demand

Consider another scenario that builds off the one where there were many small manufacturers buying boxes with great regularity. Suppose that these buyers are all in the same business. For example, they make pickles. They need boxes to ship their pickles. But suppose that pickle demand for these local manufacturers is highly unstable, and the instability affects each of them in a similar way. Suppose that the box plants cannot observe pickle demand conditions. Furthermore, each box plant cannot observe how much production is occurring at its rival's plant. In normal demand conditions, each box plant expects to receive 500 bid solicitations each quarter. But a given pickle manufacturer may decide not to make any award in a given quarter if demand conditions are sufficiently depressed.

Suppose that a box plant submits bids over the course of a quarter that are at the joint-profit-maximizing price. If it observes that it has won approximately 250 of 500 solicitations, then it will continue to hold to that price. But, if it observes that it has won 125 of 500 solicitations, then the box plant has some serious questions to address. Are the pickle manufacturers experiencing a negative demand shock, or has the other box plant undercut the joint-profit-maximizing price to obtain more awards, or is some of both occurring?

By assumption, the box plant in question is unable to determine the cause for the reduced number of contract awards. As a consequence, a box plant will reduce its bid below the joint-profit-maximizing price and move it toward the marginal cost of production. To see this, note that if the box plant does not react based on the belief that bad outcomes are attributable to negative demand shocks and not the conduct of its rival, then the rival would take advantage of this belief by undercutting the high-priced box plant.

Scenario 6: Box Plants with Strategic Buyers

In our final scenario, we alter scenario 3 by supposing that the buyers are not passive. Buyers now take strategic actions to reduce the price they pay for the commodity offered by the box plants, especially if the bid price seems high. When a strategic buyer receives unexpectedly high bids from the box plants, the buyer has several options. The buyer may inform one box plant that it will get the award in entirety if it cuts its bid by, say, 10 percent and that otherwise the other firm will get the award. At the same time, the buyer may be telling the other box plant something similar. The buyer may inform one box plant that its bid was higher than its rival's (suggesting to that box plant that it was undercut by the other box plant) and that it hopes it will be more competitive when offered an opportunity to bid in the future. The buyer may tell each box plant that it will award the contract for a long period of time if one of the box plants is willing to cut its bid price by 20 percent. The buyer has a number of ways to send signals to the box plants and to make attractive offers to the box plants that are disruptive to tacit coordination.

In scenario 3, the large number of passive buyers creates an environment in which tacit collusion can succeed. However, when those buyers are strategic, as in this scenario, tacit collusion is made more difficult. When buyers are strategic, a larger number of buyers, each of diminishing importance to the box plants, are required for tacit collusion to succeed as compared with the case of passive buyers.

The strategies a buyer can use to disrupt tacit coordination may be more effective if there are three or more box plants because then if the buyer creates the impression there have been deviations from coordination, each box plant faces uncertainty about which of its rivals might have deviated.

1.4.3 The Role of Explicit Collusion

Scenarios 4, 5, and 6 show that when purchases are sufficiently large and infrequent, or demand is sufficiently uncertain, or buyers are strategic, it may not be possible for firms to elevate prices with only tacit collusion. These scenarios show that even though firms are engaged in repeated interaction over time, they may not be able to accomplish fully collusive outcomes. With enough lumpiness or randomness or difficulty interpreting responses from buyers, as in scenarios 4, 5, and 6, respectively, a firm often cannot rely on repeated play to discipline its rivals. Without communication and transfers, the sellers are left in a tough spot in terms of trying to achieve elevated prices and profits. Deviations induced by self-interested profit maximization will creep into their conduct, and joint profits will fall short of monopoly levels. (See the appendix to this chapter for a formalization of these results.)[27]

Explicit collusion gives the firms the additional tools of communication and interfirm transfers. If the box plants have access to communication and interfirm transfers in scenarios 4, 5 and 6, then they may be able to achieve the joint-profit-maximizing price.

In scenario 4 with the large buyers, the two box plants can agree on bids to submit as well as subcontracting agreements for sharing the work that comes from these lumpy awards.[28] Most box buyers are unconcerned about who actually manufactures their boxes as long as the contract awardee bears full responsibility for all aspects of the contract award, so subcontracting is not typically problematic. If it is, then

---

27. As shown in the appendix, the difficulties associated with sustaining successful tacit collusion when buyers make purchases infrequently or demand is uncertain can be seen formally in Tirole's (1988, ch. 6.7.1, pp. 262–65) exposition of Green and Porter's (1984) model of tacitly collusive behavior.

28. The 2002 EC decision in *Food flavor enhancers* describes how the producers of food flavor enhancers confronted very lumpy purchases. There were three buyers in this market that represented over 50 percent of total purchases in the European Community. To avoid issues associated with the lumpiness of these procurements, the major produc-

it is still possible for the two box plants to make sure that the work is shared in a relatively equal way. If one box plant has won a recent large contract, then the other box plant can win the next one. The two box plants can make sure this happens through communication about the bids each will submit. If the lumpiness of the awards creates a temporary inequity in profits for the two firms, this can be resolved with explicit cash transfers, or some other kind of interfirm transaction that results in an equivalent transfer. If the firms are not confident in their ability to enforce appropriate transfers after a procurement, the transfers can be arranged prior to the procurement.

In scenario 5 with uncertain demand, communication results in each box plant submitting bids equal to their joint-profit-maximizing price. Communication in this context also includes monitoring of one another. By monitoring one another's production, each box plant is able to determine with certainty that a reduced number of awards came from a negative demand shock for pickles rather than being undercut by the other box plant.[29] With so many awards each quarter, even in poor demand conditions, it is unlikely that there will be a need for transfers between the firms.

In scenario 6 where buyers are strategic, communication could allow the box plants to monitor their bids, sales, and production.[30] With transfers they could rectify any asymmetries in the division of the collusive gain.

---

ers of food flavor enhancers went to the smaller producers before the solicitations by the big buyers had arrived and reached explicit agreements to buy product from the smaller producers, at specified prices, in exchange for the small producers' submitting nonwinning bids at these procurements. In the EC decision, these ex ante purchase agreements are referred to as "counterpurchasing agreements."

29. There are many cartel cases where noise seems to be a predominate concern. Monitoring mechanisms can be employed to disaggregate noise into its component parts, identifying how much is attributable to undercutting by other cartel firms. Once such monitoring mechanisms are in place, the undercutting incentives are largely eliminated. For many cartels there is a substantial involvement of trade associations, substantial investments in incremental monitoring, and sometimes the involvement in the conspiracy of an external monitoring firm. See the appendix to chapter 6 on third-party facilitation.

30. "In respect of multinational constructors, the cartel faced a danger that these customers would benefit from diverging prices among countries. In the words of Morgan: 'The cartel members were concerned that large OEMs who had unified purchasing policies would be able to exploit export price differences across Europe by purchasing all of their requirements from a single, cheap source of supply. In response, the cartel adopted special rules to cover the harmonisation of prices to OEMs. As a result, the cartel agreed product prices for sales to individual OEMs, which were not calculated by reference to any country.'" (EC decision in *Electrical and mechanical carbon and graphite products* at para. 125)

1.5 Lingering Price Effects of Explicit Collusion

As an example of cartels that faced difficulties elevating profits through mere reliance on recognized mutual interdependence but for which explicit collusion allowed the successful elevation of prices, consider the vitamins cartel. Results based on vitamins' price data before, during, and after the period of admitted collusion show a substantial increase in price from the cartel, but they also show a period of lingering effects on price from the cartel conduct after the period of explicit collusion ended. Returning to figure 1.1, we see that prices for vitamin A acetate 650 feed grade fell to approximately their pre-cartel levels within two years after the end of collusion. As shown by Kovacic et al. (2007), this trend applies more generally to vitamin products with more than two cartel members. Kovacic et al. (2007) consider thirty vitamin products. On average, the prices of these vitamin products were approximately 25 to 30 percent lower prior to the plea period than at the plea-period maximum.[31] For cartels with three or four members, prices typically fell back to pre-cartel levels within two years after the end of the plea period. However, for the vitamins products with only two producers, prices remained close to their maximum collusive levels for several years after the end of plea period.

Lingering effects of the conspiracy were present for all vitamin products. However, even though the firms had experienced a long period of explicit collusion and clearly understood the collusive implementation of increased prices, without communication and interfirm transfers, elevated prices were difficult to sustain except for products with only two producers.[32]

"Given the global character of the citric acid market and the use of the DEM and USD as benchmark currencies, the value of the exchange rate between the two was critical to the establishment of sustainable and competitive prices, particularly to avoid trans-shipments between the two areas. Pricing decisions were taken by the cartel members in the light of this important consideration." (EC decision in *Citric acid* at para. 93)

31. The prices used in Kovacic et al. (2007) are seven-month centered moving averages, so the "maximum plea-period price" is the maximum of these seven-month centered moving averages.

32. On the lingering effects of collusion beyond the period of explicit collusion, see Bernheim (2002), Harrington (2004b), and Kovacic et al. (2007).

1.6 Price Formation Process

We argued above that in certain environments explicit collusion allows the elevation of prices, while tacit collusion does not. In this section, we take a closer look at price formation by considering the details of a procurement process. Many cartels, at the most micro level of their operation, must engage in bid rigging to accomplish their goal of elevating prices for their products.[33]

Suppose that a buyer acquires one input through the simultaneous consideration of bids from four potential suppliers. Each of these suppliers has a cost for the provision of the object. Suppose the costs of the four suppliers are $Cost_A = 2$, $Cost_B = 6$, $Cost_C = 7$, and $Cost_D = 10$. Suppose that each supplier knows not only its cost, but also the costs of all other suppliers.[34] Suppose that the object is bought by means of a sealed-bid procurement, where bidders simultaneously submit sealed bids, the low bidder wins, and that bidder is paid the amount of its bid by the buyer for providing one unit.

Acting independently and without collusion, supplier A would submit a bid of 6 while suppliers B, C, and D would each submit bids slightly above their own costs.[35] The bid of 6 is the highest bid that supplier A can submit and not be subject to undercutting by the other suppliers. Supplier A would win the procurement and provide the item to the buyer for a price of 6.

Suppose that some subset of bidders collude. These colluding bidders meet in a room prior to the procurement and agree that all but one of them will stay in the room and not attend the procurement. At one extreme, if no colluding bidders comply with the agreement to stay in the room, we say that there is no monitoring. At the other extreme, if all but one member of the cartel stay in the room, we say there is perfect monitoring.

---

33. During the operation of the vitamins cartel, when customers solicited bids through their procurement processes, the cartel participants had to discuss their individual bids to determine among themselves the ultimate winner and the price the winner would be paid for the relevant vitamin product.
34. This simplification avoids the issue of how to get bidders to truthfully report what they know.
35. If a supplier submits a bid equal to its cost, then it earns a zero payoff from victory at the procurement. By bidding slightly above cost, a bidder would earn a positive payoff should it win.

1.6.1 Difficulties Sustaining Collusion without Monitoring

Collusion between A and B, but not C, produces a collusive gain of 1 because the cartel wins the procurement at a price of 7 rather than 6. The colluding firms need to divide this collusive gain between them. For example, they might consider dividing it so that each gets a payoff of 0.5 above what it would have gotten in the absence of collusion. However, if monitoring is not perfect and supplier B is not prevented from entering a bid—namely, B can leave the room even though they had agreed to stay—then by bidding a small amount below 7, B will win the procurement and earn a payoff of slightly less than 1. This is better than a payoff of 0.5. If B's bidding behavior is not monitored, B has an incentive to cheat on an agreement specifying that it should not bid, or that it should bid an amount greater than 7.

In the absence of monitoring, supplier A may be able to alter the division of the collusive gain to deter cheating by supplier B, but to do that supplier A must offer supplier B almost the entire collusive gain. If bidding is in 0.01 increments, then bidder A has to offer bidder B a payment of 0.99 while keeping only 0.01 of the collusive gain for itself. It may not be in bidder A's interest to engage in collusion for such a small payoff, but in the absence of monitoring, no smaller payment to B will keep B from deviating.

If the cartel consists of A, B, and C, but not D, and the agreement is that B and C will suppress their bids, allowing A to win at a price of 10, then by the logic above bidder B would need to be paid 3.99 to be satisfied with a bid above 10 (by cheating and bidding 9.99, it would have profit of $9.99 - 6 = 3.99$). This leaves bidder A with a collusive payoff of 0.01 again. But what about bidder C? Bidder C has an incentive to cheat that has not been addressed, and bidder A has nothing left to offer C to avert deviant behavior. There is not enough collusive gain to avert cheating by both B and C. The cartel of bidders A and B might be barely sustainable but the cartel of A, B, and C is not sustainable because there is not a sufficient collusive payoff to overcome the incentive for deviations by both B and C in the absence of monitoring.

1.6.2 Effective Collusion with Monitoring

Under perfect monitoring, the cartel is able to prevent bidding by all cartel members except the one designated to win the procurement. In this case, with a cartel of A and B, if supplier A makes a take-it-or-leave-it offer to supplier B for the right to be the one that bids at the procurement, then B is happy with any positive payment because reversion to noncollusive play results in a zero payoff for B. If we consider a more even division of the bargaining power, then it is natural to think of A paying B the amount 0.5 to stay in the room while bidder A goes to the procurement and bids 7. Suppliers A and B are then each better off by 0.5 relative to noncollusive play.

If supplier C joins the cartel of A and B, then with a reasonable notion of the division of bargaining power, A might pay B an amount 1.5 and C an amount 1 in exchange for their staying in the room while A wins the procurement with a bid of 10.[36] Supplier A wins at a price of 10 (versus 6 under noncollusive bidding) and pays out a total of 2.5 to its co-conspirators, leaving it with a collusive gain of 1.5 relative to noncollusive behavior. Thus, although a cartel of A and B was difficult to sustain without monitoring, and a cartel of A, B, and C was impossible to sustain without monitoring, either cartel can be effective with perfect monitoring.

This example illustrates the details of how the price to a buyer is increased through collusion, as well as some of the factors affecting the size and effectiveness of cartels. We address these issues in detail later in the book, with part II focusing on cartels and part III focusing on bidding rings.

1.7 Economic Rationale for the Illegality of Explicit Collusion

Typically, economists advocate noninterference in the marketplace. Economists are quick to note that government intervention is usually detrimental to the economy. There are exceptions. One of those is antitrust policy.

As we noted earlier, a cartel of producers reduces output in order to increase prices and profits.[37] The reduction in output and the higher prices result in a decrease in surplus to consumers. (A consumer's

36. Adding C to the cartel increases the winning price from 7 to 10 and so increases the collusive gain from 1 to 4. Sharing the additional collusive gain of 3 among the 3 colluding firms means giving 1 to each firm. Forming a cartel with just A and B creates a collusive gain of 1. Sharing that gain between A and B means giving 0.5 to each firm. Adding these up, B gets a payment of 1.5 and C gets a payment of 1. These payments are the Shapley values of the bidders. In fact, bidding rings often use a procedure called a nested knockout for allocating items won at an auction and dividing the collusive gain where the payments are the bidders' Shapley values. See Graham, Marshall, and Richard (1990).
37. We focus on collusive efforts to increase prices and decrease quantities. However, a cartel may take actions that increase the colluding firms' abilities to price discriminate, resulting in the firms producing more than prior to collusion, but with increased profits through the increased extraction of consumer surplus. For expositional simplicity, in many places in the book we discuss cartels as increasing prices and decreasing quantities without including this caveat.

surplus is the difference between his or her willingness to pay and the amount he or she actually pays for a good.) The increase in profits for the colluding firms is not big enough to offset the decrease in consumer surplus. Thus, on whole, collusion damages the economy. In part, the antitrust laws exist to protect the economy from the damage of forgone surplus that would emerge from collusive behavior.

Put somewhat differently, when a cartel increases prices, some consumption will not take place that would have taken place when the firms were acting noncollusively. The mutually beneficial transactions that would have occurred without collusion that are foregone because of the elevation in prices by the cartel are a true social loss.

An additional motivation underlying the illegality of collusion is that it undermines the reliance on competitive processes, especially in environments where buyers are informationally disadvantaged relative to sellers. Buyers want to rely on competition as a policing force in the marketplace.[38] When sellers are acting competitively in submitting bids at a procurement, buyers have confidence that they are getting the best possible offers. If buyers knew that all sellers were colluding, then buyers would have no confidence that procurements would produce the best possible offers, and they would know that they need to resort to more costly, time-intensive acquisition practices. As buyers reallocate resources from productive activities to the activity of procurement, there is a social loss. In addition, at the margin, the increased procurement costs may cause buyers to substitute away from products where suppliers are colluding or even exit certain lines of business, which is also a social loss. A market-based economy relies on the assurance of genuine competition and the integrity of competitive processes. Cartels undermine that fundamental assurance.

1.8   Cartel Detection

The Five Forces diagram in figure 1.2 can be used as a guide to identify product/market/industries that are more prone to collusion than others. Specifically, when considering all of the Five Forces, product/market/industries where increments to expected profits are largest

---

38. A policing force imposes discipline on those who would otherwise act in a relatively unconstrained manner. Without the pressure of competition, a supplier would do its best to extract payments and other favorable terms from buyers. Competition among suppliers restrains each supplier in its efforts to extract surplus from buyers. In this sense competition is a policing force.

from the suppression of interfirm rivalry are more susceptible to collusion. The history of cartels is suggestive and consistent with the Five Forces diagram. In industries where there are high barriers to entry, there are poor substitutes for the product of the industry, buyers and suppliers do not have much bargaining power against the firms of the industry or that bargaining power can be mitigated through collusion by sellers, and interfirm rivalry is intense, then the firms in that industry have much to gain in terms of expected profit increments from the suppression of interfirm rivalry.

Returning to the vitamins industry, vitamin A was made essentially by three firms in the 1990s. There were no good substitutes for vitamin A, the products made by different firms were chemically identical, and customers acquired vitamins through procurements where price was the major determinant of the procurement award. Managers in industries with these characteristics would find collusion to be quite profitable. In addition, by instituting a high-powered incentive scheme for managers that is tied directly to substantial incremental increases in current profits, a firm in such an industry could find managers drawn into explicitly collusive conduct.

Enforcement authorities and market participants want observable conduct that tells them whether a cartel is operating. Of course, cartel members know the value of stealth as well as the cost of nonstealthy conduct. Cartels try to make their actions look indistinguishable from noncollusive conduct. Nevertheless, there are actions and outcomes that are indicative of collusion. In the law and economics literature, these actions are referred to as "plus factors."[39] Many commonly mentioned plus factors associated with collusive conduct could also be consistent with unilateral conduct. However, there are some plus factors that could not be reasonably explained as being consistent with unilateral conduct by market participants. These are called "super-plus factors."[40] We begin to develop the concept of plus factors in chapter 4 and deepen the development in part IV.

1.9   Outline of the Book

We begin the book with an examination of collusion in practice (part I) using three narratives: a story of a cartel, a story of a bidding ring,

---

39. Posner (2001, pp. 79–93) offers an enumeration of plus factors. See also Gellhorn and Kovacic (1994).
40. See Kovacic et al. (2011).

and a story of a parent company concerned about detecting collusion at its divisions. Although fictitious, these narratives are each rooted in the inner workings and details from actual cartel cases.

Next we consider the economics of cartels and the economics of bidding rings (parts II and III, respectively). The two parts are organized symmetrically. The first chapter of each part discusses the pure suppression of rivalry in the context of a cartel and a bidding ring, respectively. The second chapter of each part addresses the collusive structures that are needed for the successful implementation of the suppression of rivalry. The final chapter of part II examines cartel conduct to enhance profits once the cartel has successfully suppressed interfirm rivalry among its members. The final chapter of part III looks at the issue of how auction and procurement design can make collusion by bidders more or less difficult. In part IV we discuss how economic evidence can be used to detect collusion for a cartel as well as a bidding ring. Part IV concludes by addressing the concern regarding future collusion that could emerge from a merger.

1.10 Appendix: Factors Affecting the Sustainability of Tacit Collusion*

Tirole (1988, ch. 6.7.1, pp. 262–65) provides an exposition of Green and Porter's (1984) model of tacitly collusive behavior—the model is one of tacit collusion in that the equilibrium identified does not, in theory, require communication or transfers. However, Green and Porter viewed their model as requiring explicit collusion to implement:

It is logically possible for this agreement to be a tacit one which arises spontaneously. Nevertheless, in view of the relative complexity of the conduct to be specified by this particular equilibrium and of the need for close coordination among its participants, it seems natural to assume here that the equilibrium arises from an explicit agreement. (Green and Porter 1984, p. 89, n. 5)

Although Green and Porter formulate their model in terms of quantity competition, Tirole restates the model in terms of price competition. Two firms produce a homogeneous product at constant marginal cost. In each period, the firms choose prices. All consumers purchase from the low-price firm. If the firms set the same price, half the consumers purchase from one firm and half from the other.

In each period, with probability α there is no demand for the product sold by the firms, and with probability $1 - \alpha$ there is positive demand. The realizations of demand are independently and identically distributed over time. Both firms have discount factor δ.

A firm that does not sell anything in a particular period cannot observe whether there was no demand or whether there was positive demand but its rival charged a lower price.

Similar to Green and Porter, Tirole looks for an equilibrium of the repeated game in which there is a tacitly collusive phase and a punishment phase. (Although Tirole refers to the "tacitly collusive phase" as simply the "collusive phase," we refer to it as tacitly collusive because it does not require communication or transfers.) In the tacitly collusive phase, the firms charge the monopoly price until one firm makes zero profit, which would be observed by both firms. This triggers a punishment phase in which the firms charge a price equal to their marginal cost for T periods, where T can be infinite. After the punishment phase, the firms return to tacitly collusive pricing.

As Tirole shows in his expression (6.16), no firm would wish to undercut the price in the tacitly collusive phase if and only if

$$1 \le 2(1-\alpha)\delta + (2\alpha-1)\delta^{T+1}. \tag{1.1}$$

Thus, the tacitly collusive equilibrium requires that the discount factor δ be sufficiently large, the length of the punishment phase T be sufficiently long, and the probability of no demand α be sufficiently low. Firms must place sufficiently high weight on the future, and the length of the punishment phase must be sufficiently long, that the future loss of profit triggered by a deviation outweighs the current-period benefit from the deviation. If α is high, firms view a punishment phase as likely to be triggered by periods with no demand, regardless of whether they deviate, and so they might as well deviate.

If we modify Tirole's model so that consumers make purchases only every L periods, then inequality (1.1) becomes

$$1 \le \delta^{L-1}(2(1-\alpha)\delta + (2\alpha-1)\delta^{T+1}). \tag{1.2}$$

Thus, when consumers make purchases less frequently, successful tacit collusion requires a larger δ, larger T, and/or smaller α than when consumers make purchases more frequently. If buyers make purchases in lumpy and infrequent intervals, then tacit collusion becomes harder to sustain.

To relate this back to the scenarios in chapter 1.4, if we view (1.2) with $L = 1$ as the relevant requirement for scenario 3, then the difficulties associated with sustaining tacit collusion in scenario 4 correspond to an increase in L and the difficulties associated with sustaining tacit collusion in scenario 5 correspond to an increase in α. Scenario 6 corresponds to the case where buyers consciously act on L and α to disrupt tacitly collusive outcomes.

I   Collusion in Practice

The economics literature addresses component parts of cartel and ring behavior. In addition, case studies and legal decisions often provide a close look at individual cartels and rings. However, in both these bodies of work, the intuitions for how the component parts come together as a coherent whole can be obscured. In part I, using the expositional device of narratives, we construct coherent descriptions of the functioning of a cartel and a ring. Although the stories of part I are fictional, they are rooted in actual cartel and ring cases, as indicated by the numerous footnotes provided throughout the narratives. In addition, we offer a third narrative describing the detection of a cartel from observed conduct and outcomes.

2   Narrative of a Cartel

2.1 The Story Begins

Consider an industry with four firms, where two of the firms are divisions of major multi-product parent corporations and the division managers are essentially independent and autonomous decision makers.[1] There is no real threat of entry because of the capital intensive nature of the industry in conjunction with the learning-by-doing nature of the production process. There are no reasonable substitute products for the commodity made by these firms. No suppliers have any degree of bargaining power against any of the firms, and the same is generally true for buyers, although there are some large European buyers. The commodity that the firms make is sold internationally. It is relatively inexpensive to transport—it has a high value to weight ratio. The commodity made by any firm is physically and chemically identical to that made by any of the other firms. Each firm has a sales force and distribution network that allows it to sell its product worldwide. One of the firms has a substantial production facility in East Asia, another firm has production in western Europe, another in eastern Europe, while the fourth has production solely in the United States.[2]

Some of the firms might be communicating at an early stage to try to reach some "understandings" on pricing and markets. Some of these bilateral discussions have a minor effect, but the sales forces of each

---

1. This corporate structure plays a role in the exposition in chapter 4.
2. This description fits the stylized facts of the vitamins industry at the time of its cartelization. To give an example with four firms, there were four manufacturers of vitamin E 50% adsorbate feed grade in 1990: Hoffmann-La Roche, BASF, Rhône-Poulenc, and Eisai, all participated in the cartel. For a summary of the vitamins industry and description of the cartel, see Marshall, Marx, and Raiff (2008, especially app. A).

firm continue to seek incremental market share by competing against the other firms on the basis of price.[3]

The world economy experiences a slowdown, and each firm finds itself with ever more excess capacity and an increasingly hungry sales force. Prices start to tumble as each firm goes after new business as well as the business held by each of the other three. In a relatively short period of time, none of the firms is earning a profit that it views as satisfactory.[4]

2.2 Initiation of the Cartel

The largest firm of the four asks for a meeting to discuss the state of the market.[5] The other three are reluctant because they are aware that antitrust laws look dimly on such meetings.[6] It could be at the location of an accounting or consulting firm that specializes in helping firms with such discussions.[7] Or, it could be after the conclusion of a trade association gathering.[8] The conversation quickly turns to the currently

---

3. The EC decision in *Soda-ash—Solvay* applies to the period 1987 to 1989, but prior to that, as stated in the decision at para. 40, "During 1986 Solvay realised that CFK was applying a policy of price cutting in order to retain or regain market share."

4. Related to Biotin: "By the early 1990s the price of biotin was declining. Representatives of Roche had been telling Japanese companies during their regular visits to Japan that they should cooperate with Roche and avoid unnecessary competition. During their individual visits, on technical matters, to Tanabe the Roche executives had started tentatively to explore the topic of target prices for biotin. Tanabe refers also to later meetings in March and May 1991 in which Roche 'tried to introduce target prices.' In Europe Roche's solicitations were expressed in blunter terms: according to Merck, Roche insisted that it (Merck) should come to a 'biotin meeting,' in which Merck should represent BASF since the latter took almost all Merck's production under coproduction arrangements; as a non-producer of biotin, BASF was not invited. The first known multilateral meeting of the five producers was held in Lugano, Switzerland, on 14 October 1991 at the initiative of Roche who chaired the proceedings. The participants were representatives from: Roche, Lonza, Merck, Sumitomo, and Tanabe." (EC decision in *Vitamins* at paras. 484–87)

5. As described in footnote 4 in this chapter, in biotin "Roche insisted that it [Merck] should come to a 'biotin meeting.'" (EC decision in *Vitamins* at paras. 484–87)

6. As described in footnote 4 in this chapter, cartels have often chosen to meet in Switzerland.

7. The EC decision in *Organic peroxides* at para. 92 describes the role of AC-Treuhand, a Zurich-based entity, that "organised meetings of the members of the agreement, often in Zurich." On third-party facilitation, see the appendix to chapter 6.

8. Related to amino acids: "ADM further proposed that the producers attend trade association meetings quarterly to adjust their price and sales volumes according to their agreements. It explained how forming an industry association could provide a seemingly legitimate, but artificial, reason to meet, and thus conceal the fact that purported competitors were secretly meeting to discuss prices and sales volumes. ADM described

ruinous nature of competition in the industry and the need to curb the price-cutting actions that underlie the problem.[9]

The largest firm explains that everyone will be better off if prices are elevated and continue to rise over the next several years. The smallest firm is skeptical, but it too sees that given the current state of affairs, its profits are not satisfactory. If it were making an acceptable profit, it would probably break off the conversation at this point. But the intense interfirm rivalry that has been brought on by the poor state of the market has essentially eliminated profits.[10]

---

how to have 'official' and 'unofficial' meetings. ADM explained that while attending an official industry association meeting, one person would book a hotel suite and quietly notify the others, and then they would secretly meet to discuss prices and sales volumes away from the official meeting. The participants agreed to proceed in this way." (EC decision in *Amino acids* at para. 122) Also, as indicated at paras. 112–113, the amino acid producers' association was established explicitly to serve the cartel's purposes.

Related to citric acid: "The timing of the cartel meetings was usually set to coincide with those of the general assembly of the trade association ECAMA since all cartel participants were members of this association. The companies would typically meet the evening prior to the official [European Critic Acid Manufacturers' Association (ECAMA)] meeting." (EC decision in *Citric acid* at para. 87)

Related to carbon brushes: "SGL also lists several meetings of the AEGEP as forums that were used for cartel meetings in the early nineties." (EC decision in *Electrical and mechanical carbon and graphite products* at para. 174) Further, "What can be deduced from the available evidence is that a number of meetings of the ECGA Graphite Specialties Electrical and Mechanical Committees coincided with meetings of the cartel's Technical Committee. . . . A similar correlation exists between ECGA General Assembly or Board of Directors meetings and Summit meetings of the cartel, as evidenced by the ECGA meetings on 23–24 October 1997, 20 April 1998, and 17–18 May 1999, all of which were used by the cartel to organise Summit meetings. It would therefore appear evident that cartel members took the opportunity of official ECGA meetings to meet, often both before and after the ECGA meeting, among themselves to co-ordinate their anti-competitive activities. Indeed, for at least some members of ECGA, the usefulness of the existence of ECGA, or at least of its Graphite Specialties Committee, appears to have been largely determined by its function of providing a legitimate cover for meetings of representatives of the members of the cartel. After Carbone Lorraine had left the cartel by the middle of 1999, a Technical Committee meeting of the cartel on 4 October 1999 discussed the question 'Is the umbrella of E.C.G.A. still be needed [sic]?'" (EC decision in *Electrical and mechanical carbon and graphite products* at para. 177)

9. "On the subject of the exchange of information between [high-level representatives] . . . BPB stated that, at that meeting, the representatives of BPB and Knauf 'reached an understanding that it was in the interests of BPB, Knauf and the industry as a whole (including, ultimately, the interests of consumers) for the ruinous price war to end and for producers to attempt to compete at more sustainable economic levels.'" (EC decision in *Plasterboard* at para. 55)

10. According to the EC decision in *Vitamins* at paras. 293–95 related to vitamin B$_5$: "The background against which the cartel was formed, suggests Daiichi, was a steady drop in prices for vitamins of the B complex during the 1980s and the weakness of the dollar in 1989 to 1990, leading to zero profitability for Roche in these products."

The large firm starts to flesh out the details of how to successfully elevate prices, and the other three are willing to listen.[11] Some of their willingness stems from the fact that the large firm is known to have successfully elevated prices in some of its other product areas, and the three firms have heard that this came from cooperation among rivals that was spearheaded by the large firm.[12]

The large firm points out that its plan will not work unless the firms are willing to act in solidarity to accomplish higher prices. Such solidarity will require regular communication.[13] Information will need to be shared among the firms. Some of this information would be zealously guarded by each of the firms if they were just acting alone and not trying to cooperate. They need to talk about particular customer accounts, particular geographic areas of the world, and how to divide the world market among themselves.[14] They need to talk about the

11. According to the EC decision in *Vitamins* at para. 567, "the collusive arrangements in the various vitamins were not spontaneous or haphazard developments, but were planned, conceived and directed by the same persons at the most senior levels in Roche and the other undertakings."

12. According to the EC decision in *Vitamins* at para. 2, Roche participated in the cartelization of all twelve vitamins considered in that decision, and the start dates range from September 1989 for vitamins A and E to May 1993 for carotinoids.

The firm Ajinomoto spearheaded the cartel in *Food flavour enhancers*, which the EC decision dates from November 1988 to June 1998, and then later was a key player in the cartel in *Amino acids*, which the EC decision dates from September 1990 to June 1995.

The firm SGL Carbon AG was involved in the cartel in *Electrical and mechanical carbon and graphite products*, starting at least in October 1988, then in the cartel in *Graphite electrodes*, starting at least in May 1992, and then in the cartel in *Specialty graphite*, starting at least in July 1993. The EC decisions date the ends of the cartel periods as December 1999, March 1998, and February 1998, respectively.

13. All of the cases we consider in this section describe regular meetings by the cartel members. For example, "The holding of regular and frequent meetings between the participants was a hallmark of the cartel's organisation. Between March 1991 and May 1995 around 20 multilateral meetings were held between the companies on matters directly related to the cartel." (EC decision in *Citric acid* at para. 86) As another example, in the EC decision in *Organic peroxides* at para. 353, one of the principle aspects of the cartel agreement involves "participating in regular meetings and having other contacts in order to agree to the above restrictions and to implement and/or modify them as required." Essentially identical language appears in the EC decision in *Graphite electrodes* at para. 110.

14. The following EC decisions indicate that the cartel allocated customers, geographic areas, and/or market shares: *Amino acids* at paras. 57, 68, 211; *Carbonless paper* at para. 81; *Choline chloride* at para. 64; *Citric acid* at para. 158; *Copper plumbing tubes* at para. 449; *Electrical and mechanical carbon and graphite products* at para. 219; *Food flavour enhancers* at paras. 65, 68, and 172; *Graphite electrodes* at para. 71; *Industrial and medical gases* at para. 101; *Industrial tubes* at para. 195; *Interbrew and Alken-Maes* at para. 243; *Methylglucamine* at para. 43; *Organic peroxides* at para. 353; *Plasterboard* at paras. 72, 126, 229; *Sorbates* at para. 107; *Specialty graphite* at para. 130; *Vitamins* at paras. 2, 590; and *Zinc phosphate* at para. 214.

implementation of higher prices, including the specific actions needed to elevate prices.[15] They need to figure out how to handle disagreements and grievances among themselves.[16]

2.3 Market Share Division

The large firm advocates a worldwide market share allocation.[17] The large firm has been monitoring the others through trade statistics that are readily available from governments around the world, trade associations, and private firms that specialize in the collection of such statistics.[18] It has determined that the market shares for the firms in the previous year were 50%, 25%, 15%, and 10%.[19] The large firm proposes

15. The following EC decisions indicate that the cartel implemented price increases: *Amino acids* at para. 53; *Carbonless paper* at paras. 135, 233; *Choline chloride* at para. 64; *Citric acid* at para. 158; *Copper plumbing tubes* at para. 449; *Electrical and mechanical carbon and graphite products* at para. 219; *Food flavour enhancers* at paras. 66, 172; *Graphite electrodes* at para. 50; *Industrial and medical gases* at para. 101; *Industrial tubes* at para. 195; *Interbrew and Alken-Maes* at para. 243; *Methionine* at para. 74; *Methylglucamine* at para. 43; *Organic peroxides* at para. 353; *Plasterboard* at para. 2; *Rubber chemicals* at para. 187; *Sorbates* at para. 281; *Specialty graphite* at para. 130; *Vitamins* at paras. 2, 590; and *Zinc phosphate* at para. 214.
16. The EC decision in *Organic peroxides* at para. 92 describes the role of the firm AC-Treuhand as including that they "acted as a moderator in case of tensions between the members of the agreement and encouraged the parties to find compromises. AC Treuhand would try to stimulate the parties to work together and reach an agreement. '*The message from AC Treuhand was that it would get worse for the participants if they discontinued the discussions.*'" (italics in original) See also the appendix to chapter 6.
   In citric acid, "After 1993, the cartel decided to hold more technically orientated meetings, known as 'Sherpa' meetings, in order to resolve certain grievances and market 'difficulties.'" (EC decision in *Citric acid* at para. 86)
   As described in Stocking and Watkins (1991, p. 333), one of the incandescent electric lamp cartel's two most important administrative agencies was the Board of Arbitration. "The Board of Arbitration, consisting of a Swiss professor of law, a Swiss federal judge, and a technical expert on international cartels, arbitrated all disputes among cartel members, particularly patent claims, royalty payments, and the like."
17. "BASF has described in some detail the September 1989 meeting in Zurich which involved the setting up of the cartel in vitamins A and E. On the first day senior executives responsible for vitamin marketing in each company, together with some product managers, identified the size of the market for vitamins A and E and then agreed the allocation between the four producers of the world and regional markets on the basis of their respective achieved sales in 1988." (EC decision in *Vitamins* at paras. 162–63)
18. The EC decision in *Organic peroxides* at para. 91 describes AC-Treuhand as "a Zurich based entity providing, amongst other things, services such as collecting statistics to enterprises." See the appendix to chapter 6.
19. Related to the vitamin D₃ cartel, "The first meeting, held probably on 11 January 1994 in Basel, was attended by Roche, BASF, and Solvay. They focused in this initial meeting on determining total world demand for vitamin D₃ and their individual shares. A consensus was reached that their respective shares were Solvay 41%, Roche 38% and BASF 21%." (EC decision in *Vitamins* at para. 462)

that these shares be an ongoing allocation of the market for each of the firms.[20]

At this point in the conversation, the three other firms disagree with the allocation. They each assert that their share is larger. The large firm has an accounting/consulting firm present at the meeting that specializes in organizing firms in this manner.[21] The accounting/consulting firm reviews the numbers for the other three. After some debate, the revisions of the market share allocations settle at the following: 48.5%, 25.5%, 15.3%, and 10.7%.[22] The three smaller firms assert that there are regional issues to consider. The firm with production in Asia states a desire for a larger percentage of the Asian market than its worldwide share. There are similar statements made about Europe by two other firms. The large firm notes that there will be efforts made to respect regional customers, but that the overall adherence to the worldwide market share allocation is what really matters.[23]

The large firm explains that there will need to be very regular reporting of production and sales figures to the cartel so that the progress of the market share allocation can be tracked.[24] As the world market changes, as it grows and contracts both worldwide and regionally, there will be perturbations in the sales numbers.[25] Each firm needs to

20. See footnote 17 in this chapter. Also, the EC decision in *Vitamins* at para. 167 states that for vitamin E for 1988, worldwide achieved sales were Roche 46.5%, BASF 28.1%, Rhône-Poulenc 15.2%, and Eisai 10.2%.

21. See the appendix to chapter 6.

22. The EC decision in *Vitamins* at para. 168 states that the worldwide sales figures for 1988 "may have been slightly adjusted to give the allocated quotas." It is not uncommon in the EC decisions to see cartel market shares defined down to 1/10 of one percent. For example, in the EC decision in *Carbonless paper* at para. 99, it is noted of cartel documents that "The market share and growth figures are given with an accuracy of one decimal place."

23. According to the EC decision in *Vitamins* at para. 521, "Variations in share were permitted from region to region provided the overall quota was not exceeded; any excess above quota would have to be offset by compensatory purchases from the aggrieved party."

24. "The managers who attended the European regional meetings had weekly telephone contact in order to monitor the agreements on pricing and sales volumes and to discuss individual customers. Every month they exchanged the volumes of vitamins A and E sold in each national market. Roche provided the others with the monthly sales of Eisai in the European market as a whole rather than for each country." (EC decision in *Vitamins* at para. 188)

25. "There was to be 'parallel development of sales and market share,' i.e., quotas were adjusted in volume terms to take account of increased demand while maintaining the same percentage shares and targets set each year by region. Sales would be monitored and the necessary corrections made quarterly." (EC decision in *Vitamins* at para. 395)

report in at least monthly with production and sales numbers, otherwise it will be increasingly difficult to make sure that by year-end the firms have achieved their allocated market shares.[26] As one firm moves a little ahead and another falls somewhat behind, customer accounts that are in the process of being bid will need to be reallocated from the former to the latter.[27] This will be accomplished by explicitly deciding on the bids to be submitted for these accounts.[28] The large firm explains that bids must be coordinated for all customer accounts if the cartel is to elevate prices.[29] It notes the need to coordinate all bids prior to

---

"'If the exchange of figures shows that the sales of a party in any country have exceeded the quota for any category then that party will modify its sales policy in succeeding months with the object of arriving eventually at a tonnage for the whole of the calendar year which does not exceed his percentage quota.'" (EC decision in *Organic peroxides* at para. 85)

26. "ADM named Ajinomoto as the office to which each lysine producer would provide monthly sales figures. Ajinomoto's job would be to keep track of the figures so that the producers could make adjustments in their sales to limit the overall annual sales to the agreed maximums." (EC decision in *Amino acids* at para. 122).

27. "There was a discussion between Sewon and ADM concerning the supply to each other's customers in the United Kingdom." (EC decision in *Amino acids* at para. 158).

"In 1994 the rapid increase in demand for vitamin E for human consumption necessitated a revision of the quota allocated to Rhône-Poulenc. To maintain its agreed 16% share of the overall market, Rhône-Poulenc had to increase its sales in the animal feed sector. The producers agreed in August 1994 that the Rhône-Poulenc share of the feed segment be capped at 21%; if the agreed increase in quota in that area did not however give Rhône-Poulenc its full 16% overall, the other two European producers would purchase product from it to compensate for the shortfall. Compensating purchases were made by Roche in 1996 and by Roche and BASF in 1997." (EC decision in *Vitamins* at para. 225)

28. "Customers in specific national markets were regularly allocated by agreeing that the other participating undertakings would offer higher prices than the undertaking to which the customer was allocated." (EC decision in *Choline chloride* at para. 99).

29. "In this last respect, by agreeing that the other companies would offer higher price quotes than the company to which the customer was allocated, the price agreements for individual customers served not only to maintain or increase prices to those customers, and thereby ultimately to that national market, but also to maintain the agreed customer allocations and thereby ultimately the agreed market shares." (EC decision in *Choline chloride* at para. 99)

"Each customer's largest supplier (in terms of sales) set its prices slightly below the target prices agreed with the competitors to make sure that the customer in question made the contract with this supplier. The aim was to prevent shifts in market share at the expense of the incumbent. If, during the negotiations a customer pointed out that a competitor had made a lower-priced offer, the incumbent contacted its competitor and asked for an explanation. If the competitor indeed won the contract and thus gained market share, the losing supplier sought to offset its loss with another customer by offering a lower price than the competitors. In order not to jeopardize the overall success of the coordinated price increase, this supplier informed the competitors that it would apply a lower price than agreed only because this allowed it to offset the market share lost from another customer." (EC decision in *Rubber chemicals* at para. 67)

submission.[30] It notes that this is a high-level activity and cannot be easily delegated within each firm due to the legal issues around their agreement.[31]

2.4 Price Increases and Announcements

The large firm begins discussing pricing and the implementation of price increases. They first review the nature of their customers. Most customers of these firms, especially the large ones, acquire the product through a bidding process. Once a year the customers request bids from three or four of the firms and select a winner based on price and past performance of the firms in servicing their account. But because the suppliers are largely equivalent in terms of service, most of the weight in the evaluation of the bids is placed on price.

30. "Notes by Carbone Lorraine show how Carbone Lorraine, as customer leader, co-operated with Morgan and Schunk to regularly rotate which company would win tenders organised by the Régie Autonome des Transports Parisiens (RATP) in France for a particular type of current collector shoe. Information concerning the bids made by each company cover the period 1983 to 1992. In one table, Carbone Lorraine traces which company won which bids from April 1989 to November 1991 and which company should win which bids in the next three years to arrive at an equal number of bids won by the end of 1994. Another table indicates that a bid scheduled to be won by Carbone Lorraine had to be given to Schunk as compensation for other models." (EC decision in *Electrical and mechanical carbon and graphite products* at para. 141)

"Morgan has provided examples of order confirmations of bids agreed between itself and Carbone Lorraine in 1997 regarding the customer GEC Alsthom, showing that the prices agreed did indeed lead to orders by the client. An example of a complete cycle of bid rigging has also been provided by Carbone Lorraine. The cycle starts with a tender issued by the Régie des Transports de Marseille (RTM) of 27 October 1998. Bids are requested for a number of types of carbon brushes and current collectors. Based on contacts with competitors, Carbone Lorraine then compiled a comparative table, indicating which companies won which bids and for which quantity and price in past years, and co-ordinating with them the bids each would make for the new tender. The agreed winning bids are circled. Carbone Lorraine also prepared a table indicating each company's turnover for each type of product covered by the tender, probably to ensure that the agreements made were 'fair' in terms of total turnover. After having reached agreement with competitors on the prices to be quoted, Carbone Lorraine instructed its sales representative on 16 November 1998 to quote to RTM the prices agreed with competitors. These were indeed the bids that Carbone Lorraine effectively made. Finally, an order from RTM confirms that Carbone Lorraine won exactly the bids it had agreed with competitors. These examples show that the cartel was indeed highly effective in achieving results in the market in respect of tenders, in particular by public transport companies." (EC decision in *Electrical and mechanical carbon and graphite products* at para. 151)

31. A "basic principle" for the graphite electrodes cartel was that "decisions on each company's pricing had to be taken not by the commercial managers but by the Chairman/General Managers only." (EC decision in *Graphite electrodes* at para. 50).

The four firms know that buyers often have divisions within their companies that are devoted to procurement. Procurement is an expensive administrative activity, and the procurement division in any company has a budget constraint. The procurement division must decide how and where to allocate its scarce procurement resources. When confronting unexpectedly high bids, the procurement division is likely to devote considerable resources to resist the price increase.[32]

Resistance to price increases may occur in a number of ways. For example, if the procurement division usually asks for bids from only two or three of the firms, they may instead open the bidding up to all four producers. They may attempt to buy product from third-party vendors such as brokers or dealers, although the viability of this alternative depends on how tightly the four producers are controlling supply to third parties. When evaluating the bids of the four producers, they can try to play one off against the other. For example, one of the bidders may be told that they are not lowest, but if they were to drop their bid by $.50 per kilogram, then they would be a likely winner. Similar statements may be made by the buyer to the other bidders as well. Without cooperation and established communication among themselves, each of the bidders will then wonder if it can secure the account for just a small price decrease. When times are bad, this may be very tempting. Also, if members of a sales force are on incentive pay that is tied to quantity, the drop in price may occur almost immediately.[33]

32. "That not all customers simply accepted the announced price increases, is evidenced by a fax of 30 April 1996 from the London Underground Ltd. (LUL) to Morgan, stating: 'Unfortunately your price increases are well above the current rate of inflation (i.e., 2.7%) and a full explanation is required. I also note from our files that at a meeting here on 21st September (when LUL again expressed dis-satisfaction with your pricing and stock-holding policy) Morganite agreed to respond within 3 weeks with a full breakdown of costs. This did not happen and we find ourselves no further forward in our relationship than we were this time last year. I would be pleased if you will now provide the information requested together with the factors underlying this year's increase, i.e. increased costs of materials, wages, etc. supported by relevant indices or letters from suppliers.'" (EC decision in *Electrical and mechanical carbon and graphite products* at para. 109)

"The five companies evaluated the impact of the agreed price levels and exchanged information on the acceptance of the price increases in the different regions." (EC decision in *Amino acids* at para. 81)

33. "During this meeting, ADM alluded to the importance of a company controlling its sales force in order to maintain high prices, and explained that its sales people have the general tendency to be very competitive and that, unless the producers had very firm control of their sales people, there would be a price-cutting problem." (EC decision in *Amino acids* at para. 98)

The large firm explains that each of the four firms needs to make announcements to the entire marketplace about price increases.[34] These price increases should be published in leading trade publications for all to see.[35] Most important, the people in the customers' procurement divisions need to see these announcements. The large firm explains that the announcements need to be motivated by some kind of market condition that has recently changed. It explains that this is not an issue because there are many factors changing in the world market each and every day. They will be able to offer the following kinds of "explanations" for a price increase: factor input prices have gone up, demand has increased in a particular region, inflation outpaced expectations, exchange rate fluctuations have been adverse to the producers, new regulatory compliance costs have mandated a price increase, transport costs have increased due to an increase in oil prices, and so on. The large firm explains that there will always be some "explanation" from this menu and that the firms will need to coordinate on one or two before announcing their price increases.[36]

34. See the EC decision in *Amino acids* at paras. 53 and 265 and the EC decision in *Carbonless paper* at paras. 135 and 233. See Marshall, Marx, and Raiff (2008) analyzing price announcement behavior for the vitamins cartel and providing a theoretical model of collusive price announcement behavior.

35. "The parties normally agreed that one producer should first "announce" the increase, either in a trade journal or in direct communication with major customers. Once the price increase was announced by one cartel member, the others would generally follow suit. This way the concerted price increases could be passed off, if challenged, as the result of price leadership in an oligopolistic market." (EC decision in *Vitamins* at paras. 203–204)

"In practice, the new target prices were effectively announced to customers, usually through the specialised press." (EC decision in *Methionine* at para. 278)

36. "With regard to justifications for price increases, a local meeting in the Netherlands on 19 December 1995 came up with the following agreed explanations to 'justify' an impending price increase: 'Explanation for 4% price increase 1. Environmental requirements cost extra. 2. Increase [in price] of raw materials 3. Wages [increased by] 3%.'" (EC decision in *Electrical and mechanical carbon and graphite products* at para. 108)

"After this, they entered into a detailed price discussion concerning Europe. They decided a minimum of DEM 4,25/kg as the European price, and set the prices by each currency. These prices were to be applied for deliveries from 27 April to late June. Afterwards, a price of DEM 4,50 was to be announced. The participants agreed on the explanation to be given to buyers." (EC decision in *Amino acids* at para. 164)

"Producers of cartonboard have usually attempted to justify a proposed price increase to their customers by reference to increases in the costs of raw material, energy, transport, etc." (EC decision in *Cartonboard* at para. 19)

The large firm continues by noting that price announcements should not be simultaneously announced.[37] In addition, the announcements should not always originate with one firm, but rather firms should take turns being the first to announce, with the others following with the same price announcement within a week or two, the exact timing will be decided in cartel meetings.[38] The large firm explains that there will be time, perhaps a month or more, between the announcement date and the date at which the price increase becomes effective.[39]

The large firm also notes that there cannot be any disguised price cuts. Year-end rebates, discounts for defective products, waiving shipping charges, and free samples, to name a few, are all disruptive to the cartel and unacceptable unless agreed to ahead of time by all members, with monitoring in place to ensure compliance.[40] However, the large firm notes that larger buyers are not going to pay the same

37. The EC decision in *Rubber chemicals* at para. 187 describes the cartel's "implementation of the agreed price increases by sequential announcements to customers and/or public, the timing, order and form of which had been previously agreed upon between the competitors."

"An example of differentiated timing of the introduction of price increases is provided by the local meeting concerning Germany of 14 December 1999, where it was agreed: 'Timing: S [Schunk in this case]: 10.03.2000; S.G.L.: 31.03.2000; Mor [Morgan]: 10.04.2000.'" (EC decision in *Electrical and mechanical carbon and graphite products* at para. 107)

"At the general cartel meeting of 2 February 1995 the participants also agreed on a system for launching the price increases according to which AWA would lead the price increases and others would follow. As stated in the minutes: 'AWA will lead announcement of following increases per market. To follow, Koehler AG, Zanders, Stora, Sappi, Torras.'" (EC decision in *Carbonless paper* at para. 233)

38. The EC decision in *Citric acid* at para. 158 describes the cartel as "designating the producer which was to 'lead' price increases in each national market."

The agreement described in the EC decision in *Organic peroxides* at para. 353 included "designating the producer which was to 'lead' price increases in each national market."

The EC decision in *Rubber chemicals* at para. 235 provides this explanation: "It is quite normal that a leader of a price increase loses some market share, which is a risk that the undertaking in question voluntarily assumes in collusive situations like those in question in these proceedings. In this case, by taking turns in leading the price increases implemented in 2000 and 2001, Bayer, Crompton/Uniroyal and Flexsys could level out some of these risks and losses."

39. See Marshall, Marx, and Raiff (2008) providing the data on the timing of price announcements and effective dates for price increases for a range of cartelized vitamin products.

40. The EC decision in *Specialty graphite* at para. 352 describes the cartel as "fixing of trading conditions (premiums, discounts, billing currency, exchange rates)."

See the EC decision in *Industrial and medical gases* starting at para. 240 on the imposition of minimum shipping charges.

price as the smaller buyers.[41] It is natural to discriminate prices based on the size of the account. The large firm notes that they will coordinate on these discounts at the time of discussing their bids. Overall, the large firm notes that any component of pricing that has not been pre-cleared in a cartel meeting will be viewed as a violation of the agreement.[42]

Much of the careful coordination of price increase announcements is designed so as to have customers accept, and not resist, price increases. The large firm explains that it wants the procurement divisions investing their scarce resources in lowering the prices paid for other commodities, not the one they are selling. If a procurement division can demonstrate to a CFO of a company that the price increase was unavoidable by citing increase announcements in the trade press that are uniform across all producers, then resistance is unlikely.[43] Still, the large firm notes that how much and how frequently the price can be increased without generating resistance by buyers is a delicate issue that will require ongoing discussion by the four.[44]

41. "Merck states, 'Moreover, a price increase for the coming year was typically negotiated. It was agreed to increase by agreed percentage points both the list price for MG (established anew annually), which applied at least in Europe to smaller customers . . . , as well as the individually-negotiated prices applicable to larger customers (key accounts).'" (EC decision in *Methylglucamine* at para. 84)
  The EC decision in *Electrical and mechanical carbon and graphite products* at para. 219 states that the cartel "agreed on certain surcharges to customers, on discounts for different types of delivery and on payment conditions."
42. "No party will give prices lower than any agreed minimum prices for any product to any new customer; or reduce prices for any product to existing customers without prior discussion with the other two parties." (EC decision in *Organic peroxides* at para. 85).
43. "When BASF's customers resisted the increase, Roche supported the rise by also announcing an increase to DEM 46/kg, announced in 'Ernährungsdienst' of 13 June 1998. According to Daiichi, the concerted increase was unsuccessful because of customer resistance and the huge differential between D-calpan and the equivalent in DL-calpan." (EC decision in *Vitamins* at para. 325)
44. "At the general cartel meetings the participants decided in principle on timing and the amount (in percentage form) of the price increases for each EEA country. They agreed on several consecutive price increases and for some months ahead." (EC decision in *Carbonless paper* at para. 84)
  "Participants envisaged having a stepped increase in prices from USD 0,81/lb, to USD 0,95/lb, to USD 1,10/lb, and, if possible, finally to USD 1,20/lb." (EC decision in *Amino acids* at para. 107)
  "Aventis states, 'A discussion would follow on prices, in particular whether one of the parties had the intention of increasing its price and to what extent. None of the parties proposed significant price increases as it was understood that a product manufactured since 1956 could only support a gradual and slight increase.'" (EC decision in *Methylglucamine* at para. 85)

2.5   Sales Force Issues

The large firm reiterates that resistance by buyers is not good for the four firms because there is a good chance of a mistake by one of the four in the form of a price cut when there is substantial buyer resistance. The large firm explains that this stems from the nature of their sales forces.[45]

The large firm then notes that, up to this point, acting unilaterally each of their sales forces have largely had incentives to expand market share. Ideally, the sales forces at each firm would have incentives to increase profits. However, the sales forces do not trust their management's attribution of cost to a sale, so the compensation of the sales forces is rooted in the revenue from sales. Acting unilaterally, if any firm encumbers its sales personnel from closing a deal with a relatively small price concession, they will risk losing its best sales personnel to a competitor who authorizes them to grant price concessions to close deals. As a consequence, the commissions for all sales personnel have been largely tied to the quantity sold (subject to some limits on the extent of price concessions). In aggregate, this means the sales staff at each firm is rewarded for the acquisition of market share.

The large firm explains, in a somewhat sarcastic tone, that they cannot put out memos to the sales forces that elaborate on the nature of the agreement among the four firms. Rather, the large firm notes that each of the firms must immediately change the incentives for the sales forces. They must implement and clearly articulate a "price before tonnage" incentive scheme.[46] The sales forces will no longer be

---

45. See footnote 33 in this chapter.

46. "In their 'top-level' meeting in Zurich in September 1989, the divisional chairmen of Roche, BASF and Rhône-Poulenc had agreed to a policy of 'price before volume.'" (EC decision in *Vitamins* at para. 200)

"An illustration of the utilisation of the price targets is provided by Roche's 'pricing sheet' for vitamins A and E issued to the business units in March 1991. The objective for vitamin A was to increase prices in CHF by 5% to 10% for 1991 while balancing out the USD/DEM price differential to discourage brokers. While Managers are instructed to hold the worldwide market at 48%, they are ordered to put "price target before quantity/market share target: do not overshoot quantity by not achieving price target" c.f. the 'price before tonnage' maxim." (EC decision in *Vitamins* at paras. 206–207)

"The key to the success of the price initiatives from 1988 onwards (as the producers realized) was maintaining a near balance between production and consumption. All members of the [Presidents' Working Group (PWG)] were concerned that the relaunched price initiatives should not be undermined by substantial increases in the volume sold. This was referred to by Stora as a 'price before tonnage' policy (Stora Article 11 reply of 14 February 1992). It meant the major producers could agree on price increases in the PWG

rewarded for increasing market share. Rather, their incentives will be tied to obtaining the desired pricing on customer accounts. The large firm notes that there will be deviations from this as the sales forces adjust to the new incentives, but that the four can work out those deviations both "on the fly" and at year-end if need be.[47]

2.6 Redistributions

The large firm then explains the nature of redistributions among the four firms. If at year-end they have not achieved their worldwide market share allocations, then a "true-up" will be required.[48] The large firm offers an example. The agreed share allocations are 48.5%, 25.5%, 15.3%, and 10.7%. Suppose that at year-end the realization is 48.5%, 26.5%, 14.3%, and 10.7%. Namely, firm 2 has sold a full percentage point more than its allocation and firm 3 has sold a full percentage point less than its allocation. Then the true-up requires that the second firm buy 1 percent of world market sales from the third firm at current market prices. The large firm explains the beauty of this arrangement and thus, in part, the beauty of the market share agreement. First, the third firm is made whole per the agreement—it will have sold 15.3 percent at the cartel price. It views the true-up as fair and equitable, and sees no reason to take any kind of action that would disrupt cartel stability, such as stealing customers from the second firm by cutting price. The second firm is not happy. It is buying a large amount of a commodity at market prices that it can make in its production facilities

---

with some certainty that they would be successful. The agreement reached in the PWG during 1987 included the 'freezing' of the west European market shares of the major producers at existing levels, with no attempts to be made to win new customers or extend existing business through aggressive pricing." (EC decision in *Cartonboard* at paras. 51–52)

47. The EC decision in *Industrial and medical gases* at para. 161 indicates that a cartel member, AGA, issued internal instructions to its sales force "to focus on implementing the 5% price increase with existing customers and explaining that competitors could be expected to do the same. Were attacks by competitors nevertheless to lead to price concessions, such concessions should be reported to the management."

48. "The information for the whole year was maintained on a cumulative monthly basis to ensure that each party kept to its agreed market share; if one was seen to be selling more than its allocated quota, it would have to 'slow down' sales to enable the others to catch up. If at the end of the year a producer was substantially ahead of its quota, it had to purchase vitamins from the others in order to compensate them for the corresponding shortfall in their allocation." (EC decision in *Vitamins* at para. 196)

True-ups are described in the EC decision in *Organic peroxides* at para. 85 as: "compensation may be made at the underseller's discretion by the purchase of product/s at prices which reflect the loss of profit suffered by the underseller."

for far lower cost. But the incentive is clear—do not get ahead of your share allocation because you will find yourself having to be on the buy side of a costly true-up. The large firm points out that this keeps everyone in check with regard to the incentive to steal business from one another. At the end of the year, the theft of business from any of the other three is just going to result in a costly true-up for the thief; thus, the theft is without incremental profit.

The large firm notes that there will be other times when they will need to compensate one another. For example, the large firm notes that it wants to launch an ad campaign that advocates the benefits of their product for pregnant women.[49] The large firm notes that all four will benefit from this ad campaign, but without an agreement in place, the large firm does not want to bear all the costs of the ad campaign while garnering only its market share of the benefits. Now they can share in these industrywide expenses.

The large firm explains that simply sending cash to one another is not good, but nothing precludes them from engaging in interfirm transactions at nonmarket prices that are the equivalent of sending cash.[50] For example, suppose that a factor input for the product in question sells currently for $10/kg. If each of the other three firms buy the input from the large firm at $30/kg, they are transferring resources to the large firm.

In addition to this mechanism for transferring resources, the large firm explains that they are particularly fond of using seemingly innocent litigation for this purpose. For example, the large firm explains that they might set up "standard" business contracts with one another and then sue each other for breach, using settlements as a way to move resources among themselves. The large firm explains that no one ever objects to costly litigation being resolved by settlement, and the terms are legally kept private by mutual consent, thus providing a way to transfer resources with essentially no possibility of detection. The large

49. "Roche had kept the promise it had made when it set up its own folic acid production facility to double world demand for folic acid, but Takeda had also worked hard at creating new sales routes." (EC decision in *Vitamins* at para. 371)

50. "In 1993, the parties realised that a US producer, Coors, had a larger production capacity for vitamin B_2 than they had estimated in 1991. In order to prevent Coors from disrupting their arrangements by the export of its production surplus, Roche and BASF agreed that the former would contract to purchase 115 tonnes of vitamin B_2 (representing half of Coors's capacity) in 1993. BASF in turn would purchase 43 tonnes from Roche; the burden was thus to be shared in the same 62:38 proportion as their quotas." (EC decision in *Vitamins* at para. 287)

firm explains that later in the working of the cartel they will introduce cross-licensing of patents to assist with interfirm transfers as well,[51] but this is a more advanced topic and not needed right now. The large firm asks that the accountant/consultant remind them to introduce the use of cross-licensing in the second year of the cartel.

The large firm finally notes with regard to interfirm transfers that there is a large customer in Europe. The customer accounts for almost 5 percent of the entire European market. The large firm notes that there will need to be much discussion prior to submitting bids for that business.[52] The procurement division of this buyer is extremely aggressive and savvy. The large firm notes that the four firms may need to engage in what the large firm calls a "counterpurchasing agreement" before the bidding.[53] Namely, the large firm may need to buy a large quantity of product from one or more of the other three even before the bids are submitted to ensure that there are no deviations with respect to the agreed bids at the procurement.

2.7   Questions and Answers

After dinner the large firm reviews the general principles of their agreement: ongoing communications to implement price increases and reduce buyer resistance to price increases, modification of within-firm incentives, division of the collusive gain through a market share allocation with redistributions to address deviations from the agreement, and monitoring compliance through regular exchange of information. The large firm also notes that it has the capacity to make almost the entirety of world output on its own. The large firm notes that it can aggressively target the current customers of any of the other three or just sell so much quantity on the market that the world price

---

51. See Priest (1977).

52. The EC decision in *Food flavour enhancers* at para. 65 describes the cartel's aim of "allocating large clients in Europe."

53. See the EC decision in *Food flavour enhancers* at paras. 64, 69, 112, and 122. For example, para. 69 states: "In order to protect their sales to these major European nucleotides users, Takeda and Ajinomoto also entered into agreements with their main competitors whereby Takeda and Ajinomoto purchased product from their competitors in exchange for which the respective competitors would limit their sales to the main European nucleotides users. As Cheil puts it, 'The Japanese companies (Takeda and Ajinomoto) were to buy nucleotides from Cheil and Miwon (Daesang) respectively. In exchange, the Korean producers were supposed not to sell to the European 'big three' and were to restrict quantity to Japan.'"

tumbles.[54] But, after making this statement, the large firm notes that this is not anything it desires. It is not good for itself and not good for the other three. By cooperating, as the large firm has described, they will all benefit.

The three smaller firms have a number of questions.

• *Question 1:* Why do we have to communicate and meet so much? Why can't we simply set a production quota for each firm at the beginning of the year and agree that no one will breach their allotted production?

• *Answer 1:* It will not work. First, we cannot wait to check back with each other once a year to see if we are all complying with the agreement. There will be violations, some of us will be quite perturbed, and the redistributions required to true-up after one year might be so large that we are unwilling to do them. Also, as the market moves during the year, a set quantity may not be appropriate. If demand suddenly shifts out, no one is going to be content producing a low level of output per their allocation. If demand shifts back, then the allotted quantities will be excessive, and we will want to adjust them downward. How will we do that if we are not meeting and we have not agreed on market shares but only set production quantities? If we produced an agricultural commodity, it might make sense to specify a total acreage to plant for each of us at the beginning of the year and then let the market do what it does.[55] But we are not confronting an agricultural market with a single uniform price and with buyers who are used to price volatility. Our buyers expect some regularity in price, and they will fight sudden price jumps.

• *Question 2:* How can I rely on the information reported by the other firms? I am not saying that they are liars, but we can all see the incentive to misreport our production and sales numbers and thereby chisel on the agreement.

• *Answer 2:* Partly, we will rely on everyone's realization that misrepresenting information could potentially lead to the disintegration of the

---

54. "AWA's financial and industrial weight enabled him to say that if any of these increases were not passed on AWA would make it its business to push the market right down by applying a price policy that would leave most people high and dry. He showed quite clearly what he was capable of by crushing Binda in Italy." (EC decision in *Carbonless paper* at para. 104)

55. See for example, the description of the rubber industry in Stocking and Watkins (1991).

cartel. Also our accountants/consultants will be doing their best to verify the data you report. You will be confronted with import/export statistics as well as data made available by agents of the accounting/consulting firm who are monitoring the trucks and railcars leaving each of your production facilities. Each of us might be able to get away with a minor misrepresentation, but there will be some explaining to do if your numbers are much less or consistently less than what our accountants/consultants are recording from their sources. If necessary, we can arrange for audits of each other's information.[56]

• *Question 3:* Some cartels post bonds and then use cash penalties rather than using true-ups.[57] Do we need to do that?

• *Answer 3:* If our products were sufficiently differentiated that one firm could not pass the other firm's product off as its own or if transport costs were extremely high, then cash penalties might be preferred over true-ups. But in our case, we can rely on true-ups and other transactions to correct any deviations from agreed-to market shares.

• *Question 4:* We are all aware of antitrust laws. How can we avoid prosecution? We are aware of amnesty programs. How can we trust one another not to "rat out" the cartel?

• *Answer 4:* There are several components to the response. First, our accountant/consultants will keep all records. The accounting/consulting firm will reimburse all of us for all travel expenses when we get together to discuss cartel business.[58] Never submit cartel meeting

---

56. "Indeed, in the French market meeting held on 6 December 1994 there was some disagreement between the cartel members on the accuracy of price increase and volume information exchanged in the course of the meeting. In order to verify the figures submitted, [an AWA employee], who doubted the figures supplied by Sarrió (Torraspapel), had asked and received permission to audit the information on Sarrió's sales volumes on Sarrió's premises." (EC decision in *Carbonless paper* at para. 106) (Note: AWA was the largest carbonless paper producer in Europe.)

"The auditors of each producer certified the total sales of pipes during the year, and the certificates were then exchanged among the cartel participants." (EC decision in *Pre-insulated pipe* at para. 33)

57. See Stocking and Watkins (1991, pp. 183, 190) on the steel cartel's use of a "common fund." See Stocking and Watkins (1991, pp. 232, 253, 264) on the Aluminum Alliance's use of "guarantee deposits" that were proportional to the members' sales quotas. See Stocking and Watkins (1991, p. 337) on the incandescent electric lamp cartel's payment of penalties guaranteed by the deposit of "indemnity funds" at a Swiss corporation. Finally, see *U.S.* v. *American Linseed Oil Co.*

58. As described in the EC decision in *Organic peroxides* at para. 92, AC-Treuhand "reimbursed the travel expenses of the participants, in order to avoid traces of these meetings in the companies' accounts." For more on the role of third-party facilitators, see the appendix to chapter 6.

receipts to your firm for reimbursement. Send them to the accounting/consulting firm. That firm will also issue special cell phones for us to use. We will frequently meet in Switzerland, but that will be fine because we will be creating a technical subcommittee of our trade association within the next few days that will be located close to our accounting/consulting firm. If ever asked, our Switzerland trips are to address the important issues on the agenda of that subcommittee. When we meet, no one should take notes. The accounting/consulting firm will keep track of everything.

Let me also note that a large number of cartels have functioned for years without being detected, all the time enjoying high profitability. It is natural to be nervous about what one observes in terms of prosecutions, and authorities boast of each one, but actual apprehensions and prosecutions of cartels are relatively small.[59]

But suppose we do get apprehended one day in the future. Then there will be lots of excitement and commotion, and we will be talking to lawyers frequently. However, in the end, after paying all fines, if we do things right for the next few years, we will be much further ahead financially than if we do not form a cartel now. You hear of triple damages, but the fact is that no one pays triple damages. At best, it is a threat, but it is never realized. Finally, you may be concerned about the threat of jail time. It is a remote possibility, but I think everyone in this room can endure the hardship of a minimum security facility for a brief period. In all honesty, each of us takes bigger risks in terms of potential prosecution with regard to other aspects of our business decisions such as environmental law, product liability, insider trading, or consumer fraud, to name a few. It is our job to walk up to the boundar-

59. As reported in *The New York Times,* "When Kuno Sommer, head of marketing in the vitamins and fine chemicals devision of Roche, a key participant in the meetings on citric acid, was questioned by Federal agents in March 1997, he denied that there was any price-fixing in vitamins. Federal agents later discovered, according to the Government's settlement documents, that before the 1997 interview, Mr. Sommer had 'met separately with at least two other high-level Roche executives. At the end of those meetings, it was understood by the individual that if Sommer was asked about Roche's participation in a vitamins cartel, Sommer would lie and deny that such a cartel existed.' By that time, private antitrust lawyers had already begun their own investigation in hopes of winning a huge settlement. Among their findings was a memo Mr. Sommer had written in September 1993 that suggested a continuing price-fixing scheme. 'Good experience with citric acid,' Mr. Sommer wrote before a meeting with Archer executives. 'Next opportunity B₂. We think it's worth that we explore all possibilities of cooperation. Let's explore cooperation product-by-product.'" ("Tearing Down The Façade of 'Vitamins Inc.'" *New York Times,* October 10, 1999).

ies of what is, and what is not, legal and discretely venture across the line if we think it is in the best interest of our shareholders. The cartel proposed here is just one such discrete venture.

We could also consider forming an export association to cover our communications. In the United States, if firms making a particular product can demonstrate that their export activities will have no bearing on U.S. commerce, then they can form into a legal cartel for the purposes of export. The firms in the export association can discuss and reach agreements about a whole range of issues, where these communications and agreements would be per se violations of the antitrust laws in the United States. Because their discussions and agreements are targeted at foreign countries, the activity is legal within the rules of U.S. export associations. What specifically can be discussed? Examples of activities that may be certified include joint establishment of export prices; exclusive agreements with domestic suppliers and/or foreign representatives; joint export marketing/selling arrangements among domestic competitors; allocation of export markets, territories, or customers; refusals to deal; exchanges of business information; and the joint licensing of technology.[60] Once an export association has been formed, then the members can talk about all of these issues with regard to any foreign country. It is a rather trivial matter for us to choose a single foreign country and designate it as meaning "United States." We will have, to a great extent, cover from antitrust laws through the export association in doing so. And law enforcement agencies would have a remarkably difficult time to learn that, say, "Costa Rica" meant United States for all of us.

• *Question 5:* We each have production facilities in different countries and regions of the world. Why don't we declare those regions as being the sole property of the cartel member who produces there and then divide up the rest of the world by market shares?

• *Answer 5:* With some other cartels this would make sense. It is often more difficult to monitor the activities of firms within their home countries because import/export data are not relevant. If the value to

---

60. See the website of the U.S. Department of Commerce's International Trade Administration for information on the Export Trade Certificate of Review: "The Export Trade Certificate of Review provides substantive federal antitrust protection and procedural benefits to U.S. firms interested in collaborating on export activities. By coordinating with one another under the legal protection of this program, U.S. firms can reduce their shipping costs, boost their negotiating power, fill large export orders, and develop long-term export business." (http://trade.gov/mas/ian/etca/index.asp, accessed October 7, 2011)

weight ratio of our product were low, and transport costs were a big issue, we might allocate home countries to domestic producers.[61] Also, home country allocations are a good way to threaten firms if you think that deviations might be likely.[62] Firms in many industries have good marketing and distribution in their home country, but these essential factors are less well developed for them in foreign countries. Attacking a firm on its home turf is certain to get its attention. In this industry, we have a high value to weight ratio, and we have relatively sophisticated marketing and distribution resources worldwide. Thus, a home country allocation does not seem appropriate. Although we will all do our best to respect home producer incumbency, we must not lose sight of the fact that our worldwide market share allocation is what really matters.

• *Question 6:* The market share allocations make me nervous. Can't we just agree on price increases and leave it at that? Then we do not have to exchange so much information, and we do not have to meet so often.

61. Choline chloride has a low value to weight ratio (see the EC decision in *Choline chloride* at para. 39), and cartel participants agreed to "allocate markets worldwide among the participating undertakings, including an agreement that the North American producers would withdraw from the European market." (EC decision in *Choline chloride* at para. 64).
    "Furthermore, at least in 1991, Ajinomoto, Kyowa and Sewon agreed to the home-market principle, i.e., that the local producer should sell as much as possible in its own region." (EC decision in *Amino acids* at para. 211)
    The EC decision in *Food flavour enhancers* at para. 65 describes "respecting each other's markets" as an aim of the cartel.
62. "The other participants said that if Sewon persisted in implementing its increase, then they would all increase their sales as well. Moreover, ADM threatened to increase its sales on the Korean market from 1000 t per year to 5000 t per year if Sewon persisted in raising its worldwide sales to 50,000 t. ADM also said that it could force the standard price of lysine down to USD 1,30/kg in order to force Sewon back to the negotiating table." (EC decision in *Amino acids* at para. 148)
    "The multinational nature of the industrial gases groups is also important because, as has been shown in the analysis of the market structure in Part I section A.5(c) there is abundant information in the Commission's file that retaliation against competitors which 'steal' customers by undercutting prices is a normal feature in the industrial gases industry. There is also evidence that such retaliation is not necessarily confined to the Member State or region where the 'aggression' was committed. On the contrary, many undertakings consider such retaliation most effective if carried out on a broad basis, preferably on the home market of the 'aggressor' in question. Therefore, an undertaking in the industrial gases sector in the Netherlands which participated in the infringements and failed to respect the agreements depicted in this Decision risked retaliation not only in the Netherlands but in other Member States as well." (EC decision in *Industrial and medical gases* at para. 372)

- *Answer 6:* This will not work. Let's review some basic things. There is a demand curve for our product. It is relatively inelastic, but it still slopes downward. The demand curve does not sit still through time. It moves around, and it does so in a way that is hard to predict. At any point in time, we can set a price, or we can set a total quantity to produce by all of us, but we do not have the luxury of setting both. However, we can set a price and then whatever the corresponding quantity demanded turns out to be, now and over the next year, we can divide that among ourselves per a market share agreement. Note that we cannot set a price and then also set a fixed quantity to divide among us, unless someone has a crystal ball that will tell us market demand conditions over the entire next year.

Suppose that we only agree on a price. My firm wants to sell as much as it can at that price. So do each of your firms. That is bound to lead to price degradation. We have to do something beyond just talking about prices. We have to introduce something that we all perceive as fair but that will also address our natural incentives to chisel on our agreement. That is one of the beauties of the market share allocation. With good monitoring of one another, anyone who chisels on the market share agreement by trying to sell beyond their allotted share will confront a true-up in the near future where they are buying product from another firm at the cartel price. Our joint commitment must be to four things: the price we set, the market share agreement, the complete revelation of relevant information to one another, and the willingness to redistribute gains and losses should issues arise. This foursome will work. Without a market share agreement, we should all go home and return to business as usual, ruinous noncollusive competition among ourselves.

- *Question 7:* Do we need to use the accountant/consultant? I do not want there to be yet someone else involved with this. Can't we do this business entirely among ourselves?

- *Answer 7:* It can be done without the services of the accounting/consulting firm. But that would be a poor choice. If we insist on that, then a couple things must be kept in mind. First, we will be leaving a paper trail as we meet to discuss cartel business. Everyone will need to do what they can to reduce that paper trail.[63] Shred documents as

---

63. "For this period, price, discount and volume agreements were always concluded orally, either during meetings or by phone. After instructions had been passed on, written notes were destroyed. If anyone sent notes to one of the participants, this person was reminded by phone to destroy the paper." (EC decision in *Copper plumbing tubes* at para. 129)

soon as possible. Keep notes to a minimum. Second, one of us will need to take on the role of being the central collector and depository of information. That firm will be incurring some extra expenses, so we will need to think about providing that firm with payments that otherwise would have gone to the accounting/consulting firm.

- *Question 8:* What about a competitive fringe? When we raise prices, we are potentially going to see some effort by others to enter our industry.
- *Answer 8:* Our market share agreement will apply to the relative shares among the cartel members. If the competitive fringe is small, we can live and let live. If the competitive fringe grows large, we will figure it out as we go. One possibility is to preemptively buy out the competition.[64] If we anticipate growth of the competitive fringe, we can take steps to encumber that growth.[65]

We need to think about potential entry as we consider our price increases. We may all agree that we can increase price by some amount, say 20 percent, but if that increase induces substantial entry into our industry, then we have probably pushed the price increase too hard. We will revisit this issue regularly.

- *Question 9:* Isn't the price announcement strategy, which involves the public announcement of identical price increases, going to catch the eye of law enforcement?
- *Answer 9:* Public law enforcement can only detect a cartel if one of us admits to being in a cartel and presents the law enforcement authorities with condemning documents. There is no industrial equivalent of the NYSE's Stock Watch program, which looks for insider and other illegal trading. The DoJ, FTC, and EC have no resources to monitor price announcements, capacity utilization, market shares, or anything else over a broad range of industries.

Furthermore, we will always prepare for questions from law enforcement authorities at our cartel meetings. We can defeat any investigation into our pricing conduct by the competition authorities by invoking the defense of oligopolistic interdependence and citing "justifications" for

64. The EC decision in *Organic peroxides* at para. 353 describes one principle aspect of the cartel as "the co-ordinated acquisition of competing companies which were not part of the agreement."
65. The EC decision in *Graphite electrodes* at para. 110 describes one aspect of the cartel as "limiting the transfer of technology outside the cartel."

price increases, where the "justifications" have been discussed and agreed upon at our last cartel meeting. We will have our story straight before we are asked, in anticipation of being asked.[66]

• *Question 10:* Do we need market leaders for the various regional and national markets?

• *Answer 10:* It depends. Assigning a cartel leader for individual customers can make sense if the customers are large.[67] We may consider this in the future.

• *Question 11:* In reviewing some of the U.S. Department of Justice and European Commission decisions regarding cartels, it seems clear that there is no one set formula for running a cartel. *Cartonboard* and *Food flavour enhancers* had some noticeably different components to their cartel mechanisms than what is being proposed for us. Why are these components not relevant for us?

• *Answer 11:* We will draw upon the experiences of all cartels. The accounting/consulting firm will be a big help in that regard. They have assisted numerous cartels in many industries. Their knowledge about what works, and what does not work, far exceeds the highly censored and incomplete information in U.S. Department of Justice and European Commission decisions.

You mentioned *Cartonboard.* That is a 24/7 production process where firms are either producing full-out or nothing. That production process has a big impact on the implementation of a collusive agreement. A supply restriction can only be implemented by shutting down production facilities. This is a highly visible and lumpy way to restrict supply. In *Cartonboard,* once the supply restriction had been in place, much less monitoring of production was required because firms just return to 24/7 production. Our production process is not 24/7. We have much greater flexibility in terms of weekly capacity utilization. As a consequence, monitoring of one another is much more important for us.

---

66. The EC decision in *Cartonboard* at para. 73 describes how cartel members believed they could use oligopolistic interdependence as a defense for certain of their actions. For the text of this paragraph, see chapter 4.3.

Recent research by Marshall, Marx, and Raiff (2008) identifies differences between noncooperative and collusive price leadership.

67. On the assignment of market leaders or account leaders, see the EC decisions in *Industrial tubes* at para. 195, *Copper plumbing tubes* at para. 449, and *Electrical and mechanical carbon and graphite products* at para. 219.

You also mentioned *Food flavour enhancers*. That cartel confronted a small number of very large purchasers. The central cartel problem was how to construct credible and stable ways to avert cheating by cartel members. In that case, undercutting the cartel and winning a contract from a firm that purchased 25 percent of total output would be difficult to correct after the fact. Even our largest buyer is relatively much smaller, and they purchase frequently. We have to be concerned about the temptation to cheat, but the payoff is small relative to what it was in *Food flavour enhancers*. Therefore, the counterpurchasing agreements that occurred in *Food flavour enhancers* are something that we will probably not do except perhaps for our largest customer, although the accounting/consulting firm understands when and how to do them, and they may recommend that we consider them at some future date.

- *Question 12:* If we are criminally prosecuted, what will the economic experts be looking for with regard to establishing civil damages?
- *Answer 12:* They will likely be looking for a benchmark period where they can be fairly certain we were not colluding. They will use the benchmark period to create a but-for prediction of prices during the period in which we admit collusion. There are two aspects of this that we will use to our advantage should we get to that point.

First, the public authorities want big criminal fines. But, to get us to agree to big criminal fines, we will want to specify a number of things such as the period of the collusion, the buyers who were affected, the product scope of our agreement, and perhaps the geographies where the cartel operated. The public authorities will likely yield to our requests with regard to the latter components of a plea agreement because they want the big criminal fines, but these latter components will be structured in a maximally disadvantageous way for civil plaintiffs so that, in aggregate, what we pay in criminal and civil fines will be much lower.[68]

---

68. "Canada added that in its experience in negotiations of plea agreements and fines the competition authority might be willing to narrow the scope of the guilty plea in light of possible subsequent civil action, and might seek a relatively higher fine to compensate for the reduced charge to ensure that the fine was adequate in light of the volume of affected commerce. In the consent agreement the level of the fine might appear distorted because the trade off struck between lesser charge and higher fine might not be apparent to the outside observer." (Organisation for Economic Co-operation and Development, Working Party No. 3 on Co-operation and Enforcement, October 13, 2006, "Private Remedies: Class Action / Collective Action, Interface Between Private and Public Enforcement," DAF/COMP/WP3/M(2006)2/ANN3 at para. 45)

Second, we need to purge from our records all information that would allow a reasonable estimate of a but-for price from a benchmark period. All older transaction data needs to be discarded, or transferred to our accountant/consultant, who can archive it should you need it for some purpose in the future. You will not be able to access that data without going to the firm's Swiss location and working there.

3   Narrative of a Bidding Ring

3.1   Preamble

This chapter deals with collusion at auctions by bidding rings. Bid rigging is a violation of the Sherman Act for both auctions and procurements. A large amount of bidding in the United States occurs at auctions, especially ascending-bid auctions.[1] For example, tobacco, timber, art, antiques, the assets of many bankrupt firms, and numerous other commodities are sold via ascending-bid auctions.[2]

In this chapter, we provide a fictional account of a bidding ring operating at an ascending-bid auction. Footnotes indicate similarities between our story and known bidding cartels, including stamps,[3] antiques,[4] machinery,[5] and real estate.[6]

In the previous chapter, we focused on cartels. In order for an industrial cartel, such as the vitamins cartel, to implement a collusive scheme,

1. First-price sealed-bid auctions and procurements account for a significant amount of economic activity as well. Bidder collusion is common at these. In chapter 1, we provide an example of collusion at a first-price sealed-bid auction. Compared to first-price sealed-bid collusive mechanisms, mechanisms for collusion by bidders at ascending-bid auctions provide a better vehicle for explaining how bidders accomplish the suppression of competition.
2. Theoretical results for ascending-bid auctions also apply to procurements conducted via "reverse auctions," where the bids decline until there is only one supplier willing to provide the good at the indicated price.
3. *NY et al.* v. *Feldman et al.*, 210 F. Supp.2d 294 (S.D.N.Y. 2002) (hereafter, *NY* v. *Feldman*).
4. *U.S.* v. *Ronald Pook*, No. 87–274, 1988 U.S. Dist. LEXIS 3398 (E.D. Pa. April 18, 1988) (hereafter *U.S.* v. *Ronald Pook*).
5. *U.S.* v. *Seville Industrial Machinery Corp.*, 696 F. Supp. 986 (D.N.J. 1988) (hereafter *U.S.* v. *Seville Industrial Machinery*).
6. *District of Columbia, ex rel. John Payton, Corporation Counsel* v. *George Basiliko, et al.*, No. 91–2518, 1992 U.S. Dist. LEXIS 1260 (D.C. February 10, 1992) (hereafter *District of Columbia* v. *George Basiliko*).

it typically must orchestrate cartel bids at procurements. That said, no one would characterize the vitamins cartel as a bidding ring. A bidding ring's central focus is the suppression of competition at an auction or procurement. Typically, a bidding ring "squares up" the allocation of the collusive gain shortly after each auction or procurement through side payments or interfirm arrangements such as subcontracts or joint ownership. The line between bidding rings and cartels becomes blurry when, for example, colluding bidders use a bid-rotation scheme that relies on a market share agreement to determine which bidders are supposed to win particular procurements.[7]

Overall, colluding firms will strive to do what is minimally necessary to be profitable. For vitamin producers, rigging bids alone would not be adequate to prevent deviant conduct by cartel members because each firm would have an incentive to secretly sell additional product outside of the context of standard procurements. A market share agreement, with the associated monitoring and redistributions, eliminates this incentive. In other environments, rigging bids may be all that is required. For example, if a seller offers a fixed number/type of items at an auction without reserve, then secret deals to purchase incremental units are not relevant.

3.2   The Instruction Begins

We describe a fictional bidding ring that frequently participates at auctions to acquire items. The items might be stamps, used industrial metal-working machinery, antiques, or a number of other products. For the purposes of this exposition, we focus on antiques.[8] Our use of the example of antiques is solely for expositional purposes, and much of what we discuss in this chapter illustrates fundamental principles of bidder collusion.

The members of our bidding ring frequently appear at antique auctions in a particular geographic area to attempt to acquire items from estates. An experienced member of this ring, an antiques dealer, has an employee that he wants to train to represent the firm at the auctions as a member of the bidding ring. The experienced member of the ring provides a tutorial for the employee in which he explains the funda-

---

7. One example is the electrical contractors conspiracy, which is sometimes referred to as the "phases of the moon" conspiracy. See Richard A. Smith, "The Incredible Electrical Conspiracy," *Fortune*, April 1961, 63, 132–80, and May 1961, 63, 161–224.
8. A bidding ring of antiques dealers was prosecuted in *U.S.* v. *Ronald Pook*.

mental principles of the ring. The experienced bidder begins his instruction as follows.

3.3 Two Motivations for the Ring

I do not want you to take any notes today. We are going to talk about a number of things regarding auctions and how our firm buys antiques at auctions. Just listen and I will let you know when it is appropriate to ask questions. To start with, I am going to talk generally about why this is important to our business. Then we will move on to the details of how things operate.

You probably have not noticed, but at some of the auctions you have attended, there is a group of antique dealers who are not bidding as individuals, but rather as a group. The antique dealers in this region have a bidding ring. In a nutshell, we suppress competition among ourselves to keep auction prices lower. There are two central motivations for our behavior. I will call these scenarios 1 and 2.

3.3.1 Scenario 1: Symmetric Information Regarding Quality

Suppose a Chippendale highboy is being sold.[9] It is a good reproduction and somewhat valuable, but nevertheless a reproduction. I recognize that some refurbishment will be required to bring out the full value of the piece. It is clear that other dealers will know the piece is a reproduction. Some other dealers who have similar pieces already in stock will have a very low value for the item. Those who think it would be a good addition to their inventory will have higher but different values because dealer costs of refurbishment will differ.

Collectors attending the auction will have much less ability to cost-effectively refurbish an antique, especially a large piece like a highboy. Thus, the dealers will have a cost advantage even though a collector will typically have a higher value than the dealers once the piece is refurbished.

By bidding as part of a ring, we protect the return to our investment in refurbishment capability as well as our investment in our retailing ability (showroom, customer contacts, etc.). Furthermore, given the large number of pieces that come up at a typical auction, demand among collectors is more random than among dealers. A given dining

9. A "highboy" is a tall chest of drawers. A specific highboy was a focus of some of the court argument in *U.S. v. Ronald Pook*, p. 4.

room set may be of no interest to any collector in the bidding audience, but some group of dealers will always be willing to take the item into inventory. By forming into a ring, we suppress the competition among ourselves for pieces for which we are essentially the only bidders present.

3.3.2 Scenario 2: Asymmetric Information Regarding Quality

Suppose that the item being sold is an authentic Chippendale highboy circa 1780 that was made by a renowned Boston craftsman. If it is obvious to almost everyone that this is an authentic period piece, then we are essentially in scenario 1, where dealers and collectors have similar information and dealers have relatively minor differences in their values for the piece based on differences in their costs of refurbishment.

But suppose that it is not obvious that this is an authentic period piece. Suppose that the highboy has been listed incorrectly in the auction bulletin as a reproduction and, furthermore, that the piece is in somewhat rough condition. My inspection reveals that some bad reconditioning has been done in the past that has diminished the value of the piece, but the reconditioning has also made the piece appear to be a basic reproduction to all but the most trained and experienced eye. Based on my expertise, I know what it is going to take to get maximal value from the highboy. Three of our antique dealer competitors, who have equivalent expertise to me with regard to pieces like this, will almost surely also recognize it as an authentic piece.[10] However, no one else will recognize it as an authentic piece.

In this scenario, the four expert dealers would forfeit the returns to their expertise if we bid against one another at the auction. Additionally, our competitive bidding would convey our assessment of the authenticity of the piece to the less expert dealers and collectors, who would then enter the competition against us. Naturally, in the normal course of business, I would not volunteer an assessment of the authenticity of the item as if it were a free piece of information, but when expert dealers bid competitively against one another, that is exactly what we do.

The Chippendale highboy might be worth $2,000 if it were not an authentic period piece, but if two expert dealers bid against one another,

10. Cassady (1967, p. 180): "Probably the expert making the original discovery would be able to guess the identity of the knowledgeable individuals among the antique dealers known to him."

driving the price up to $25,000, we tell the auctioneer, all the collectors, and everybody else at the auction that we have made a determination that this is an authentic period piece of high quality. By bidding against one another, we have diminished our own profits and provided a free appraisal to everybody in the market, and thereby empowered others to bid because we removed concerns about authenticity. To protect our informational advantage and secure the appropriate return on our hard-earned expertise, we agree not to bid against one another.

The majority of the volume we encounter falls under scenario 1. However, although scenario 2 is far less common, it can be quite profitable. Overall, by bidding as part of a ring, we protect the return to our expertise and investments, which in scenario 1 relates to refurbishment and in scenario 2 concerns the actual nature and quality of items.

3.4   Ring Logistics

We will now go through the logistics of what we do in the ring. The ring has been around for many years and its membership is quite fluid.[11] Essentially, almost every antique dealer in this region of the country is a member of the ring.

3.4.1   Ring Bidding

The auctions we attend are largely oral, ascending-bid auctions. During these auctions, you will observe that a number of different dealers place bids, but when any ring member bids, no other member of the ring will raise the price. If one ring member drops out of the bidding, then some other ring member may enter, but two ring members will not bid against one another. That simple bidding rule suppresses competition among ring members, and it allows us to win every item for which a ring member has a higher value than the bidders outside the ring. If a ring member has the highest value for an item among all bidders at the auction, then the ring will win the item.

Once a member of the ring wins an item, then the ring determines its final ownership. A member of the ring who wins an item at the main auction does not own it. A ring member who wins at the auction has an obligation to pay the auctioneer for the item because the auctioneer views that person as the owner of item. But a ring member winning an

---

11. This is a characteristic of rings at many ascending-bid auctions. This is unlike cartels, as well as rings at first-price auctions.

object must bring the object to what is called a "knockout" after the auction to allow others in the ring the opportunity to obtain ownership of that item. Ultimate ownership is determined at the knockout. (Knockouts were used in *U.S. v. Ronald Pook*,[12] *U.S. v. Seville Industrial Machinery*,[13] *District of Columbia* v. *George Basiliko*,[14] and *NY* v. *Feldman*.[15])

12. As stated in *U.S. v. Ronald Pook*: "When a dealer pool was in operation at a public auction of consigned antiques, those dealers who wished to participate in the pool would agree not to bid against the other members of the pool. If a pool member succeeded in purchasing an item at the public auction, pool members interested in that item could bid on it by secret ballot at a subsequent private auction ('knock out') . . . . The pool member bidding the highest at the private auction claimed the item by paying each pool member bidding a share of the difference between the public auction price and the successful private bid. The amount paid to each pool member ('pool split') was calculated according to the amount the pool member bid in the knock out." (*U.S. v. Ronald Pook*, p. 1)

13. The mechanism used by the industrial machinery bidding ring of *U.S. v. Seville Industrial Machinery* in the period after 1970 was similar to that used in *U.S. v. Ronald Pook*. Some dealers of used industrial metal-working machinery from the New York, New Jersey, Pennsylvania, and Connecticut area regularly formed a ring to suppress bids at bankruptcy/liquidation auctions. The auctions typically used an ascending-bid format. If a ring member won an item at the main auction, that member was obligated to bring it up for sale at another auction which occurred after the main auction that was attended by only ring members. The results of this latter auction process, called a "knockout," determined the ultimate ownership of the item and the division of the collusive gain. (Prior to 1970 members of the ring were given an opportunity to make vague indications of interest prior to the auction, and then only the ring organizer submitted bids at the auction based on his educated guess about the likely high value for the object from among the ring members.) (*U.S. v. Seville Industrial Machinery*) See also Marshall and Meurer (2004).

14. The decision for the real estate bidding ring in *District of Columbia* v. *George Basiliko* states: "the defendants and the co-conspirators discussed and agreed . . . not to compete with one another to win the bid; selected a designated bidder to act for the conspirators . . . ; discussed and agreed on specific payoffs that conspirators present would receive for not bidding, or discussed and agreed to hold a private, secret auction among themselves after the designated bidder won the public real estate auction . . . ; in many instances, held a secret auction in which the conspirators bid solely among themselves to acquire the property for a price higher than the price paid by the designated bidder at the public real estate auction and agreed to divide the difference between the public real estate auction price and the secret auction price by making payoffs among the conspirators; arranged by contract or other means for the secret auction winner to take title or ownership of the property; and made the payoffs that they had agreed to make." (*District of Columbia* v. *George Basiliko*, p. 6)

15. In the collectable stamp bidding ring of *NY* v. *Feldman*, "The ring used an internal auction or 'knockout' to coordinate bidding. Ring members would send a fax or supply a written bid to an agent (a New York taxi and limousine driver employed by the ring), indicating the lots in which they were interested, and what they were willing to bid for them in the knockout auction. The taxi driver would then collate all the bids, determine the winner of each lot, notify the ring as to the winners in the knockout and send the bids to another ring member who would coordinate the sidepayments after the target auction was concluded. Depending on who actually won the knockout, the taxi driver

3.4.2   Ring Knockout

I will now explain how the knockout works. Suppose that members of the ring have won fifty items at the auction: highboys, lowboys, sofas, love seats, dining room sets, mirrors, lamps, tables, and chairs. After the auction is over, all of the items are brought to the knockout for determination of ultimate ownership among members of the ring. The knockout is a separate auction that is conducted after the main auction. The only participants at the knockout are ring members.

Often, I assume the role of the auctioneer at the knockout. I am also a bidder as a member of the ring. The knockout auctioneer calls up the first item that was won at the main auction by the ring. Suppose that is a Federal-style dining room set that sold for $38,000 at the main auction. The knockout auctioneer solicits what are called "bonus bids." These are bids from ring members in excess of $38,000.

Suppose I enter a bonus bid of $1,000. If the bonus bidding stopped there, then I would have to reimburse the original buyer the $38,000 that he paid for the item, plus I would have to put $1,000 "into the hat." I will explain what we do with the money that goes "into the hat" in a moment.

Suppose instead that the bonus bidding does not stop at $1,000, but rather ends with my bid of $20,000. Then I pay the ring member who won the item at the main auction $38,000, and in addition I put $20,000 "into the hat." If there is no bonus bidding, then the ring member who won the object at the main auction keeps it and nothing is put into the "hat."

As we go through this process for the remaining forty-nine items, we build up a lot of "hat" money. At the end of the day, the "hat" money is divided up among all the members of the ring.

At the last auction we went to, there were ten members of the ring and the "hat" money was approximately $500,000. That money was divided equally, so we each walked away with $50,000 in "hat" money.

---

would, usually, either bid for the winner in the target auction, using the bid supplied in that auction as the upper limit, or organize for another auction agent to bid for the winner on the same basis. In the language of auction theory, the knockout was conducted using a sealed-bid format, with the winning bidder getting the right to own the lot should it be won by the ring in the target auction. The winning bid in the knockout set the stopping point for the ring's bidding in the target auction. Since bidding in the target auction was handled by the ring's agent, monitoring compliance with this policy was not a problem. Sidepayments were used by the ring to compensate ring members for not competing for a lot, when the ring was successful in winning that lot." Asker (2008, p. 4)

Without a ring, much of that money would have been paid to the auctioneer. Instead, it was kept within the ring.

A wonderful part of the process is that we do not need to have any discussion ahead of time about who is planning to bid on what, the maximum price we are willing to bid up to, or anything else. The rule for bidding at the main auction is extremely simple—if any member of the ring is bidding on an item, then no other member of the ring bids against him or her.

Nested Knockout

There are some subtleties associated with the knockout that we need to cover. Antique dealers are all different. I am a relatively powerful, wealthy, experienced dealer. There are others who are far less experienced, far less wealthy, and do not know as much. Everybody who is a dealer makes a contribution to the ring by not bidding at the main auction. But those contributions are different. My contribution is much bigger than that of a less experienced dealer. To capture that in terms of the payoff we get from suppressing our bids, we sometimes run a "nested knockout."[16]

A nested knockout can be illustrated in a simple example. Suppose that there are three powerful, experienced, wealthy dealers, while there are seven lesser dealers. The items we won at the main auction go to the knockout, where the three dealers who are more experienced and wealthy form a ring using the same rules as at the main auction in terms of the implementation—if any member of this inner ring of three is bidding at the knockout, then neither of the other two bids. If one of the seven not in the inner ring wins the item at the knockout, then we apply the same rules as before—bonus money is put into the "hat" and divided equally on that item. But, if one of the three from the inner ring

---

16. Cassady (1967, p. 182): " . . . not only is there a ring whose purpose is to eliminate competition in the public auction, but a ring within the ring for the purpose of paying off unimportant members on the basis of a modest enhancement in price, thus leaving most of the advantage to those in the inner circle."

In the court's decision in the matter of *U.S. v. Seville Industrial Machinery*, there was an expression of astonishment at the lack of cooperation among members of the cartel. The court noted that the cartel had subcartels and that the subcartels would often bid collusively against those not in the subcartel at the knockout. Subcartels were often nested, namely a subcartel within a larger subcartel within another, and so on, where there would be as many knockouts as levels of nesting. The court viewed the subcartels as a kind of collusive cannibalism: "If the evidence presented in this case is indicative of the ethics of this or any segment of the business community, then we should weep for its existence and fear for its future." (*U.S. v. Seville Industrial Machinery*, p. 993)

wins the item, then bonus money still goes into the "hat" and is still divided up, but after the knockout there will be a second knockout, where only the three dealers in the inner ring participate. The items at this second knockout will be those items that these three won at the first knockout. At the second knockout, the three inner ring members bid competitively in terms of bonus bids.

As an example, suppose that at the main auction $38,000 was paid for the item. Suppose that one of the inner three wins the item at the first knockout for a $5,000 bonus bid, and at the second knockout there was a $10,000 winning bonus bid. The first $5,000 gets divided equally among all ten bidders participating in the ring. The next $10,000 of bonus bid is divided among the inner three only. It is in this way that we ensure that the payoffs from participation in the ring are commensurate with the contribution of each individual to the profitability of the ring.

Some rings prefer to use a sealed-bid knockout, where the high bonus bidder wins, but the payments to each ring member depend on their bonus bids. In this case, the effects of a nested knockout can be achieved directly.[17]

Knockout Bidding Incentives

There is another subtlety of the bidding at the knockout that you need to know. You have to be careful what you reveal during the bonus bidding process. If you convey to the other bidders that we have a customer interested in a particular Federal-style dining room set, perhaps by being somewhat anxious or making some open comment about how this would be great for us to acquire, it is guaranteed that you are going to be run-up in bonus bidding at the knockout as ring members attempt to extract as much of our profits as possible. Because

17. As shown by Graham, Marshall, and Richard (1990), these payments can be designed so that each ring member receives its imputed Shapley value (a measure of its contribution to the ring).

The knockout scheme used by the stamp cartel described in Asker (2010) was conducted using a variant of the nested knockout studied by Graham, Marshall and Richard (1990). "Sidepayments were used by the ring to compensate ring members for not competing for a lot, when the ring was successful in winning that lot. . . . Thus the sidepayments involve ring members sharing each increment between bids, provided that their bids are above the target auction price. Half the increment is kept by the winner of the knockout, and the balance is shared equally between those bidders who bid equal to or more than the 'incremental' bid. The sidepayments were aggregated and settled on a quarterly basis." Asker (2010, pp. 727–28)

of this, you must not convey information of any sort about our level of interest in an item.

Because of the incentive to run-up the bonus bidding, there can be "overbidding" at the knockout.[18] Even if I am not interested in an item, I may bid up the bonus bid just because I get a piece of it. If I think the probability is low enough that I would actually win something, but I can increase my payoff a couple thousand dollars by putting in a bonus bid, that is something I will do. This incentive is there for everybody, so you get over-bidding at the knockout. Although everybody will say how lousy the item is and how much work it will take to make it right, you must ignore that. It is just talk to keep the bonus bidding under control.

3.5 Ring Membership

You might have noticed a few months ago that there was someone who appeared at an auction and was bidding quite aggressively for certain items. This was a dealer who had come in from a different region of the country. Prices were ascending to levels that made us extremely uncomfortable for a number of reasons. First, we do not like paying that much for the items. Second, we were conveying to the entire group of bidders that the set of items being auctioned that day were largely authentic period pieces. If that continued that could hurt us on all items being sold during the auction because it would become clear that the estate from which they came was one where the previous owner had made substantial investments in authentic period pieces.

After three or four had gone off at high prices, a couple of us walked over to the out-of-town dealer and had a conversation with him. We explained that we were running a bidding ring and that he was invited to participate. After some brief discussions, that dealer stopped bidding on all future items unless it was clear to him that no other ring member was interested. By quickly including the out-of-town dealer, we were no longer providing free appraisals to everyone at the auction, and we were no longer cutting dramatically into our profits.[19]

---

18. Cassady (1967, p. 182): " . . . the buyer of an item in the final round may pay as much for it in the end as if he had bought it in open competition at the public auction, because he may use up his dividend in overbidding at the settlement."

19. See Graham and Marshall (1987), especially "Fact 4" on pages 1220–1221. See also Cassady (1967, p. 180): " . . . individuals have to be compensated in some way for their willingness to withhold bids and to keep their knowledge to themselves."

3.6   Auctioneer's Response

You may be concerned about the response of the auctioneer at the main auction to the presence of a ring. The auctioneers we face are typically not oblivious to the fact that they are confronting a ring.[20] They understand that dealers are not bidding against one another. Nevertheless, at the end of many auctions, they will offer the ring the use of the auction hall to conduct the knockout. Sometimes auctioneers will engage in behavior like "quick knocks," awarding items to non-ring bidders before the bidding has completed, or employing a "protecting bidder," who is somebody they can point to for an incremental bid for an item should the ring start to substantially eat into their revenues. But most of the time, auctioneers realize that rings have many opportunities to bid at a lot of different auctions in this geographic area. If the ring is sufficiently unhappy with an auctioneer, they can choose not to show up at that auctioneer's sales. The ring is a strong bidder and the withdrawal of ring participation is a major revenue blow for an auctioneer.

Sometimes when the auctioneer is selling items on a consignment basis, getting 5 to 10 percent of the revenue from the sale, the auctioneer can be lured into joining our ring.[21] This can be terrific for profits. Here is how that might work in practice. Suppose that the auctioneer was going to set a reserve price of $20,000 on an item and that the ring would have been willing to pay up to $25,000. The auctioneer's commission on that might be $2,000. If we think the bidding competition will be weak, we might offer the auctioneer $3,500 to $5,000 to drop the reserve price to $5,000. We would arrange this prior to the auction with nothing in writing. Some auctioneers are quite resistant to getting involved (they may be court-appointed as part of a bankruptcy or the liquidation of an estate), but others are quite agreeable.

3.7   Implementation of Sidepayments

Let us talk about the actual implementation of the side payments. We do not want a paper trail associated with ring members writing each

---

20. See Marshall and Meurer (2001, pp. 358–59) for a discussion of strategic conduct by an auctioneer to combat rings.
21. An analogous situation occurred where a consultant was hired to function as the procurer for a city and the award was made to a firm that was a business associate of the consultant. (*K. Buddie Contracting Inc.* v. *Seawright*, 595 F. Supp. 422 D.C. Ohio, 1984)

other checks with memo lines reading "payoff for ring activity." Instead, you might have noticed that the ring members are constantly suing one another. We sue one another over any number of things. Breach of contract is a frequent one. Almost none of this litigation is meaningful.[22] All we are doing is stating a complaint, filing it through our attorneys, and settling under strict confidentiality. In this way, I settle up the side payments from the knockouts that I owe other ring members under cover of a litigation settlement. We have attorneys who are agreeable to handling our business in this way. They look away, but we do not really care about any of that. If they were ever challenged by the bar, they would simply say this was a legitimate piece of litigation, and that costly court time and court resources were avoided through settlement. These are standard arguments offered for settling rather than litigating. Also, the settlements can and should be done under seal. Overall, this mechanism provides complete cover for settling up the knockouts.

3.8 Questions and Answers

At this time let me ask you if you have any questions.

• *Question 1:* What if we win an item at the auction but do not take it to the knockout?

• *Answer 1:* There is obviously an incentive for ring members not to take items won at the main auction to the knockout; however, this is the most egregious behavior possible within the ring. That behavior will be severely punished. Dealers behaving this way will be kicked out of the ring. Out-of-town dealers who might not find getting kicked out of our ring as a serious punishment are the real threat in this regard. When we ask out-of-town dealers to join our ring, we insist that they not bid until they are certain no other ring member has an interest. If they want to acquire an item, we prefer they do it through the knockout, where there is no threat that they will "walk" with the item.

• *Question 2:* What is an example of a major mistake that I could make representing our firm within a ring?

• *Answer 2:* You have to know who is in the bidding ring. With regard to the main auction, you cannot put yourself in a position where the bidding is progressing, you suddenly start to bid, and only then find

---

22. For the use of litigation settlement to facilitate bidder collusion within the context of bid protests, see Marshall, Meurer, and Richard (1994).

out that you are bidding against a member of the ring. That is a bad outcome. The other members of the ring will be extremely upset, and then they will ask who is going to pay for the money you threw away. I do not want to answer that question. You must understand at all times at the main auction whether a bid is from a ring member or not.

• *Question 3:* You had mentioned that joint ownership happens among members of the ring. Can you tell me a little more about why that happens and how that helps the functioning of the ring?

• *Answer 3:* Sometimes it is a budget constraint issue and sometimes a mechanism for risk sharing, but that could happen whether or not a ring is at the auction. It can also facilitate the functioning of the ring. Suppose there are two dealers, myself and another dealer, who have a narrow expertise in the value of a certain item. The two of us know a group of collectors that nobody else knows, and in addition we have studied a particular narrow set of items to understand their value to this group of collectors. Any bidding that the two of us undertake against one another is going to reveal our information to the general bidding public. Similarly, bidding between the two of us at the knockout will cause other ring members to run up the bonus bidding. We can solve the problem through joint ownership and thereby avoid the awkwardness of having non-nested rings.

• *Question 4:* What do we do with government authorities that start investigating us? As best as I can tell, we are in violation of antitrust laws by engaging in this activity. What do we do, what do we say, what do we not say?

• *Answer 4:* First, do not answer any questions without our lawyer present. Second, you are not going to be talking about anything other than participating in an auction. We all participate in auctions. Even with a ring there is lots of bidding at an auction. Furthermore, I do not know if you noticed this, but in the early parts of the auctions, when the items are first ascending in value, many members of the ring are bidding against one another.[23] These are largely low meaningless prices. No one is going to actually pay $3,000 for a $23,000 Chippendale highboy. However, once we get to some price where we think we have a legitimate shot of owning the item, we stop the meaningless

---

23. Cassady (1967, p. 181): " . . . a well-organized ring provided for simulated competition at lower price levels."

competitive bidding because beyond that point it would be eating into our profits. That meaningless competitive bidding has several functions, but one of these functions is to provide a credible basis for saying that we were bidding against one another at the main auction. Also, in this economy, it is still not a crime to buy low. This is a big part of how we all function in any industry. There is no need to defend buying low or selling high.

There is a delicate matter that we have to pay attention to with regard to enforcement. Let's suppose that I am going to the auction and am bidding on behalf of a customer who wants a 1820 Chippendale highboy. They know the item is being sold at that auction. Further suppose that I am the high bidder at the main auction, where the bidding stopped at $3,000 and I am functioning in a ring. And suppose that the knockout bidding goes way up, ending at $20,000. If there are ten members of the ring and I walked away with the item for a $20,000 bonus bid, then I end up paying a total of $21,000 for the highboy. The auction price is going to be made public, so the buyer that I am representing is going to know I paid $3,000 for the item at the main auction. It is a little hard to explain that I actually paid $21,000 for the item when all was said and done. That is the delicate thing that requires some work. Keep in mind that the presence of a ring at these auctions is not a mystery. It should not come as a surprise except to the least experienced bidders in the room.

• *Question 5:* I thought collusion was inherently unstable because there was always a strong incentive to cheat on the collusive agreement. Why does our ring work so well? Specifically, why has this ring persisted for generations with an open membership policy and a very simple operating rule with seemingly no defection?

• *Answer 5:* That is an excellent question. You need to keep in mind that most of the auctions in which we participate are ascending-bid auctions where we can observe the identities of bidders as they submit bids. Unlike many stories you hear about the instability of cartels, this auction format is particularly conducive to collusive behavior. Suppose again that there is a Chippendale highboy, an authentic piece, that I and other dealers have recognized as such. I know that I am willing to bid up to, say, $82,000 for it. The rules that we are using at the auction mean the following: I am willing to bid up to $82,000 acting noncooperatively and I am willing to bid up to $82,000 while functioning within a ring. Hopefully, because of the ring, I do not have to bid that high.

Many people think in terms of standard sealed-bid auctions or posted-price markets when they think about the instability of cartels. Because I am willing to bid up to my maximum value for the item at an ascending bid auction, which is the same regardless if I am bidding collusively or noncooperatively, there is nothing anybody can really do to cheat, except win an item and not bring it to the knockout, which they can do exactly once because that conduct results in them being expelled from the ring.

• *Question 6:* I want to understand better about who gets to join the ring and who does not get to join. Suppose that another dealer from out of town starts bidding against the ring. It is my understanding that we invite that individual to join the ring. But what about some of the brokers who never have any inventory but are only there bidding for collectors and users of antiques? Are they always invited to join the ring?

• *Answer 6:* Pure brokers, those who never inventory any items and only buy for specific customers, are never members of the ring.[24] If they are invited and say "yes," then the ring does not want them; and if they are invited and say "no," then the ring very much wants them. So they are never asked and are not part of the ring. That needs some explanation. Either brokers have a customer for the items in question or they have no customer. If they have a customer, then their willingness to pay for the item is much higher than even the strongest ring member. If they have no customer, then their willingness to pay is zero. If a broker is part of the ring and bids at a knockout, then all other ring members know that the broker has a customer. Thus, the other ring members artificially bid up the price at the knockout to extract the broker's surplus. The extraction is so extreme that brokers who are trying to acquire items for customers prefer noncooperative conduct to joining the ring. However, if a broker has no customers, then that broker is not helping the ring suppress the price paid at the main auction yet is getting part of the "hat" money. The extreme valuations of brokers—either zero or some very high amount—results in them not participating in the ring. There is no animosity about this—it is just the way it is.

• *Question 7:* Items are not always sold by ascending-bid auctions. Sometimes there are sealed-bid auctions where the high bidder pays

24. See Marshall and Meurer (2004, p. 109).

the amount of his or her bid. Does the ring function during those auctions and does anything change in terms of its operation?

• *Answer 7:* That is a good question. Everything I have told you so far is for ascending-bid auctions where the identities of bidders can be observed. To this day, even with modern technology, that is a frequent type of auction that we encounter. Let's talk about sealed-bid auctions, where the high bidder wins and pays the amount of its bid.[25] Those auctions are problematic for us in terms of organizing and running the ring. I do not know if someone has a brother-in-law or some other agent going to these auctions as a bidder trying to undercut the ring.[26] Why might they do that? Ring members reduce their bids at a sealed-bid auction in order to secure a collusive gain, and there is no capacity for the ring to respond to a higher bid in real time. That is the nature of the auction being sealed bid. Suppose that someone I do not recognize wins at the auction. That could just be an outside bidder or, alternatively, it could be the agent of a ring member where the deviant ring member is trying to capitalize on the suppression of bids by the ring. This makes a ring a more difficult proposition at a sealed-bid auction. If you have all the bidders in the ring, then it is a fairly simple matter to run a ring at a sealed-bid auction. If there is any possibility that there are others outside the ring, then things get more complicated. If you know the identity of all serious bidders outside of the ring, then you know that if anybody outside the ring bids other than one of the serious nonring bidders, they must be an agent of someone in the ring. Then things become easy again because it is simple to monitor whether there was cheating within the ring. In the absence of knowing all of the identities of serious outside bidders, it is a difficult process to enforce the ring agreements and prevent cheating by members of the ring during the auction.

25. See Marshall and Marx (2007), especially corollary 1 and the subsequent results, discussing limitations of collusion at sealed-bid auctions.
26. See Marshall and Marx (2007), especially proposition 5 versus corollary 5.

4 Narrative of Cartel Detection

4.1 Preamble

In this chapter, we discuss the process of inferring collusion from economic evidence. As the basis for the narrative in this chapter, we return to the four colluding firms introduced in chapter 2. We assume that those four firms actually formed the proposed cartel and that they have been successfully operating for three years. As in the narrative of chapter 2, our focus is on industrial cartels, where the colluding firms produce an intermediate good to be sold to other firms.

We suppose further that one of the colluding firms is the division of a parent corporation and that the parent does not know that its division manager is a member of a cartel, although several other separate divisions of the parent have been found to be involved in price-fixing conspiracies in recent years.[1]

The parent has noticed that the division's profits have increased substantially in recent quarters and that prices for the division's product have also ascended at an unprecedented rate. The parent company uses high-powered incentive schemes to reward division managers for increasing profits, but the parent is increasingly concerned about public perceptions as well as repeated liability exposure from the involvement of division managers in price-fixing conspiracies.

The general counsel's office of the parent corporation has approached an economic consultant to help the parent corporation understand how

---

1. In *Vitamins*, the primary conspirators colluded in multiple vitamin products. Akzo Nobel was named in EC decisions as a participant in cartels in *Choline chloride* and *Organic peroxides*. ADM was named in EC decisions as a participant in cartels in *Amino acids* and *Citric acid* and was charged with price fixing in *In re High Fructose Corn Syrup*, 361 F.3d 439 (7th Cir. 2004). SGL Carbon AG was named in EC decisions as a participant in cartels in *Graphite electrodes*, *Electrical and mechanical carbon and graphite products*, and *Specialty graphite* (isostatic and extruded).

it might detect collusion by division managers in the future, especially the division that was one of the four firms in chapter 2. The consultant is well versed in the history of cartel cases, the mechanisms used by practicing cartels, the economic theory regarding collusion, and the econometrics relevant to cartel detection.

The consultant has provided the firm with chapters 1 and 2 of this book as background reading. The consultant is offering a one-day seminar to the firm. Those in attendance will include high-level managers from the parent corporation as well as attorneys from the parent corporation's office of the general counsel.

4.2   The Seminar Begins

Thank you for inviting me to spend this day at your firm to discuss the detection of a cartel. I am an economist, not an attorney. Several members of the firm's office of the general counsel are in attendance today. They can provide the legal implications of the Economics that I offer.

Let me begin by emphasizing that, as discussed in chapter 1, there are strong incentives for collusion, and as discussed in chapter 2, the organization and operation of effective collusion is a soluble problem for many products. Today I am going to review what division managers would need to do to implement and run cartels, with the focus on observable conduct and outcomes to detect their potential participation in a cartel.

Our common experience as individual consumers from buying things in stores at posted prices is not relevant for understanding purchasing by your corporate customers. When you buy toothpaste, or chicken, or socks, you pay posted prices. You do not negotiate at the cash register. You do not run procurements.

In contrast, the buyers of your firm's products use competitive processes to aggressively pursue price discounts and value enhancements. If a competitor of yours offers a price discount, it will not be on a sign in front of their corporate headquarters. The price cut will be offered in secret. Buyers may tell you that such secret price cuts are being offered by competitors, even when they are not, in order to induce you to offer secret price cuts. For the kinds of products you sell, if it costs $2 to make a unit and the profit-maximizing price to sell a unit is $3, and this is also true for your competitors, then it is likely that competitive forces will push the price paid by buyers close to $2, not $3. In this environment, collusion can increase profits. If your firm directly communicates with rival firms and reaches an agreement about pricing, along with ways to monitor compliance of those agreements, and also agrees to undertake interfirm transfers should issues arise with the agreement, then the price that will be realized for the product will be closer to $3 per unit.

You, as a parent corporation, provide high-powered incentives for division managers to increase their profits. There is little that a division manager within your company can do, given the nature of your industry and products, that is more effective at increasing profits quickly than engaging in collusion. Collusion has a guaranteed payoff if it is well organized and implemented, and the payoff can start to be realized in one quarter. Product marketing, service improvements, and investments in cost reductions have an uncertain return that take longer to realize, often much longer, than collusion.

The detection of collusion based on economic evidence can be difficult because some of the actions required to suppress interfirm rivalry also have legitimate noncollusive rationales. My understanding is that you, as a parent corporation, want to be cautious about interfering with the judgment of your managers. You do not want to do things that would have a chilling effect on the managers' ability to make profits for the company. Thus, you would not want to take actions based on economic evidence that allows only the weak inference that managers are engaged in collusion. You might instead consider a standard similar to that used for criminal liability, under which you only take action if the evidence supports an inference that there is a high probability of collusion. That said, certain type of economic evidence can provide a strong inference of collusion.

4.3   Taxonomy of Cartel Actions

To be effective at increasing profits through the suppression of interfirm rivalry, the members of a cartel will undertake certain actions. The exact nature of these actions is dependent on the associated product, market, and industry. The cartel firms will have as their primary mission the elevation of profits. But this immediately forces them to confront the market reality that to elevate price, they must reduce the quantity sold in the market. For the kinds of products made by your firm, a cartel might address this by gradually and persistently increasing price, while using a market share agreement to implement the quantity restriction.[2] As firms pursue ever higher prices, the fixed market shares can only be maintained if the firms restrict supply.[3] If the cartel firms have agreed to raise prices this quarter from $10 per unit to $11 per unit, then a firm with a 20 percent market share will implement the new price and not sell any more quantity than what yields them a 20 percent market share, or else they will need to make amends with other cartel members. Incentives for a sales force to pursue sales beyond their allocated market share can be mitigated by adjusting sales force incentives to emphasize pricing discipline over market share.[4]

The cartel firms must monitor one another to make sure that no member is secretly cheating and selling beyond its share, but such monitoring is a soluble problem with reporting, surveillance (to spot-check reports), and the use of statistics provided by government agencies and port authorities.[5] As buyers try to disrupt price increases with aggressive procurements and allegations that suppliers have offered secret deals, the cartel firms will need to communicate to make sure that all maintain compliance with the agreement.[6] If unintentional deviations occur, then redistributions may be needed, but the cartel will have agreed to the nature and method of such interfirm transfers at the cartel's inception.[7] For example, end-of-year transactions may be required to make sure all firms have achieved their agreed market shares, where those who have unintentionally oversold their shares buy product at market prices from those who have undersold their shares.[8]

The economics literature emphasizes the need for a threat of punishment to support cartel behavior, where the primary threat is simply the threat of reversion to noncollusive behavior. This threat may not be articulated as a well-defined punishment strategy by cartel members, but rather as an "I give up" capitulation by key members if they cannot get the cartel to function effectively.[9]

2. See chapter 2, footnote 14.
3. Similarly prices can only be increased within the confines of a customer allocation or geographic allocation if firms restrict supply.
4. See chapter 2.5.
5. See chapter 2, footnote 18, and chapter 2.7, questions 1 to 3.
6. See chapter 2.7, questions 1 and 2.
7. See chapter 2.6.
8. See chapter 2, footnote 48.
9. The use of reversion to pre-collusive play as a punishment for deviations from collusion is explicitly mentioned in congressional testimony involving dyestuffs manufacturers. The testimony includes a letter from a foreign sales manager of a dyestuffs

Once a cartel gets interfirm rivalry under control, the cartel firms will turn their attention to other sources of profit, such as conduct that dominant firms would undertake against smaller firms in the industry.[10]

Overall, there are nine broad baskets for the conduct of a cartel.[11]

1. Raise prices above what they would have been without the conspiracy.

2. Reduce total industrywide quantity below what it would have been without the conspiracy.

3. Take steps to reduce resistance by buyers to price increases.

4. Change within-firm incentives so as to inhibit interfirm competition and foster higher prices.

5. Allocate the collusive gain among members.

6. Redistribute gains and losses among members so as to maintain compliance with the agreement.

7. Monitor compliance with the agreement and communicate regularly regarding all relevant features of the conspiracy that require discipline.

8. Stand ready to abandon collusive conduct if some cartel members continually engage in substantial noncompliant conduct.

9. Once interfirm rivalry has been suppressed successfully, seek additional profits through activities such as dominant-firm conduct.

The detection of collusion using economic evidence involves identifying economic evidence in these nine categories of cartel conduct. The inference problem is complicated by the fact that some economic evidence can have both noncollusive and collusive explanations. Smart cartels are well aware of these inference problems. The European Commission made note of this phenomenon in its 1994 decision regarding the *Cartonboard* conspiracy when it described the cartel's careful orchestration of conspiratorial price announcements to market participants:

---

manufacturer stating: "You and your contemporaries should be in a position to establish market prices based upon definite strength determination of color, which prices should be followed by you if such an understanding is reached. But, if you have any indication that a contemporary is not adhering to such prices, then immediately revert to the prices prevailing before any arrangements were established." (S. Comm. on Patents, Hearings before the Committee on Patents on S. 2303 and S. 2491, Part 5, p. 2424, 77th Cong. 2nd Sess., May 13 & 16, 1942)

10. For an expanded discussion of this point, see chapter 7.

11. These are drawn in part from Kovacic et al. (2011).

Had they been challenged, the producers could as a result of this elaborate scheme of deception have attributed the series of uniform, regular and industry-wide price increases in the cartonboard sector to the phenomenon of 'oligopoly behaviour'. They could argue that it made sense for all the producers to decide of their own volition to copy an increase initiated by one or other of the market leaders as soon as it became publicly known; unlawful collusion as such would not necessarily be indicated. Customers might well suspect and even accuse them of operating a cartel; and given the relatively large number of producers, economic theory would be stretched to its limits and beyond, but unless direct proof of collusion were forthcoming—and they went to some lengths to ensure it was not—the producers must have had hopes of defeating any investigation into their pricing conduct by the competition authorities by invoking the defence of oligopolistic interdependence. (EC decision in *Cartonboard* at para. 73)

As in the case of the *Cartonboard* conspiracy, a smart cartel may take actions to give the appearance that the competitive process is still functioning, even though it has defeated the competitive process as a policing device to the benefit of the cartel members. However, as I will discuss with you today, certain economic evidence can be used to infer the existence of collusion.

4.4 Economic Evidence of Collusion

The product division that you have asked me to analyze in depth for today's talk has experienced increased prices and profits in recent quarters. Rival firms have also experienced increased prices. There are only four firms that make this product, there are high entry barriers, and there are no good substitutes. It is natural and expected that these four firms would recognize their mutual interdependence and price accordingly. Without collusion, it would not be unnatural for there to be some parallel movements in prices between rivals.

We will discuss circumstantial economic evidence of collusion above and beyond parallel movements in prices. Some economic evidence can be powerful in allowing a strong inference of collusion; however, other evidence can be quite weak. Some pieces of economic evidence are weak individually but quite strong when considered in conjunction with other pieces of economic evidence. For example, there might be a conduct that would be consistent with unilateral actions by firms in the face of depressed market demand and a separate conduct that would be consistent with unilateral actions by firms in the face of rising demand. However, the simultaneous observation of both of these conducts might be inconsistent with unilateral conduct and lead to the strong inference of collusion.

In general, the identification of what types of economic evidence provide a strong inference of collusion requires information about the relevant product, market, and industry. For example, certain types of interfirm transactions might have a natural noncollusive explanation in one product/market/industry but not in another.

One type of economic evidence that would provide the strong inference of collusion would be the observation that transaction prices are elevated above the levels predicted by a reliable predictive econometric model that accounts for all material noncollusive effects on price.

In order to calculate whether prices are elevated relative to noncollusive conduct, one estimates what the price would have been had there not been a cartel. This is often referred to as the but-for price —but-for the existence of a cartel, what would the price have been?

To isolate the effect of collusion on price, one approach is to construct a model that reliably predicts price variation during some set of circumstances where we can be reasonably assured conduct is noncollusive. If the model predicts price movements in this benchmark accurately, then it can be used to predict what prices would have been during the period of collusion. However, this requires an assumption about a period of time, a geographic location, or a product space that is not influenced by the cartel and thus can be used as a reliable benchmark.

One way to do this analysis well requires a predictive econometric model that accounts for demand and cost factors specific to the product, market, and industry. None of these factors can be potentially manipulable by a cartel if they are to be included in the predictive model. This model would be used to predict prices during a time period when collusion is suspected. If this prediction is significantly less than the actual price, then this analysis would lead to the strong inference of collusion. This is an exercise that the parent corporation can undertake for any or all of its product divisions.

As shown in figure 1.1, the actual price of vitamin A650 is well above the but-for price. Suppose that BASF asked me in 1991 to construct a predictive model for vitamin A650 in order to see if its vitamins division was potentially engaged in collusion. Without any acknowledgment of a cartel by the vitamins division at BASF, I would need to try some conjectures for a benchmark period. One such conjecture would be that the cartel began sometime in 1989, another could be that it started sometime in 1990. What I would see from the predictive model is that the prediction of price was rapidly diverging from the actual price in late 1990 and early 1991. This would be a red flag to the BASF parent corporation that a cartel was likely in operation.

Other examples of economic evidence that would need to be evaluated within the context of a particular product/market/industry include the relative fixity of market shares and, separately, the nature and character of price announcements, such as their regularity, the number of firms announcing the same price in a short period of time, and the length of lead times between the announcement of a price increase and the date at which it becomes effective.[12] However, instead of delving into these and others, I think it would be best to open the floor to questions.

4.5   Questions and Answers

• *Question 1:* I do not understand what you mean by economic evidence supporting the strong inference of collusion. If we do not observe such evidence, does that mean the product division is not participating in a cartel?

• *Answer 1:* Let me clarify by reviewing some basics of logic and conditional probability. *If A then B* is not equivalent to *if B then A*, and it is also not equivalent to *if not A then not B*, but it is equivalent to *if not B then not A*. As an example, *if something is a crow then it is black* is not equivalent to saying that *if something is black then it is a crow*, and it is not equivalent to saying that *if something is not a crow then it is not black*, but it is equivalent to saying that *if something is not black then it is not a crow.* So, in this light, let me answer your question regarding cartels and economic evidence. *If we observe economic evidence supporting the strong inference of collusion, then a cartel is likely* is not equivalent to *if we do not find economic evidence supporting the strong inference of collusion, then a cartel is unlikely.*

For example, suppose that we do not observe a shift in the within-firm incentives of the sales force to "price before volume" such as that described in chapter 2.5. This does not imply the absence of a cartel. There could be many reasons that this shift was unnecessary given the nature of the product, market, and industry. For example, it could be

---

12. See chapter 2.4.

that the division manager has to directly set and sign off on all bids solicited by potential customers. With that type of direct control on pricing, there may be no need to shift the incentives of the sales force. In terms of conditional probability, the key feature of economic evidence that supports the strong inference of collusion is that the probability of observing that evidence in the absence of a cartel is quite low. That feature implies that the probability of a cartel given the evidence is quite high.

• *Question 2:* With regard to the particular econometric exercise that you highlighted, how do we know what to include in or exclude from the predictive model? It seems to be a completely legitimate claim by division managers that the model is not tracking actual prices because some key variables have been omitted.

• *Answer 2:* The variables in the model should be determined in consultation with the division manager and his or her staff. Let the division manager tell you what is important to the determination of the product price. Let all of those things have a chance to be included in the model provided they are not manipulable by a potential cartel. Let the model select, using an objective criterion, which of those to include and which to exclude to produce a best predictive model in the benchmark period. The only things not included as candidates in the model are intangibles and unanticipated shocks. But, if these are really important in influencing price, then that is a perfectly fine discussion to have with the division manager.

• *Question 3:* Many of our product managers have joined trade associations. These trade associations typically request that our divisions report information on a quarterly basis such as production, sales, capacity utilization, expansion plans, exports, inventories, and much more.[13] Furthermore, at the trade association meetings, our division managers meet with rivals to discuss industry-related issues. The trade association attorneys are present, but we are always concerned about the interaction that goes on given that all rivals are gathered together. Also, the division managers often report that special subcommittees have been established to look at specific problems. All of this makes us nervous as the parent corporation, but it seems that to enjoin participation in such meetings is to competitively disadvantage our divisions. What are your thoughts on this?

13. See chapter 2, footnote 8.

• *Answer 3:* Trade associations are often involved in pro-competitive activities such as resolving industrywide coordination and public good provision issues for industry members, but your concerns are warranted. Unless there has been substantial prophylactic training about the legal pitfalls of anti-competitive conduct, managers of rival firms gathered for a trade association meeting may find themselves discussing mechanisms and logistics for the suppression of interfirm rivalry. Given the noncollusive benefits of participation in a trade association, you do not want to prohibit participation in them, but you must accept the responsibility of forewarning your managers of the antitrust liability from certain kinds of interaction with rivals.

• *Question 4:* One of our divisions participates in an export association. Is this a conduct that leads to the strong inference of explicit collusion?

• *Answer 4:* Government approved export associations are legal, but if I wanted to run a cartel and could set up an export association, I would definitely do so.[14] The U.S. Department of Commerce at its website provides a description of what a hypothetical export association can legally do.[15] The actions described there are nothing short of collusion. Granted, the conducts must be targeted at overseas markets, but it is not reasonable to assert that the firms participating in this legal collusion would forget all of those discussions when it came time to function in the domestic market.

14. See the answer to question 4 in chapter 2.7.
15. See the sample application for an Export Trade Certificate of Review at the website of the U.S. Department of Commerce International Trade Administration (http://trade .gov/mas/ian/build/groups/public/@tg_ian/documents/webcontent/tg_ian_002211 .pdf) (accessed October 7, 2011), which is reproduced, in part, in the discussion of export trade associations in the appendix to chapter 7.

II Economics of Cartels

Rivalry is costly to firms. Industry profits are negatively affected by interfirm rivalry—this is the center force in Porter's Five Forces. Although the suppression of rivalry increases profits, the suppression of rivalry has many challenges associated with it. For example, the suppression of rivalry typically creates an external benefit for firms that are not participating in a cartel, and so firms may prefer not to join. Also, there are numerous pricing, allocation, and enforcement issues that need to be resolved in order for a cartel to be effective and thus successful in elevating profits for members. Without addressing those issues, a cartel will encounter substantial problems.

As mentioned in the preface, our focus is on industrial cartels, where the colluding firms produce an intermediate good to be sold to other firms.

Part II proceeds as follows. Chapter 5 focuses on the effects of the suppression of rivalry. Chapter 6 addresses the implementation of the cartel agreement. This chapter is built around the discussion and analysis in Stigler (1964) of the structures required to implement a successful cartel. Chapter 7 considers how a cartel that has successfully suppressed rivalry among members may be able to further enhance profits by acting on the remaining four perimeter forces identified by Porter.

5   Suppression of Rivalry by Cartels

Rivalry among firms in an oligopolistic industry consists of any firm-specific investments or actions that enhance a firm's product in the eyes of customers relative to products of other firms in the industry. Interfirm rivalry can occur in both price and nonprice terms. Any component of price can be a potential source for price-based rivalry, including payment terms, rebates, quantity discounts, shipping costs, and a myriad of other components of price. Nonprice rivalry can occur in advertising and marketing, research and development, product innovation and differentiation, and components of quality such as product reliability, product durability, customer service, and timeliness of delivery.

5.1   Basics

5.1.1   Role of Rivalry

Oligopolistic sellers of a product know many things that buyers of that product do not know. Sellers typically interact with many buyers and deal with all aspects of production and market conditions. They know what factors affect the costs of production. They know how exchange rate fluctuations affect the market for the product. They know general demand conditions in the market better than a buyer. They know better than a buyer what capacities are coming online and going offline, and how these changes will affect the market. They know how foreign producers can affect the market better than a buyer. Overall, sellers are typically better informed about many aspects of the product, market, and industry than a buyer.

Despite buyers' informational disadvantage, buyers have the advantage that they can use rivalry among sellers to elicit information from the sellers. A buyer may not know if a price of $100 is too high, but if a procurement produces a bid of $30, and no bids above $40, this tells the buyer that $100 was too high. A buyer who believes that the product in question should have a useful life of 1,000 hours, but obtains bids specifying a useful product life from between 1,800 and 2,000 hours, has learned that 1,000 hours is too low. A buyer who thinks that a contract awardee should be on site for a service-call within 24 hours of a breakdown, but who obtains bids for service call turnaround of between 4 and 6 hours, knows that it need only be down for one-quarter of a day and not a full day. In these cases, buyers learn much about products and market conditions through supplier rivalry.

Without rivalry, buyers have little defense against the informational advantages of sellers. Buyers need rivalry, as expressed through competitive processes, to protect themselves against suppliers who are informationally advantaged.

5.1.2 Competitive Processes

Competitive processes can take many forms. Buyers can conduct procurements. Or buyers can have discussions with suppliers sequentially over a long time, perhaps selecting a seller after careful review of this information. If a seller wants to be awarded the business of a buyer, then it offers a better value proposition to the buyer than any other seller.

There are two misconceptions regarding competitive processes that are important to dispel. First, as a rule, buyers do not buy from the low-price supplier only to find out later that there are important additional dimensions for them beyond price. Buyers understand how to use interfirm rivalry to elicit the information they need and make award decisions that account for all contractual features that are important to them. Buyers understand that rivalry can occur on both price and nonprice terms. A price is defined for some unit of value, such as a price per gallon of 87 octane gasoline pumped by the purchaser at a particular gas station at a particular time. One can think of a price as having a numerator and a denominator, with the dollar price being in the numerator and the nonprice components of the product, including quantity and quality, being in the denominator. Purchasers want the price per unit of value to be low—they are concerned about both the numerator, where small is good, and the denominator, where large is good. Interfirm rivalry drives down the overall price per unit of value, taking into account both numerator and denominator.

Second, a "strategic alliance" between a buyer and seller does not imply that the buyer has abrogated all use of competitive processes. Strategic alliances are about encouraging relationship-specific investments, not throwing all rents into the hands of one or the other party in the relationship.

Even though buyers actively use interfirm rivalry to police their procurements, any firm has only limited resources to devote to procurement processes, implying that the acquisitions of some products receive more attention and scrutiny than others. If a procurement is conducted for a product and the price spikes up, then the procurement division is likely to devote additional resources to the acquisition of that product, perhaps suspending the first procurement and rescheduling a new one so that a previously unqualified foreign supplier can be vetted for participation in the procurement process. A procurement division solves an optimization problem across all procurements given its resource constraints.

Sellers recognize the reliance of buyers on competitive processes and make substantial efforts to emerge victorious as the awardee. A supplier, recognizing that it faces competition from the other suppliers in the market, and understanding the market and its own position within the market, attempts to submit a bid that is viewed as "best" by the purchaser.

If an account is not won by a firm's sales staff, there is usually a postmortem done by upper management to understand why. The sales force that was in charge of the procurement will often be asked if they submitted a competitive price, if they made it clear that the firm's service was top notch, if they highlighted the newly designed products of the firm, and if special deals with regard to shipping and volume purchases were put forward. In other words, upper management will ask the sales force whether they made every effort to demonstrate that their firm's product was a superior value proposition as compared to what other firms in the industry were offering. This postmortem evaluation is the firm's review of its comparative place with respect to rivalry in the industry.

Many corporations in an industry are evaluated comparatively. Market shares of each firm in an industry are among the easiest quantities to measure. Observing that a firm's market share has fallen is an immediate source of concern among shareholders and an investing public. This creates a powerful force for interfirm rivalry as well. This all being said, at the end of the day, profits are what matters. Each seller wants to increase its profits, but as depicted in Porter's Five Forces diagram, interfirm rivalry stands as a major force in the way of doing so within many industries.

5.1.3 Suppression of Rivalry

Mitigating or eliminating rivalry sometimes involves increasing the dollar price (the numerator), and in other cases it involves decreasing the quantity,[1] quality,[2] or some other attribute (the denominator).

There is a common folklore among antitrust practitioners that cartels are more likely to form in environments where competition is focused on the dollar price, with the product attributes held fixed.[3] It is unclear how to evaluate this assertion. Cartels are more likely to form when the suppression of interfirm rivalry has a higher expected yield in terms of profitability for member firms than other profit-enhancing activities. Cartels focus on elevating the price per unit of value. This leads them to consider not just the elevation of price, but also the diminishment of the unit of value. For example, the incandescent light conspiracy focused, in part, on the reduction of the life of lightbulbs, which was an action designed to decrease the denominator.[4] The common folklore that cartels are more likely to form when competition is focused on price may arise because it may be easier to detect cartels that focus primarily on price and more difficult to detect cartels that focus on diminishing the unit of value.

1. Bath gel manufacturers, including Sara Lee Corp., Colgate-Palmolive Co., and Puig Beauty & Fashion Group SL, were fined by the Spanish competition authority, CNC, for their roles in a price fixing conspiracy. "The toiletry manufacturers agreed to raise the price for bath and shower gels by more than 15 percent, hiding that collusion from consumers by packaging their products in smaller containers but keeping the price for each bottle the same, the CNC said." (Melissa Lipman, "Spain Investigates Colomer Role in Bath Gel Cartel," *Law 360*, February 16, 2010, p. 2)

Procter & Gamble and Unilever were fined $456 million by European Union regulators for fixing prices of powdered laundry detergent together with Henkel in eight EU countries. "The cartel was started when the companies were in joint talks on how to cut down on packaging, said the EU's Competition Commissioner Joaquin Almunia. 'They used this environmental initiative to agree on market share and to agree on not reducing the prices even if the packages were smaller,' Almunia said." ("EU Fines Unilever, P&G for Detergent Price-Fixing," *CBSNews Business*, April 13, 2011, available at http://www.cbsnews.com/stories/2011/04/13/ap/business/main20053476.shtml, accessed April 13, 2011)

2. The Incandescent Electric Lamp Cartel coordinated a reduction in the life of their lightbulbs. (Stocking and Watkins 1991, ch. 8)

3. See Posner (2001, pp. 69–79).

4. See footnote 2 in this chapter.

Effective collusion suppresses interfirm rivalry and thereby increases seller profits and decreases buyer profits, but it also subverts the use of competitive processes to police the marketplace. If a buyer learns that sellers are functioning as a cartel, the buyer is unlikely to adhere to the competitive processes it was using previously. By finding competitive processes that are more effective at policing the marketplace in the face of collusion, a buyer can secure a competitive advantage for itself, or if other buyers have also recognized the presence of the cartel, it can prevent itself from being competitively disadvantaged.

Suppose that a buyer enters a market and must acquire a product that it has never before acquired. It qualifies suppliers and conducts a procurement. Prior to the procurement, the buyer has obtained a general idea that the price should not exceed $100 per unit, but this information is loose, at best, because the buyer cannot discuss prices paid for factor inputs with its own industry rivals without violating the antitrust laws. Unknown to the buyer, costs in the industry can be as low as $35 per unit. Six bids are obtained at the procurement, and the low bid is $39 per unit. After some further investigation and inquiry, the buyer acquires the factor input from the low bidder. Interfirm rivalry has been used successfully to police the market and generate large amounts of surplus for the buyer. If, however, the low bid had been $85 as a consequence of collusion by the sellers, then the buyer may well have ended up paying $85. The collusion would have suppressed interfirm rivalry, but the relatively uninformed buyer may have accepted the bid of $85 thinking that the competitive process was still effectively policing the market.

When interfirm rivalry is subverted, the learning process generated by competitive processes is largely defeated. If collusion is suspected, the buyer can take costly actions to attempt to resist the collusive price increase. Because buyers are left scrambling to dynamically adjust their procurement processes in an attempt to challenge the potential collusion by sellers, the damage to the economy exceeds the straightforward deadweight loss associated with elevated prices.

5.2 Buyer Resistance

Buyers use competitive processes to police the marketplace with regard to price and nonprice attributes of products that they are trying to acquire. For some purchases a buyer can rely on well-established highly liquid markets to make acquisitions. The Chicago Mercantile

Exchange has a listing of such commodities. However, for the vast bulk of purchases made by industrial buyers, procurements are frequently employed where the buyer invites qualified suppliers to submit sealed bids.

Buyers insist on suppliers having satisfied some kind of qualification process. No buyer wants to entertain offers from suppliers who lack the experience or know-how to actually provide the product in question. For example, the authors of this book should not be considered as qualified suppliers of vitamins, steel-reinforced bars, or industrial chemical products, and thus should not be, and would not be, invited to submit bids at procurements for such products.

In a simple procurement context, with minimum specifications regarding product characteristics having been stated in the bid solicitation, the bids are evaluated solely based on price. In more complicated procurement settings, the bidders may submit multidimensional bids that are scored by the buyer. It may seem that all a buyer can do in this context is determine the best bid and award the contract to that bidder. But the buyer may be dissatisfied with the bids, even the best of them, in which case the procurement award will be suspended. The buyer's dissatisfaction may be caused by incorrect or inadequate information about supplier costs and/or demand conditions or, alternatively, a suspicion of collusive conduct by suppliers.

5.2.1 Buyer Options Following the Suspension of a Procurement

Once a procurement has been suspended, the buyer has a number of options beyond its own additional investigations regarding the sellers' cost and/or demand conditions. We refer to the set of bidders who could submit bids prior to the suspension as the "historically qualified" bidders or suppliers.

1. *Identify, invite, and encourage qualification of additional bidders.* There could be suppliers in foreign countries, or relatively new entrants, who are unfamiliar to a buyer. The cost of qualifying such sellers, and the possibility of there being some unanticipated adverse outcome as a result of buying from them, may initially leave a buyer satisfied with relying on well-known historically qualified suppliers as the only invited bidders. However, a buyer's strong dissatisfaction with historically qualified suppliers' bids in a procurement may lead the buyer to invite a number of new and/or foreign suppliers to seek qualification and participate in a new procurement.

2. *Identify and pursue alternative sources of supply.* It may be the case that there are brokers or well-organized spot markets for the product that the buyer seeks to acquire. The buyer may not be satisfied with the use of these third-party markets on an ongoing basis because some aspects of the relationship with a procurement awardee are of value. But, in the short term, these alternative sources of supply can fill a gap in supply until the buyer identifies the nature of the problem with the initial bids received and/or identifies longer run solutions. The use of third-party sources also constitutes notification to historically qualified suppliers that the buyer is willing to undertake such measures rather than passively accept bids that were submitted in response to the initial bid invitation.

3. *Broaden requirements so as to include substitute products that were previously not entertained.* It may be the case that the buyer is able to reconsider whether some substitute products can satisfy its needs. For example, if a grocery store chain in 1995 was dissatisfied with the procurement results for paper bags, it could consider extending the procurement to include plastic bags as an alternative, where a new procurement would specify both, and the invited bidders would now include the producers of plastic bags.

4. *Redefine the acquisition process in an effort to elicit price/term concessions from historically qualified bidders.*
a. *Change the quantity and frequency with which purchases will be done in exchange for price/term concessions.* This measure challenges coordination among suppliers by implicitly asking the suppliers about their value of the future. By offering long-term contracts for large quantities in exchange for price/term concessions, a buyer is asking suppliers if they prefer to grab a big payoff today rather than maintain industry pricing discipline. A large payoff today, even if accepting it would be observable, may be attractive to a supplier that had been tacitly or explicitly attempting to maintain higher prices. Of course, if the initial bids are rooted in factor cost or demand factors that are not observable to the buyer, then there will not be much of a response by suppliers to such an offer.
b. *Void the procurement results and wait some time period before reconducting the procurement.* Patience is another challenge for coordination among suppliers. Voiding a procurement and waiting before reconducting the procurement implicitly asks suppliers how much they value future payoffs versus current payoffs. A buyer may have inventories of the item that allow this patience on its part. However, if the

pricing is rooted in factor cost or demand factors, making suppliers wait is unlikely to affect their bids in any material way.

c. *Reconduct the procurement with a publicly announced reserve price.* Many procurements do not have publicly announced reserve prices, although the decision by a buyer to not make any award means that an unannounced reserve price did exist. A buyer might reconduct the procurement with a public announcement of a reserve price that explicitly states their expectations for acceptable price bids.

d. *Inform historically qualified bidders about each other's bids.* It is common after receipt of bids, but before making an award, for a buyer to inform a bidder that their current bid is deficient, especially in light of the bids submitted by others. A buyer may go from bidder to bidder, making representations about the bids of rivals, seeking concessions and more favorable terms. If the initial bids are not rooted in cost and/or demand factors, but instead stem from a weak form of collusion, then the buyer may be able to obtain substantial price concessions, especially if the buyer can somehow guarantee the anonymity of the awardee.

5. *Develop internal production capabilities (vertical integration).* This is a rather dramatic step, but it may occur when there appears to be no measure that provides reasonable pricing from suppliers. It is a step that is entirely unnatural in some settings. For example, no major poultry producer is going to integrate into the production of vitamin A. However, in some circumstances the development of internal production capability may be desirable for a buyer, even if that production is less efficient than that of existing suppliers, because it constitutes a credible threat against suppliers.

5.2.2 Illustration of Buyer Resistance

To illustrate the challenge that buyer resistance poses for the suppression of interfirm rivalry, consider the following hypothetical. Suppose that a buyer invites four historically qualified sellers to submit sealed bids for the provision of a product. The four sellers submit bids as follows:

Seller A: $101
Seller B: $106
Seller C: $109
Seller D: $110

Suppose that the buyer had a prior expectation that it would end up paying no more than $92 for the product. The buyer is dissatisfied and begins discussions with the sellers, after submission of their bids, along the following lines. The buyer approaches seller B and tells it that a bid of $94 would edge out the lowest seller by a small amount and stands a good chance of winning. Seller A is told that a bid of $90 would just beat out the lowest bid and seller A would almost surely be the awardee if it lowered its bid to that amount. Sellers C and D are also provided with similar statements by the buyer, attempting to get a revision of their bids toward $90.

If the initial bids were noncollusive and rooted in actual cost and/ or demand conditions that the buyer did not understand, then the misinformation by the buyer that some seller submitted a bid in the low to mid $90s would not result in any meaningful change in bids by the sellers.

If instead the sellers were all explicitly colluding in the submission of their bids (and thus their bids were substantially above noncollusive bids), then the buyer's misinformation would be confirmed as such by the sellers through direct communication among themselves. The response of colluding sellers to this buyer resistance is the same as when sellers acted noncollusively, namely little or no change in bids.

However, if the sellers were not communicating, but instead tacitly attempting to substantially raise prices, then the misinformation by the buyer could be disruptive and result in a drop in bids, as sought by the buyer.

Suppose that the cost to make the product and provide it to the buyer is approximately $70 for all sellers and that these elevated bids are the result of explicit collusion. The elevation in the initial bids is part of the suppression of interfirm rivalry from the explicit agreement. But the discipline to communicate with and monitor one another is the second part of the suppression of interfirm rivalry because without that communication and monitoring, the buyer would be able to move the price downward by convincing each seller that its "competitors" were secretly offering the buyer better deals at each step along an iterative negotiation path.

The decision by a buyer to take some of the more costly measures described above depends on whether the product in question is relatively inconsequential to the profits of the buyer's firm. If so, then the buyer will be reticent to take extra measures, unless the price has risen to such a large extent that the buyer believes incremental investments in competitive pressure will have a substantial return in terms of price reductions. A cartel is always probing this boundary—how much to push a price increase without producing substantial buyer resistance.

The buyer may approach one of the sellers and offer to buy over an extended period if the seller provides substantial price concessions at the current time. Again, if the sellers' conduct is noncollusive and rooted in cost and/or demand conditions, then there will typically be no substantial benefit for the buyer from such a costly action. However, if the sellers are engaged in collusion (tacit or explicit), then by increasing the payoff to a seller from a contract award by lengthening the time interval between bid solicitations, the buyer creates an incentive for a potential deviation by a seller.

Such conduct by a single buyer may be largely irrelevant to sellers that are tacitly or explicitly colluding. However, if one buyer is motivated to engage in such resistance, then there is a good chance that other buyers are also motivated to do so. This motivation is created by the sellers' pricing. Specifically, if the price increase is substantial, then buyers will individually resist the price increase, where the aggregate of the individual resistances will be substantial. Cartels are well aware that their agreement to suppress interfirm rivalry is unlikely to survive intense broad-based buyer resistance and are always considering how much a price can be increased before generating that kind of reaction from buyers.

A buyer can also introduce noise into the procurement process. A decision to void a procurement with no subsequent announcement about how the buyer will acquire the product adds noise. A decision to buy from third parties adds noise for historically qualified suppliers. A decision to reconduct the procurement with a broader definition of an acceptable product adds noise. The aggregate of all such incremental noise over all buyers can be quite disruptive to any form of collusion, tacit or explicit.

A buyer can also invite a new supplier to participate in a new procurement. A new supplier will do little to improve the bids if the historically qualified supplier bids were noncollusive and rooted in cost and/or demand conditions. However, if the historically qualified suppliers are colluding, then the new supplier poses a threat to their profitability.

If the newly qualified supplier cannot be enticed to join the cartel, or in the case of tacit collusion does not yet understand the long-run nature of the bidding behavior among the historically qualified suppliers, then the new supplier is likely to reveal through its bidding that the initial bids were not rooted in cost and/or demand factors, but were elevated due to collusion. Even with extra communication and monitoring, a well-functioning, sophisticated cartel may not be able to survive an aggressive new entrant. For example, the vitamin C cartel collapsed in 1994/5 as a consequence of the entrance of noncartel Chinese producers, but the vitamin A and E cartels, which did not confront such entry, survived until 1998/9.

Overall, the suppression of interfirm rivalry has two components. First, the colluding firms have to elevate their prices to buyers through the suppression of rivalry among themselves. Second, the colluding firms have to figure out how to raise prices without eliciting substantial buyer resistance. Any cartel, at its inception, can figure out that profit maximizing prices are well above current levels, but for the cartel to immediately call out the monopoly price will typically induce such a strong reaction from buyers that the price increase will almost surely fail.

5.2.3 Porter's Five Forces Revisited

In figure 5.1, the center box, industry rivalry, has been disaggregated into cartel and noncartel firms. The arrows depict that the cartel competes with the noncartel firms, and the noncartel firms also compete with one another, but the cartel firms do not compete among themselves.

As discussed above, the suppression of rivalry by cartel firms involves the management of buyer resistance to product price increases and the management of seller resistance to downward pressure on factor prices. The light gray arrows from the right force and the left force, which point to the cartel in the center force, indicate that control of these components is an integral part of the suppression of rivalry by the cartel. We will return to this diagram in chapter 7.

5.3 Model of Price Competition without Buyer Resistance*

As mentioned above, cartels will seek incremental profits through any number of actions, where the elevation of price is but one. However, for expositional purposes it is convenient to discuss the suppression of rivalry as being focused on the elevation of price, so we will do that in what follows.

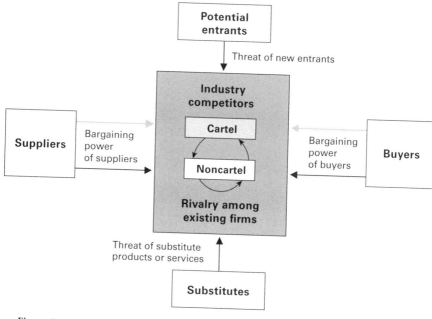

Figure 5.1
Modified Five Forces diagram to show cartel and noncartel firms. Source: Porter (1980, fig. 1.1). Adapted and modified with the permission of Free Press, a Division of Simon and Schuster, Inc., from *Competitive Strategy: Techniques for Analyzing Industries and Competitors* by Michael E. Porter. Copyright © 1980, 1998 by the Free Press. All rights reserved.

We present a model of oligopolistic competition in an industry and show how collusion among various subsets of the firms in the industry can increase their payoffs.[5] As our model of oligopolistic competition, we use a standard framework of differentiated products price competition. In this type of model, each firm chooses the price it will charge for its product. It chooses one price, and all units are sold for that price. Firms sell more if they charge less or if their rivals charge more. We assume products are differentiated, at least to some extent, so that a

5. Authors considering collusion in an environment with repeated price competition include Tirole (1988), Kandori and Matsushima (1998), Athey and Bagwell (2001, 2008), Bagwell and Wolinsky (2002), Athey, Bagwell, and Sanchirico (2004), Harrington and Skrzypacz (2007), and Gerlach (2009). For other theoretical models of collusion, see Cramton and Palfrey (1990), Demougin and Fishman (1991), Kihlstrom and Vives (1992), Raith (1996), Laffont and Martimort (1997, 2000), Sannikov and Skrzypacz (2007), Lee (2010), and Miklós-Thal (2011). On the effects of collusion on attributes other than prices and quantities, see Fershtman and Gandal (1994) and Fershtman and Pakes (2000).

firm's sales do not fall to zero if it charges a price slightly higher than that of its rivals, as would be the case in a model of Bertrand competition with homogeneous products.

We consider a model without buyer resistance to highlight: (1) the benefit to cartel firms of interfirm rivalry suppression, (2) the cartel membership decisions faced by firms in the industry, and (3) the incentives for deviations by cartel firms. Adding buyer resistance to this analysis would be analytically burdensome and distract from these three central points.

In this model, the firms in an industry compete by choosing the prices at which to offer their products. The quantity demanded from a particular firm depends on the price it sets as well as the prices set by its rivals.

For simplicity in modeling, we adopt a symmetric version of the model presented in Singh and Vives (1984), although we extend the model to allow for more than two firms.

Letting n denote the number of firms in the industry, we will work with inverse demand functions

$$p_i = a - q_i - s\sum_{j\neq i}q_j,$$

where $a \geq 1$ and $s \in (0, 1)$. In words, this equation says that firm i's price is equal to amount a, minus firm i's quantity, minus amount s times the sum of the other firms' quantities.

As one can see from these demand functions, the market price for firm i's product is decreasing in its own quantity. This is a standard downward-sloping demand curve. The market price for firm i's product is also decreasing in the quantities produced by firm i's rivals; however, because s is less than one, the impact on firm i's price of an increase in a rival's quantity is less than the impact of an equal increase in firm i's own quantity.

We assume that each firm has the same constant marginal cost $c < 1$ and zero fixed costs. Thus, firm i's payoff is equal to its price minus its marginal cost, times the quantity it produces: $(p_i - c)q_i$.

In this environment, we can calculate the equilibrium prices, quantities, and payoffs for the n firms under different assumptions about competition or collusion in the industry.[6]

6. The underlying model for our analysis of differentiated products price competition is that of Singh and Vives (1984). In that model, a representative consumer maximizes $U(q_1,\ldots,q_n) - \sum_{i=1}^{n}p_iq_i,$ where

5.3.1 Monopoly Outcome*

If there is only one firm, that firm maximizes its payoff by choosing its price p_1 to maximize its profit $(p_1 - c)q_1$, where with only one firm $q_1 = a - p_1$. The monopoly firm's profit is maximized when p_1 is equal to $p^M = (a + c)/2$. At a price of p^M, the quantity demanded is $q^M = (a - c)/2$, and the monopolist's payoff is

$$(p^M - c)q^M = \frac{(a-c)^2}{4}.$$

We can use the monopoly outcome as a benchmark as we increase the number of firms in the market.

5.3.2 Oligopoly Outcome*

A standard analysis of the oligopoly model described above involves calculating the Nash equilibrium of the game in which the firms simultaneously choose their prices. To analyze this game, we start by viewing each firm as choosing its price to maximize its payoff, holding fixed the price choices of its rivals. The Nash equilibrium is a list of prices (one for each firm) such that no firm can increase its payoff by changing its price.

Formally, a price vector $(\hat{p}_1, \ldots, \hat{p}_n)$ is a Nash equilibrium if for every firm i, $\hat{p}_i$ maximizes firm i's profit, fixing the other firms' prices at their Nash equilibrium values. In other words, if every firm other than i chooses its corresponding price in $(\hat{p}_1, \ldots, \hat{p}_n)$, then firm i maximizes its payoff by choosing price $\hat{p}_i$, and this holds for all firms. Thus, the Nash equilibrium has the property that when other firms choose their Nash equilibrium prices, a firm cannot profit by deviating from its Nash equilibrium price.

$$U(q_1, \ldots, q_n) = \sum_{i=1}^{n} \left(a_i q_i - \frac{1}{2} b_i q_i^2 - \sum_{j > i} s_{ij} q_i q_j \right).$$

Consumer surplus is $U(q_1, \ldots, q_n) - \sum_{i=1}^{n} q_i p_i$, and welfare is consumer surplus plus the sum of the firms' profits. This model generates inverse demand relations

$$p_i = a_i - b_i q_i - \sum_{j \neq i} s_{ij} q_j$$

and, assuming $b_i = 1$ for all i and $s_{ij} = s$ for all $i \neq j$, demand relations

$$q_i = \frac{1}{1 + (n-2)s - (n-1)s^2} \left[(1 + (n-2)s)a_i - s\sum_{j \neq i} a_j - (1 + (n-2)s)p_i + s\sum_{j \neq i} p_j \right].$$

Table 5.1
Noncooperative outcomes (assuming $s = 0.6$, $a = 1$, $c = 0$)

Firms in the industry	Noncooperative price	Noncooperative quantity per firm	Industry quantity	Noncooperative payoff per firm	Industry payoff
n	p^N	q^N	nq^N	π^N	$n\pi^N$
1	0.50	0.50	0.50	0.250	0.250
2	0.29	0.45	0.89	0.128	0.255
3	0.20	0.36	1.09	0.073	0.218
4	0.15	0.30	1.21	0.046	0.186
5	0.13	0.26	1.29	0.032	0.161
6	0.11	0.22	1.34	0.024	0.141
7	0.09	0.20	1.38	0.018	0.126
8	0.08	0.18	1.42	0.014	0.113
9	0.07	0.16	1.44	0.011	0.103
10	0.06	0.15	1.46	0.009	0.094

One can show in our model that the Nash equilibrium price for firm i is[7]

$$p_i = p^N \equiv \frac{(1-s)a + (1 + s(n-2))c}{2 + s(n-3)}.$$

If each of firm i's rivals sets its price equal to p^N, then firm i maximizes its payoff by also setting its price equal to p^N. We refer to these prices as the noncooperative prices. Notice that p^N increases with a and with c. This means that increases in demand lead to higher prices, and increases in marginal cost lead to higher prices.

To get a sense for how the equilibrium prices vary with the number of firms in the industry, the following table shows the values of p^N for $n = 1, \ldots, 10$ assuming $s = 0.6$, $a = 1$, and $c = 0$.

As shown in table 5.1, the noncooperative price decreases as the number of firms in the industry increases. To understand intuitively why the noncooperative price decreases with the number of firms in the industry, suppose that there is a monopolist that maximizes its

7. To see this, note that in this model firm i's quantity as a function of all the firms' prices is

$$q_i = \frac{1}{1 + (n-2)s - (n-1)s^2}\left((1 + s(n-2))(a - p_i) - s(n-1)a + s\sum_{j \neq i}p_j\right).$$

Differentiating the firms' profit expressions with respect to their own prices and setting those equal to zero, we can solve for the Nash equilibrium prices.

payoff with a price of 10 and a quantity q^M. If the monopolist were to decrease its price to 9, it would sell additional units as new customers purchase who were not purchasing at the price of 10, but it would receive 1 less for each of the q^M units that it would sell at a price of 10. If the monopolist's payoff is maximized at a price of 10, that means that the loss of revenue from the q^M units demanded at a price of 10 outweighs the revenue from additional units sold at a price of 9.

Now suppose there are two firms in the industry. Suppose that one of these two firms can sell quantity q at a price of 10. Would this firm want to decrease its price to 9? As in the case of the monopolist, the firm would receive less revenue on the q units it could sell at a price of 10 and it would gain revenue as it sold units to consumers who were not buying anything at the higher price. However, there is an additional component to the calculation. The firm also gains because by lowering its price it steals some customers from the other firm. Thus, with multiple firms in an industry, there is an additional incentive to lower price. Lowering price allows a firm to steal customers away from a rival firm. This displacement effect results in lower prices in a competitive market than in a monopoly market.

Table 5.1 also shows that the quantity produced by each individual firm decreases as the number of firms in the industry increases, but the total industry output increases. The payoff to each individual firm decreases as the number of firms in the industry increases.

When products are perfect substitutes, that is, when $s = 1$, then industry payoff is maximized when there is only one firm in the industry. However, when products are not perfect substitutes, this need not be the case because additional products bring additional differentiation, which has value to consumers.[8] As you can see from table 5.1, for the parameters assumed there, the industry payoff is maximized when there are two firms in the industry. Beyond that, as the number of firms in the industry increases, the industry payoff decreases. Similarly, as the number of firms in the industry increases, the quantity per firm decreases, the total quantity produced increases, the price decreases, and the payoff per firm decreases.

As we now show, firms in the industry modeled in table 5.1 can increase their payoffs by colluding. If the firms continue to offer their differentiated products, but coordinate their pricing decisions, they can each obtain a higher payoff than if they all act noncooperatively.

---

8. However, for s sufficiently close to 1, namely, for products that are sufficiently close substitutes, a monopoly structure maximizes industry profit.

5.4   Collusive Outcomes*

We can use the model presented above to analyze the outcome associated with collusion, where firms in a cartel coordinate prices and divide incremental payoff from collusion among themselves. Consider an industry with four firms. If two of the firms collude, they choose their two prices jointly to maximize their joint payoff, while the two noncolluding firms choose their prices individually to maximize their individual payoffs. Similarly, if three of the firms collude, those three would choose their three prices jointly to maximize their joint payoff.

Table 5.2 shows the market outcomes for an industry with four firms. The case of one firm in the cartel is the same as the case of $n = 4$ in table 5.1.[9]

To see how to read table 5.2, consider the case of 3 firms in the cartel. In that case, the three colluding firms choose a price of 0.259 and the noncartel firm chooses a lower price of 0.197. The cartel price maximizes the joint payoff of the three cartel firms given that the outside firm chooses a price of 0.197, and the outside firm's price maximizes its payoff given that the cartel firms all choose a price of 0.259. Given these prices, each cartel firm sells a quantity of 0.231 and the outside firm sells a quantity of 0.387, for a total industry quantity of 1.081. Each cartel firm has a payoff of 0.060, for a total cartel payoff of 0.180, and the outside firm has a payoff of 0.076.

The table shows that the cartel price is increasing in the number of firms in the cartel, and prices of any firms outside the cartel are also increasing in the number of firms in the cartel. Associated with the increase in the cartel prices, as the number in the cartel increases, the quantity sold by each cartel firm decreases. Although the price of any outside firms increases with the number of firms in the cartel, the effect of the increase in the prices of the cartel firms dominates, and the outside firms sell more (at a higher price) as the number of firms in the cartel increases. This is reflected in the increases in the payoff to the noncartel firms as the number of firms in the cartel increases.

In this model, the cartel price is always greater than the noncartel price. Noncartel firms benefit from the presence of the cartel because the cartel creates a price umbrella that allows the noncartel firms to increase their prices relative to the noncooperative outcome, while still undercutting the prices of the cartel members.

9. Because we assume the firms' products are not perfect substitutes for one another, the all-inclusive cartel has higher expected payoff than the monopolist in table 5.1.

Table 5.2
Collusive outcomes by cartel size in an industry with four firms (assuming $s = 0.6$, $a = 1$, $c = 0$)

Firms in the cartel	Cartel price	Noncartel price	Cartel quantity per firm	Noncartel quantity per firm	Industry quantity	Cartel payoff per firm	Cartel payoff	Noncartel payoff per firm
1	0.154	0.154	0.302	0.302	1.209	0.046	0.046	0.046
2	0.187	0.164	0.267	0.322	1.178	0.050	0.099	0.053
3	0.259	0.197	0.231	0.387	1.081	0.060	0.180	0.076
4	0.500		0.179		0.714	0.089	0.357	

As you can see from table 5.2, a firm's payoff increases from 0.046 to 0.050 when it forms a cartel with another firm, moving the industry from one with noncooperative outcomes to one with a cartel of two firms. Similarly, when a third firm joins the cartel, the two firms already in the cartel experience an increase in their payoffs, and the third firm's payoff increases from 0.053 to 0.060. When the fourth firm joins the cartel, the firms already in the cartel again experience an increase in their payoffs, and that fourth firm's payoff increases from 0.076 to 0.089. Thus, in this example, cartel members want all the firms to join the cartel and all firms want to join.[10]

We now show that this need not always be the case. It may be that some firms prefer to remain outside a cartel rather than join. This happens in the model of table 5.2 if the firms' products are sufficiently weak substitutes (e.g., $s \leq 0.1$). It can also happen when the firms differ in their quality levels. As an example, suppose there are four firms, numbered 1, 2, 3, and 4, and suppose the parameters are as in table 5.2, with the exception that firm 4's inverse demand function has a value for a of 0.85 rather than 1. We can view firm 4's product as offering lower value to consumers than the products of firms 1, 2, and 3.

Given these parameters, table 5.3 shows the prices and payoffs for the firms for different cartel membership. The per-firm payoffs assume that the total cartel payoff is divided among the cartel members according to their relative noncooperative payoff shares. Thus, for the all-inclusive cartel, the total cartel payoff is divided among the firms with 30.7 percent (= $0.056/(3 \times 0.056 + 0.014)$) going to each of firms 1, 2, and 3 and 7.8 percent going to firm 4.

As shown in table 5.3, firm 4's payoff is higher if it remains outside a cartel of firms 1 to 3 than if it joins the cartel. This can be seen from the table, which shows that firm 4's payoff when firms 1 to 3 are in the cartel is 0.034, but firm 4's payoff as a member of the all-inclusive cartel is only 0.027, which is about 20 percent less.

Table 5.3 shows that, although the all-inclusive cartel maximizes the industry payoff, once the three high-quality firms have formed a cartel, the lower quality firm does not want to join. The effects illustrated in this example can be related to cartels in industries such as vitamin C, where manufacturers Roche, BASF, Takeda, and Merck KGaA formed the cartel, but Chinese manufacturers (whose worldwide market share

---

10. For models of cartel formation games, see Thoron (1998) and Prokop (1999).

Table 5.3
Collusive outcomes in an industry with four differentiated firms (assuming $s = 0.6$, $c = 0$, $a_1 = a_2 = a_3 = 1$, $a_4 = 0.85$)

Firms in the cartel	Price				Payoff per firm (allocating cartel payoffs according to noncooperative payoff shares)			
	Firm 1	Firm 2	Firm 3	Firm 4	Firm 1	Firm 2	Firm 3	Firm 4
None	0.169	0.169	0.169	0.085	0.056	0.056	0.056	0.014
1 and 2	0.205	0.205	0.180	0.096	0.060	0.060	0.064	0.018
1, 2, and 3	0.285	0.285	0.285	0.132	0.072	0.072	0.072	0.034
All	0.500	0.500	0.500	0.425	0.105	0.105	0.105	0.027

reached 34 percent during the plea period) and other smaller manufacturers remained outside the cartel.[11]

The example provided in table 5.3 shows that, although the all-inclusive cartel maximizes industry payoffs, there may be incentives for one or more firms to remain outside the cartel. Thus, cartel membership is affected by the characteristics of an industry.

5.5 Incentives for Cheating*

In the model of collusion described above, colluding firms choose their prices jointly so as to maximize their combined payoff. But once the colluding firms identify the prices that maximize their combined payoff, individual cartel members may have an incentive to choose a different price.

For example, referring to table 5.2, if two firms form a cartel, the outcome is for the cartel firms to set a price of 0.187 and for the two noncartel firms to set a price of 0.164. Consider the incentives for one of the firms in the cartel to cheat on the cartel agreement. Suppose that the cheating firm expects its co-conspirator to set its price equal to 0.187 and for the two noncartel firms to set their prices equal to 0.164. In that case, the cheating firm maximizes its payoff by setting a price of 0.161, undercutting the other firms' prices.

We can also consider the outcome if the noncartel firms anticipate the opportunistic behavior by the cheating firm. To do this, we fix the co-conspirator's price at 0.187 and let the remaining three firms optimize individually. In this case, the cheating firm and the two noncartel firms each sets a price of 0.160, again undercutting the cartel price.

The profits from such undercutting can be substantial, as shown in table 5.4 below, which makes the assumption that the cheater and noncartel firms all optimize, given that the price of the other cartel firms is fixed at the cartel price given in table 5.2.

Table 5.4 shows the prices, quantities, and payoffs when all but one of the cartel firms adhere to the cartel price given in table 5.2, while the remaining cartel firm, the "cheater," and the noncartel firms optimize independently of one another, taking as given the price of the remaining cartel firms. The table shows the increase in payoff to the cheater relative to its payoff in table 5.2, where it is assumed to adhere to the

11. See Bernheim (2002, figs. 8.7, 8.8, and 8.9).

Table 5.4
Payoffs from cheating on a collusive agreement in an industry with four firms (assuming $s = 0.6$, $a = 1$, $c = 0$)

	Price		Quantity		Payoff		
Firms in the cartel	Cartel firm	Cheater and noncartel firm	Cartel firm	Cheater and noncartel firm	Cartel firm	Cheater and noncartel firm	Increase due to cheating
1	0.154	0.154	0.302	0.302	0.046	0.046	0%
2	0.187	0.160	0.248	0.314	0.046	0.050	1%
3	0.259	0.187	0.187	0.367	0.049	0.069	15%
4	0.500	0.295	0.069	0.580	0.034	0.171	92%

cartel price. As the table shows, the payoff to cheating on a cartel by undercutting the cartel price can be substantial.

Because of the incentive for individual cartel members to set their prices below the price that would maximize cartel payoffs, cartels face an enforcement challenge. Adherence to a cartel agreement is not necessarily in the individual self-interest of the cartel members. In order for a cartel to function, some mechanism must be established by the cartel to address this incentive for price reductions by cartel members.

5.6 Conclusion

A cartel suppresses rivalry among members and accounts for the reaction of buyers to any profit-enhancing actions the cartel undertakes. If the suppression of rivalry by cartel firms did not have to account for buyer resistance, then many cartels would dramatically increase prices at the inception of their agreement. Vigorous buyer resistance can undermine cartels by inducing secret price deviations by sellers. In the next chapter, we discuss the importance for a cartel of averting secret deviations by members and the structures cartels create to accomplish that.

Generally, membership in a cartel is desirable, but smaller firms can benefit from remaining outside the cartel by undercutting the elevated cartel price. The small firms will be able to substantially increase their sales at such elevated prices, which can be more profitable than membership. As we discuss in chapter 7, a highly successful cartel will not tolerate this kind of poaching by smaller firms.

6   Implementation of Collusion by Cartels

As described in the previous chapter, cartel firms can increase their profits relative to noncooperative behavior if they can orchestrate their actions so as to mitigate interfirm rivalry. Cartels put in place structures to coordinate behavior to secure a collusive gain and combat secret deviations by members. In this chapter, we explore Stigler's (1964) description of the components of collusive structures and then discuss each in detail.

6.1   The Central Cartel Problem and the Solution

Stigler (1964) is foundational to the economics of industrial organization, and especially the economics of explicit collusion. Stigler (1964) begins his analysis by noting that a cartel will want to increase profits through what he calls "pricing structures." By pricing structures, Stigler is referring to any profit-improving change in pricing that is agreed to by cartel members. For example, enhancements in price discrimination, relative to noncollusive pricing, may be an important part of some cartels' pricing structures.[1] For other cartels, the focus may be on increasing the prices paid by buyers without any incremental emphasis on price discrimination.

The next step in Stigler's analysis is the keystone. If a cartel agrees to a pricing structure, and the cartel is enhancing profits relative to the absence of a cartel, then each cartel member will consider whether it can secretly deviate from the agreement to obtain additional profits. Specifically, if the cartel has agreed to a price, then each member will consider whether it can secretly offer some buyers a slightly lower price, and thereby capture additional sales and additional profits. The

---

1. See chapter 1, footnote 37.

need to avert secret deviations by cartel members is the central problem facing a cartel. If there are substantial secret deviations from the cartel agreement, the cartel will fail. If the cartel can deter substantial secret deviations, the cartel can survive and potentially thrive. Thus, the focus of any cartel is the creation of structures that increase profits while averting secret deviations by members.

It is not necessary for a cartel to deter all secret deviations in order to be profitable. Some amount of secret deviations may occur and be tolerated by a cartel. However, when the secret deviations prevent the cartel's pricing structure from being implemented, the cartel suffers.

From the perspective of a cartel, the implications of unintentional deviations and secret deviations are quite different. Unintentional deviations can arise from a number of sources. For example, each firm in a cartel manages a sales staff that typically does not know that a cartel is operating. As a consequence, the sales staff may occasionally submit bids that are too aggressive or may win customers that should not have been won according to the cartel agreement. But when these mistakes are quickly acknowledged by upper management, they fall in the realm of unintentional deviations and can be addressed through reallocations of future contracts, subcontracts, end-of-period transfers through the purchase/sale of product, or other interfirm transfer methods. In contrast, secret deviations include special deals for customers that are not acknowledged by the perpetrator to other cartel members and require costly intelligence to uncover.

The economics literature since Stigler (1964) has emphasized the role of punishment strategies in supporting collusive behavior. From the viewpoint of the formal analytics of game theory, which relies on punishments to sustain payoffs above noncooperative outcomes, this is understandable. In practice, the enforcement structures, including the threat of punishment, are important, but they are only one part of the solution to the problem of secret deviations. As highlighted by Stigler, the allocation scheme of the cartel also plays an important role in averting secret deviations.

Before delving into the meaning of each of these, we present a "Stiglerian" diagram of collusive structures. Figure 6.1 summarizes the collusive structures central to averting secret deviations and generating increased cartel profits.

As shown in figure 6.1, the key collusive structures are pricing structures, allocation structures, and enforcement structures. As depicted in figure 6.2, pricing structures are designed to implement price increases

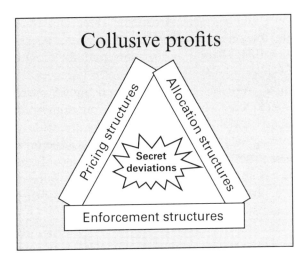

Figure 6.1
Stigler's (1964) collusive structures to support collusive profits and control secret deviations: pricing, allocation, and enforcement

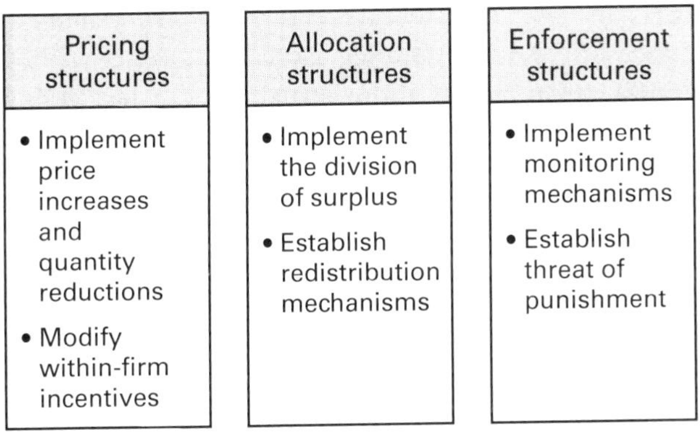

Pricing structures	Allocation structures	Enforcement structures
• Implement price increases and quantity reductions • Modify within-firm incentives	• Implement the division of surplus • Establish redistribution mechanisms	• Implement monitoring mechanisms • Establish threat of punishment

Figure 6.2
Functions of the collusive structures

and quantity reductions as well as modify within-firm incentives to support the objectives of the cartel. Pricing structures often require explicit communication among cartel members—for example, to agree on the increments by which price will be increased or to agree on artificial justifications for those price increases.

Allocation structures implement the division of the collusive gain and establish mechanisms by which cartel firms can engage in interfirm redistributions to resolve unintentional deviations. Three important allocation structures are: market share agreements, geographic allocations, and customer allocations. Allocation structures typically require monitoring of cartel behavior.

Enforcement structures are necessary to detect and punish intentional deviations. They include structures that facilitate communication among cartel members, reporting of information relevant to establishing that firms are complying with the pricing and allocation structures, and the threat of adverse action in the event of noncompliance. Trade associations are sometimes involved as a component of the enforcement structure, as are contractual provisions such as fidelity rebates with associated audit provisions in customer contracts.

A cartel's pricing, allocation, and enforcement structures jointly determine the cartel's ability to deter secret deviations and hence the cartel's profitability. Individually they are not enough. For example, an agreement about a pricing structure, without any agreement regarding an allocation and enforcement structure, will almost surely result in secret deviations to the demise of the cartel. Product/market/industry characteristics affect how the structures are implemented. For example, the presence of multi-market contact among colluding firms may contribute to the allocation structure by facilitating redistributions.[2]

The pricing, allocation, and enforcement structures must complement one another in order for a cartel to enhance its profits. For example, the implementation of an allocation structure involving a global market share agreement requires monitoring of market shares. The required level of monitoring might only be acceptable to the cartel members if it is performed by an outside auditor, so the involvement of an outside party that works on behalf of the cartel might need to be part of the complementary enforcement structure.[3]

As another example of the interdependence of the collusive structures, Stigler (1964) notes that a cartel will pursue opportunities for price discrimination to increase profits, however, allowing different prices to be charged to different customers can open the door for secret

2. On multimarket contact, see Bernheim and Whinston (1990), Evans and Kessides (1994), and Matsushima (2001).
3. For example, the EC decision in *Pre-insulated pipe* at para. 33 states that "A retired business executive . . . was engaged as a consultant to act as the 'coordinator' of the cartel." For more on the role of third-party facilitators, see the appendix to this chapter.

deviations. How far a cartel can move in the direction of price discrimination without inviting secret deviations depends on its enforcement structure. It may be profit enhancing to sell second-quality products at a discount to demand-elastic customers, but for a cartel to allow this opens the door for some members to sell first-quality products at second-quality prices, which would constitute a secret deviation.[4]

A cartel can take advantage of the additional profit derived from price discrimination if the enforcement structure allows deviations to be detected quickly and thus deters them. Even if the enforcement structure has sufficient monitoring to allow the pricing structure to involve price discrimination, it must also be coordinated with the allocation structure. The use of price discrimination can conflict with an allocation structure that calls for equal division of the collusive gain if, for example, a given cartel member typically services relatively demand-elastic customers, while another services relatively demand-inelastic customers.

Although the collusive structures of pricing, allocation, and enforcement are interrelated, these separate categories are useful to organize thoughts regarding cartel implementation. Thus, in what follows, we separately address the collusive structures for pricing, allocation, and enforcement.

4. In the *Trenton Potteries* case, bathroom porcelain manufacturers were in a cartel and undercut the cartel's price by selling "seconds" at a discount. "It was a part of the government's case to show that it was the purpose of respondents, in aid of their price-fixing agreement, not to sell second grade or class B pottery in the domestic market. The government offered evidence, including the testimony of the secretary of the respondents' association, to show that a distinct association of jobbers of pottery was cooperating in this effort, and that its secretary had tendered his active assistance to confine the sale of this class of pottery to the export trade. On cross-examination of the secretary of the respondents' association, the fact was brought out that, at one time, 20 out of 24 members were selling class B pottery in the domestic market." (*United States v. Trenton Potteries Co.*, 273 U.S. 392 (1927), p. 273) One can see that if the cartel had allowed the domestic sale of seconds, cartel members could have disguised secret price cuts by labeling first-quality merchandise as seconds. As stated in Priest (1977, p. 334), "There is no reason to believe that seconds were always an inadvertent by-product, for a manufacturer can directly control the number of defective goods produced by varying investment in machinery and skilled labor or by altering the rate of production. The manager of the Colwell Lead Company testified that his firm produced seconds upon order. Furthermore, Standard Sanitary produced no seconds at all, implying that the Arrott process [for pneumatic dredging used by Standard Sanitary] did not enable comparable production savings for seconds. Seconds might better be viewed as a substitute for nondefective goods, for which there is a distinct and differentiable demand."

6.2 Pricing Structures

We discuss three main groups of pricing structures:[5] those designed to implement price increases, including reducing buyer resistance to price increases; those designed to implement quantity reductions; and those geared toward modifying within-firm incentives.

One would not expect demand for a product to remain fixed over time. Thus, if a cartel fixes the price at which cartel firms sell their product, the quantity cartel firms sell will vary with changes in demand. Alternatively, a cartel can fix the quantity that cartel firms sell, and then the market-clearing price will vary with changes in demand. Even if demand is temporally stable, fixing both the price and quantity is redundant. Therefore, cartels either focus on increasing the price or decreasing the quantity brought to market, but not both. That said, they are connected through the demand curve.

If price is successfully increased, the quantity demanded by consumers will decrease. If the quantity produced is decreased, the price that would equate customer demand to that quantity will increase. Thus, we will discuss implementing price increases and implementing quantity reductions within the single heading of "pricing structures." For some cartels it makes more sense to focus on one versus the other in terms of implementation costs and the demands on the associated allocation and enforcement structures.

6.2.1 Reducing Buyer Resistance to Price Increases

Cartels increase per-unit prices relative to what they would have been with noncollusive conduct in order to secure a collusive gain; however, as discussed in the previous chapter, buyers will not automatically accept price increases by their suppliers. As enumerated in the previous chapter, there are actions buyers can take to resist price increases. In many industries, procurement personnel are required to explain to superiors their efforts in resisting price increases or the reasons for acquiescing.[6] However, procurement personnel have scarce resources to allocate to the buying process and cannot resist all increases for all products. The cartel therefore has an incentive to implement pricing structures that increase the acceptance of and decrease the resistance to cartel price increases.

---

5. For the initial discussion of pricing structure we put aside the issue of price discrimination. See chapter 6.2.5 on price discrimination by cartels.
6. See Marshall, Marx, and Raiff (2008).

The notion of price acceptance and resistance has received attention in EC decisions in cartel cases.[7] In the EC decision in *Cartonboard*, cartonboard producers sometimes faced resistance from converters to whom they sold their products:

There is on the other hand an upper limit in practical terms on the amount of any price increase that could be imposed unilaterally by the cartonboard producers on the converters. The converters have on some occasions resisted a proposd [sic] price increase for cartonboard on the ground that their own customers would in their turn refuse to accept a price increase for packaging . . . . (EC decision in *Cartonboard* at para. 19)

In *Industrial and medical gases*, some price increases were implemented without problems: "the report on the first quarter of 1995 states that price increases were implemented without major difficulties as of 1 January 1995."[8] This was not always the case in *Electrical and mechanical carbon and graphite products* (as described in chapter 2, footnote 32).

In what follows, we describe two components of a pricing structure that are commonly used by cartels to reduce buyer resistance to price increases: coordinated announcements of price increases and coordinated justifications for price increases.

6.2.2   Coordinated Price Announcements and Justifications
Vigorously competing noncollusive oligopolistic firms as well as tacitly colluding oligopolistic firms are both observed to publicly announce price increases.[9] Therefore, on the surface, public price announcements do not allow one to obtain any incremental understanding regarding the conduct of firms engaged in explicit collusion.

An oligopolistic firm that wants to increase its price has, coarsely put, three options. First, it can do nothing in terms of notifying customers of an intended increase in its price but, instead, just bid higher amounts at procurements. Second, the firm can privately notify customers before the procurement, where it is clear to the customers that the communication about the price increase is not public. Third, the firm can announce through group email, news releases, or stories conveyed to journalists at the relevant trade press that it is the firm's intent

---

7. See chapter 2, footnote 43, and regarding *Amino acids* see chapter 2, footnote 32. See also Marshall, Marx, and Raiff (2008).
8. EC decision in *Industrial and medical gases* at para. 147.
9. The literature on price leadership includes: Stigler (1947), Markham (1951), and Bain (1960), d'Aspremont et al. (1983), Rotemberg and Saloner (1990), Booth et al. (1991), Deneckere and Kovenock (1992), and Deneckere, Kovenock, and Lee (1992).

to increase the price for their product. Sometimes the trade press will pick up the story from the firm's website or from customers who have received a blast fax or group email.

6.2.3 Industrial Price Announcements

Our focus is on industrial cartels and not cartels that might arise in posted-price markets for the sale of retail goods. Collusion among grocery stores in a local area to elevate posted prices for everyday products that individual consumers purchase in weekly trips to the store are not our focus. We emphasize this here because of the fundamental differences between public price announcements that retail customers encounter in their weekly shopping versus public price announcements that are encountered by industrial buyers.

Retail customers think of public price announcements by grocers as discounts or sales on specific items. No retail customer expects to see a grocer advertise that the price of strip steaks has increased 20 percent in the past week. Retail customers expect to see public price announcements of price declines, not price increases. In addition, retail customers expect a public price announcement to be a binding commitment to a price by a grocer. If a price decrease is advertised, say from $6/lb to $5/lb for strip steaks, then each customer expects to pay $5/lb. No retail customer expects to be able to bargain for a lower price at the cash register when checking out of the store.

In contrast, for industrial customers, such as large poultry producers that regularly purchase vitamin premixes for their broilers, sellers announce price increases, not price decreases. Also, for industrial purchases, the publicly announced price is not a binding commitment to a price. These are not posted-price markets. The transaction price is determined through competitive processes, usually procurements. So a public price announcement is a communication to the market by a seller that may have no affect on transaction prices.

With regard to the distinction between retail markets and industrial markets, consider items in a grocery store—individual customers buy these products at posted prices as retail consumers, but the grocery stores buy these products as industrial buyers who use procurement processes to police the market.

In what follows, we consider price announcements by sellers who are vigorously competing,[10] tacitly colluding, and explicitly colluding.

10. Within the vernacular of Economics, this is static Nash competition.

Price Announcements by Competitive Firms
Vigorously competing noncollusive oligopolistic firms that have encountered a common increase in factor costs and/or a common positive demand shock will find themselves in a position where each firm independently has reached a determination that a price increase is warranted. In such a circumstance, it would be natural for at least one firm to publicly announce a price increase.

To understand this conduct, consider the alternatives. Suppose that no firm announces anything to buyers, and each buyer confronts higher bids in the next procurement that it conducts. Each buyer, with no forewarning from any seller of a price increase, would likely resist even a mild price increase because it would be concerned that its competitors are not confronting a similar price increase. Concerned about being competitively disadvantaged with respect to the cost of the factor input in question, each buyer would challenge the higher bids. However, the challenge would likely yield little to no concession in price from the sellers because the price increase is rooted in real economic factors that led to higher noncollusive prices. But buyers and sellers would incur incremental costs from the price resistance. Also, because some buyers may be concerned that they are being singled out for the price increase, they may investigate alternatives such as substitute products or foreign suppliers.

Private notification of a price increase does little to mitigate the push-back from buyers. It does provide the seller with the opportunity to justify the increase and offer whatever objective evidence is available for the justifications. But in the absence of a compelling set of justifications, a buyer will typically resist a price increase out of concern, again, that it has been singled out and that it will be competitively disadvantaged with respect to its peers.

A public announcement of a price increase, with accompanying public justifications, informs each buyer that it is not being singled out in some way for a price increase and, thus, that it will not be competitively disadvantaged relative to its peers. This mitigates the incentive for any buyer to resist a moderate price increase.

While the leading firms in an industry may publicly announce their price increases, it is often the case that smaller firms do not announce.[11] The smaller firms in the industry can try to slightly undercut the announced price, if that room exists. If they do not have room to under-

---

11. See Deneckere and Kovenock (1992).

cut an announced price by the industry leaders, then the last thing they want to do is publicly notify all buyers that they are incapable of doing so. Also, the publicly announced price, being rooted in a realized factor price and/or demand shock, will likely take effect immediately or in the near future. Lengthy delays in implementation of the price increase would typically not be consistent with the underlying root cause of the price increase being a factor cost and/or demand shock.

Price Announcements by Tacitly Colluding Firms

Tacitly colluding oligopolistic firms have many of the same motivations for using public price announcements as vigorously competing oligopolists. In addition, a public price announcement is a way for tacitly colluding oligopolists to signal one another.

A public declaration of a 10 percent increase in price by a large firm would be observed by all buyers as well as all sellers. However, tacitly colluding oligopolistic firms will be especially susceptible to buyer resistance because their announced price will typically exceed the price that would come from vigorous competition. Without interfirm communication to invalidate claims by buyers that other sellers are undercutting the announced price, a seller will confront a powerful incentive to reduce its price.

The initial announcement by a leading firm can act as a focal point for the other sellers in the market, but it cannot hold up against substantial buyer push-back. Thus, in anticipation of the consequences of substantial buyer resistance, tacitly colluding oligopolists will likely be cautious in advancing price increases that are not rooted in economic fundamentals.

Price Announcements by Explicitly Colluding Firms

Cartels commonly coordinate public price announcements by member firms. For example, international cartels in the vitamins industry coordinated announcements of price increases, including the designation of which company would lead the price increase.[12]

As another example, in *Rubber chemicals*, one of the components of the conspiracy was "issuing price announcements and price quotations in accordance with the agreements reached."[13] Similar charges have

---

12. *United States* v. *F. Hoffmann-La Roche Ltd*, Crim. No. 3:99-CR-184-R, May 20, 1999, Transcript of Plea of Guilty and Sentencing at paras. 10–11.
13. U.S. Department of Justice Press Release, "Crompton Corporation Agrees to Plead Guilty for Participating in Rubber Chemicals Cartel," March 15, 2004. Available at: http://www.usdoj.gov/opa/pr/2004/March/04_at_160.htm.

been made against firms in sorbates,[14] monochloroacetic acid and organic peroxides,[15] polyester staple,[16] high pressure laminates,[17] amino acids,[18] carbonless paper,[19] cartonboard,[20] and graphite electrodes.[21]

When the large buyers are multinational, their purchasing divisions may solicit bids from regions around the world. In this case, cartel members coordinate their bidding to avoid creating an opportunity for the multinational buyer to purchase all of its supply from a region where bids were lowest.[22]

A buyer that receives private notification of a price increase may resist because of concerns that it is being disadvantaged relative to other buyers. A public announcement mitigates this concern.[23]

Justifications

When publicly announcing a price increase, and presumably also when privately notifying buyers of a price increase, firms often offer justifications for the increase. Among vitamin manufacturers, justifications given in the *Chemical Marketing Reporter* during the cartel period included changes in exchange rates, factor prices, and demand. Cartels can reduce buyer resistance by offering plausible justifications for their price increases, but to avoid generating buyer resistance or arousing suspicion of illegal activity, it is important that cartel members coordi-

14. U.S. Department of Justice Press Release, "Top Japanese Executives Indicted in Price-Fixing Conspiracy," July 25, 2000. Available at: http://www.usdoj.gov/opa/pr/2000/July/423at.htm.
15. U.S. Department of Justice Press Release, "International Chemical Corp. Agrees to Plead Guilty, Pay Fines for Participating in Multiple Criminal Antitrust Conspiracies," March 14, 2002. Available at: http://www.usdoj.gov/atr/public/press_releases/2002/10835.wpd.
16. See *Hollinee LLC* v. *Nan Ya Plastics Corp.,* et al., U.S. District Court, Western District of North Carolina, Charlotte Division, October 2002.
17. "In Re: High Pressure Laminates Antitrust Litigation," Master File No.:00 MD 1368 (CLB), U.S. District Court for the Southern District of New York, June 18, 2003.
18. EC decision in *Amino acids* at paras. 53 and 164.
19. EC decision in *Carbonless paper* at paras. 233 and 236.
20. EC decision in *Cartonboard* at paras. 20 and 76.
21. U.S. Department of Justice Press Release, "German Company and Chief Executive Officer Each Agree to Pay Record Fines for International Conspiracy," May 4, 1999. Available at: http://www.usdoj.gov/atr/public/press_releases/1999/2411.htm.
22. Coordination of price increases across countries can be a challenge for a cartel, especially if buyers include multinational firms that would be sensitive to cross-country price differential that do not correspond to competitive conditions. See chapter 1, footnote 30.
23. Marshall, Marx, and Raiff (2008) emphasize the distinction between public price announcements and private notification by sellers to buyers. In an industry with an investigative trade press there will be no distinction because the trade press will unearth private announcements and report them.

nate on those justifications. (For examples of cartels coordinating justifications for price increases see chapter 2, footnote 36).

6.2.4 Implementing Price Increases

For industrial cartels, the implementation of a price increase often comes down to rigging bids at procurements. For large customers, the decisions regarding bidding often originate with top management who are aware of the existence of the cartel and the current cartel pricing goals. The orchestration of the initial bids requires a determination of the low bidder, their bid, as well as the bids of other cartel members. Sloppiness with regard to the submission of nonwinning bids is something that experienced cartels avoid.

After the submission of initial bids, there is often buyer resistance of various intensities. The cartel members are typically in communication with one another during that push-back so as to make sure that there are no unnecessary price concessions and that all cartel members are satisfied with the outcome. If the buyer resistance is particularly strong, it may be advantageous for the cartel to arrange for the designated winner from the cartel to offer some concessions to the buyer.

If there are noncartel bidders, then the cartel must devote even more effort and attention to communication among members as well as monitoring of members. The cartel will realize that some increased percentage of market share will be lost to noncartel firms because noncartel firms will be in a position to undercut the elevated cartel prices.

6.2.5 Price Discrimination by Cartels

Stigler's (1964) discussion of pricing structures implies that cartels try to increase profits by increasing the extent and scope of price discrimination among customers. For expositional simplicity throughout the book, we limit discussions of increased price discrimination and focus on the desire of sellers to increase prices to increase profits. Price discrimination can incrementally increase profits, but it can also cause discordancy for a cartel by creating opportunities for secret deviations.

The ability to sell both top-quality product and seconds might be advantageous in the abstract in terms of facilitating price discrimination, but in the case of *Trenton Potteries* the cartel's inability to monitor the exact quality of what was being sold created an opportunity for secret deviations that was destabilizing to the cartel.[24] The cartel had to ban the sale of seconds to maintain cartel pricing discipline. Thus, a

---

24. See chapter 6, footnote 4.

cartel may prefer to ban price discrimination in order to eliminate secret deviations.

In contrast, other cartels such as *Electrical and mechanical carbon and graphite products*, where carbon brushes were the main output of the cartel firms, established pricing schemes that facilitated price discrimination while still monitoring pricing by cartel members. In the case of carbon brushes, a carbon brush is typically designed and manufactured to the exact specifications of a buyer, so it is a highly idiosyncratic end product, although the potential component parts of a carbon brush are easily enumerated. The carbon brush cartel priced out each and every component of a brush through a scheme called "bareme" pricing. In this way, each cartel firm was able to verify that pricing was consistent with the cartel agreement, while allowing different prices for different design specification.[25] With the bareme pricing scheme in place, price discrimination could potentially be implemented without threatening the cartel agreement.

6.2.6 Implementing Quantity Reductions

As discussed above, some cartels focus on the implementation of quantity reductions for their pricing structure. If a cartel can successfully reduce quantity, then the market clearing price associated with that reduced quantity will be higher. Once quantities are reduced, no firm has an incentive to sell items at prices less than the market clearing price, so incentives for secret price cutting are eliminated. Thus, collusive structures for implementing quantity reductions can be viewed as pricing structures.[26]

Unless the distribution of quantity reductions among cartel members falls in line with the cartel's allocation structure, appropriate redistributions may need to be made.[27] Enforcement requires monitoring to ensure no cartel member produces more than its agreed-to amount.

25. See the EC decision in *Electrical and mechanical carbon and graphite products* at para. 91 and following. See also the EC decision in *Industrial bags* related to that cartel's calculation of a "converting price." (EC decision in *Industrial bags* at paras. 281 and 287)

26. European cartels identified by Mouraviev and Rey (2010) as involving quantity competition based on EC decisions include *Hydrogen peroxide, French beer, Luxembourg brewers, Far East trade tariff charges,* and *Europe Asia trades Agreement.*

27. In the Nitrogen Cartel, "Under the 1932 agreement certain members were indemnified for restricting output. Thus the Internationale Gesellschaft der Stickstoffindustrie A.G. paid 4.5 million RM to the Compagnie Néerlandaise de l'Azote for closing down a portion of its Sluiskil plant in the Netherlands and limiting its output to 15,000 metric tons of nitrogen for the year ending June 30, 1933." (Stocking and Watkins 1991, p. 160)

For a well-known example, the OPEC Cartel has operated by establishing petroleum output limits for its member countries. By suppressing the output of oil, they can increase the market clearing price for oil above what it would have been without the constraints.

The role of quantity reductions to increase prices is well understood by governmental agricultural price support programs that pay farmers not to grow certain crops or to leave fields fallow.[28]

Some production processes can be characterized as either "on" or "off," with no or limited ability to slow down and speed up production. For example, in the manufacture of linerboard, which is a component of cardboard, production lines typically run twenty-four hours a day, seven days a week. Shutting down a production line for maintenance or other reasons, and restarting it, is costly. When operating, there is limited ability to speed up or slow down a production line without compromising quality. Thus, for a product such as linerboard, if a production line is taken down for a period of time for reasons other than maintenance, which is anticipatable, that removes output from the market that cannot be replaced (except over a long period of time). Any such downtime corresponds to a reduction in total quantity, with associated upward pressure on the market price. In markets such as this, a cartel can effectively increase price by coordinating downtime above and beyond the required maintenance downtime.[29] Similarly, in these markets, a cartel can effectively increase price by eliminating inventories.[30]

As part of their pricing structure, cartels may have an incentive to manipulate capacity,[31] although this can have two effects. On the one

---

28. See "'OPEC of Potatoes' Hit with Price-Fixing Action," *Law 360*, June 18, 2010, discussing actions allegedly taken by the United Potato Growers of America Inc. and others to diminish the overall number of potatoes available to direct purchasers.

29. Cartel members in *Cartonboard* were attentive to downtime: "From the beginning of 1990, however, the industry leaders were faced with increased capacity and reduced demand and considered it necessary to concert on the need for taking downtime in the forum of the [Presidents' Working Group]. The major producers recognized that they could not increase demand by lowering prices and that maintaining full production would simply bring prices down. In theory, the amount of downtime required to bring supply and demand back into balance could be calculated from the capacity reports. For example, if machine utilization rates for the year were forecast at (say) 92%, this meant that 8% of capacity was not going to be used. It would therefore need four weeks of downtime by the industry to bring production and demand back into equilibrium." (EC decision in *Cartonboard* at para. 70)

30. In the Aluminum Alliance, "The Foundation Agreement required the Alliance to remove from the market, at the outset, all accumulated stocks of members in excess of forty tons per Alliance share and to pay £55 a ton for them." (Stocking and Watkins 1991, p. 262)

31. See Davidson and Deneckere (1990) and Staiger and Wolak (1992).

hand, reducing capacity among cartel members can support the cartel's goals because it limits the ability of cartel members to cheat on the cartel agreement by selling additional units at a lower price.[32] On the other hand, reducing capacity among cartel members can be at odds with cartel goals because it limits the ability of cartel members to punish deviators by expanding output and thereby driving down the price.

If a reduction in capacity serves the cartel's purposes, it may have an incentive to take advantage of natural opportunities to reduce capacity, such as fires or storms that damage a facility.[33] In that case, the cartel has an incentive not to restore the capacity or delay the restoration of the capacity. If the cartel can create an "unnatural" disruption to capacity, that can be valuable as well. In industries where new capacity is being built, a cartel may coordinate a delay in the construction of new capacity. Of course, in these cases some compensation may have to be made to the disadvantaged cartel member for acting in a way that benefits the cartel as a whole.

6.2.7 Modifying Within-firm Incentives

As discussed in chapter 2, colluding firms may want to modify incentives provided to their employees.[34] An agreement among high-level management to participate in a cartel and not compete aggressively against fellow conspirators sometimes needs to be implemented by a sales force that was formerly accustomed to being rewarded for stealing customers from competitors and increasing their firm's market share. The incentive of the sales force must change to reflect the cartel objectives. For example, a cartel firm might change sales force incentives to emphasize "price before tonnage," so that sales force members are incentivized to maintain the target prices provided by upper management even if, in the view of the sales force, that means forgoing sales that could be won through relatively small reductions in price.[35]

---

32. In the Magnesium Cartel, as part of an accord between Alcoa and I.G. Farben (IG) known as the Alig agreement, the firms "limited the initial capacity of any production company which might be licensed, whether jointly or separately owned, to 4,000 tons annually and gave IG a veto over any increase." (Stocking and Watkins 1991, p. 290)
33. "In December 1990 Rhône-Poulenc's vitamin E factory was severely damaged by fire. The major producers concluded that customers would be prepared to pay higher prices in the face of a product shortage, they also concluded that vitamin A prices could be increased at the same time on the back of the shortfall in vitamin E." (EC decision in *Vitamins* at para. 216)
34. See also Spagnolo (2005).
35. See chapter 2, footnote 46.

The issue of sales force incentives arose for cartels in *Amino Acids, Vitamins,* and *Cartonboard.*[36]

6.3   Allocation Structures

Allocation structures serve two primary purposes: to divide the collusive surplus and establish mechanisms for redistributions associated with unintentional deviations. The smooth functioning of a cartel can be disrupted if a cartel member believes that it is being relatively disadvantaged by an exogenous shift in the marketplace or economic environment. Thus, it can be important for the sustainability of a cartel that members' relative shares of the collusive surplus are perceived by each member as fair and equitable. No cartel firm wants a negative comparative evaluation of its profitability within its peer group. An allocation structure that is perceived by each member as fair can support the cartel goal of preventing the dissipation of cartel rents through internal dissension.

A customer allocation within a cartel assigns specific customers to specific cartel members.[37] A geographic allocation within a cartel specifies geographic areas where specific cartel members can and cannot sell

---

36. EC decision in *Amino acids* at para. 98 as well as chapter 2 footnotes 33, 46, and 49.

37. In *Electrical and mechanical carbon and graphite products,* the cartel "agreed account leadership for certain major customers, agreed to freeze market shares in respect of those customers, and regularly exchanged pricing information and agreed specific prices to be offered to those customers." (EC decision in *Electrical and mechanical carbon and graphite products* at para. 2)

In *Industrial tubes,* "The participants agreed also upon allocation of key customers and volumes supplied to them, monitored by customer leadership rules. KME has described the procedure of the customer discussions in the first few years of the functioning of Cuproclima as follows: 'A customer's identification number would be called. The manufacturers supplying that customer would answer the call and withdraw from the meeting in order to discuss how to proceed vis-à-vis this customer in terms of pricing, supply quantities and terms and conditions. If another manufacturer also wanted to supply the customer concerned, he would contact Mr. Truog. It was then up to the current supplier(s) whether to grant the manufacturer a supply share with respect to the said customer. In the event that several members simultaneously submitted an offer at the same price, the suppliers agreed that each manufacturer would tell the (usually major) customer that it was only able to deliver a limited quantity of tubes. The remaining quantities could then be supplied by the other manufacturer.' The customer allocation was also implemented by quoting artificially high prices, if a supplier was approached by a customer that was not allocated to it. In practice, according to Outokumpu, the customer situation changed rather often, but the market shares remained stable throughout the years." (EC decision in *Industrial tubes* at paras. 106–107)

product.[38] A market share allocation among members of a cartel specifies the maximum shares of within-cartel sales that each cartel member is allowed in the market for a given time period.

In a dynamic environment, one would not expect customers' demands to vary in exact proportion to one another, so the share of cartel surplus captured by the various cartel members under a customer allocation would be expected to change over time. Similarly, in a dynamic environment, one would not expect the demand in various geographic areas to vary in exact proportion to one another, so the share of cartel surplus captured by the various cartel members under a geographic allocation would be expected to change over time. However, with a market share allocation, the cartel focuses directly on the goal of keeping cartel members' shares of the cartel surplus constant over time.

A particular challenge for a cartel is that a secret deviation has a potentially big payoff when there are large buyers. In such a case, the cartel's allocation scheme may specify redistributions that reduce the payoff to secret deviations by firms in the cartel.[39]

Stigler (1964) emphasizes the role of a market share allocation in deterring secret deviations. As Stigler notes, an agreement to fix market shares and redistribute gains and losses from unintentional deviations is remarkably effective in averting secret deviations. With monitoring to measure aggregate production and sales by cartel member over the course of a year, each cartel member will want to stay on course to sell its market share, and nothing more, because selling more than its share will result in another firm selling less than its share and force the

---

38. A geographic allocation was used in *Tuscaloosa* v. *Harcros* 158 F.3d 548 (11th Cir. 1998), where providers of repackaged chlorine were alleged to have allocated contracts in geographic markets, and in *U.S.* v. *Koppers*, where two road construction firms divided the state of Connecticut between them: "Arthur Schuck, Koppers' manager of its eastern road materials district, made a proposal to Dosch-King in 1967 that the two firms divide the state between them so that Dosch-King would be the low bidder in the western part of Connecticut, where its activities were concentrated, and Koppers would be the low bidder in the eastern part, where its storage facility and distribution point were located." (*U.S.* v. *Koppers Co.*, 652 F.2d 290 (2d Cir. 1981) at para. 4)

On geographic patterns of trade and home bias in a non-collusive setting, see Hortaçsu, Martinez-Jerez, and Douglas (2006).

39. During the operation of the cartel in *Food flavour enhancers*, the European market for nucleotides was dominated by three main buyers, representing between 45 and 55 percent of the market. Although these large customers were allocated by the cartel to one or two cartel suppliers (Takeda and/or Ajinomoto), those cartel members purchased portions of the amounts supplied from other cartel members through "counterpurchase agreements." (EC decision in *Food flavour enhancers* at paras. 32, 64, 70, 81, 83, 86)

former firm to buy product from the latter at year end to "true-up" to the market share agreement. The purchasing firm has to buy product at cartel prices that it could otherwise produce on its own at a much lower cost—this is an implicit penalty for overselling one's market share.

It is commonplace for cartel members, at the inception of the cartel agreement, to use market shares during the year or two preceding the cartel agreement as the basis for the cartel market share allocation.[40] It is common for the initial market share allocation to be viewed as inalienable and nonnegotiable during the life of the cartel.[41] This treatment of the share allocation rule eliminates unproductive rent-seeking arguments about share allocations among cartel members.

Despite this advantage of a market share agreement, it also has drawbacks. In some cases, it may be difficult for a cartel to measure the production and/or sales of the cartel members and of the cartel as a whole in order to calculate the realized cartel shares. A cartel may find it easier and less costly to use an allocation structure such as a customer allocation or geographic allocation that approximates the desired allocation of shares. For example, if production and/or sales quantities are difficult to monitor, but if cartel firms can easily observe which customers each cartel member is serving, then a customer allocation may be straightforward to monitor. In addition, individual customers might be assigned to cartel firms in a way that approximates a relatively stable share allocation.

Similarly, it may be straightforward to monitor whether a cartel member's product crosses a geographic boundary. In this case, if geographic areas can be divided among cartel firms in a way that approximates the desired share allocation, then a geographic allocation might be used.

---

40. See the EC decisions in *Carbonless paper* at para. 81; *Citric acid* at para. 81; *Copper plumbing tubes* at paras. 137, 210, 350, 444; *Electrical and mechanical carbon and graphite products* at paras. 2, 128, 131, 219; *Graphite electrodes* at paras. 2, 71, 50, 110; *Industrial tubes* at paras. 79, 103–104, 107, 151, 195; *Organic peroxides* at paras. 85, 107–109, 135, 353; *Rubber chemicals* at paras. 66–67; *Sorbates* at paras. 84, 106–16; *Specialty graphite (isostatic)* at paras. 130, 141, 143, 147; and *Zinc phosphate* at paras. 2, 66–68.

41. As exceptions, in some cases the cartel agrees to an allowable range for market shares or a path of changing market shares over time. For example, the vitamins cartel agreed to a path of changing market shares between 1996 and 2002 for carotinoids. (EC decision in *Vitamins* at para. 528) For riboflavin, the cartel agreed to a range for cartel firm production levels. (EC decision in *Vitamins* at paras. 281–82)

These three cartel organizations are highlighted in Posner (1976), where he states:

If the major firms in a market have maintained identical or nearly identical market shares relative to each other for a substantial period of time, there is good reason to believe that they have divided the market (whether by fixing geographical zones or sales quotas or by an assignment of customers), and thereby eliminated competition, among themselves. (Posner 1976, p. 62)

In what follows, we provide discussion and examples of customer, geographic, and market share allocations. We then discuss the implementation of redistributions.

6.3.1 Customer, Geographic, and Market Share Allocation

Although each of customer, geographic, and market share allocations are observed in isolation, combinations of these cartel allocations are possible and observed. For example, if only one cartel member has production facilities in a country then the cartel may allocate that country to that producer (geographic allocation), but will likely apply a market share allocation in regions where there is no cartel production.[42]

Although market share allocations are prevalent among cartels, geographic allocations and customer allocations, as well as combinations of these with market share allocations, are observed in practice.[43] These

42. As stated in the EC decision in *Graphite electrodes*, "the 'home producer' (market leader) was to establish the market price in its home area and the other producers would then 'follow' (in the United States and parts of Europe, UCAR was designated the leader; SGL led the rest of Europe and the four Japanese producers were the market leaders in place in Japan and parts of the Far East)—for 'non-home' markets (export markets where there was no 'home' producer or market leader) prices would be decided by consensus—non-home producers should not compete aggressively; market shares would be allocated with nonhome producers being required eventually to withdraw from the home markets of the others (the allocation of non-home or export markets was to be decided at the regular 'Working Level' meetings)." (EC decision in *Graphite electrodes* at para. 50)

43. For legal opinion related to these cartel organizations, see *United States* v. *Suntar Roofing, Inc.*, 897 F.2d 469 (10th Cir. 1990) at para. 9, which states: "Consistent with the analysis of the Supreme Court and previous holdings of this court and of other circuits, we concur with the determination of the trial court and hold that the activity alleged in the indictment in this case, an agreement to allocate or divide customers between competitors within the same horizontal market, constitutes a per se violation of Sec. 1 of the Sherman Act. See *United States* v. *Topco Assocs., Inc.*, 405 U.S. 596, 608, 92 S.Ct. 1126, 1133, 31 L.Ed.2d 515 (1972) ("[o]ne of the classic examples of a per se violation of Sec. 1 is an agreement between competitors at the same level of the market structure to allocate territories in order to minimize competition"); *United States* v. *Goodman*, 850 F.2d 1473, 1476 (11th Cir.1988) ("customer allocation agreement alone is a per se violation of 15 U.S.C.

cartel organizations have different properties, specific to products/ markets/industries, when it comes to the ease of monitoring compliance, the need for updates to the agreement over time, the susceptibility of the cartel's sustainability to outside entry, and the variability of the share of cartel surplus captured by various cartel members over time.

A customer allocation can be disrupted by changes to the set of customers served by the market, including entry or exit by customers, or changes in the relative sizes of customers that cause the original customer allocation to no longer reflect the desired allocation of collusive surplus among the cartel members.

Similarly, a geographic allocation can be disrupted by changes in customer locations, including entry or exit by customers, changes in the relative sizes of customers in different geographic areas, changes in the regulatory or political environment (e.g., boycotts, tariffs, wars), or changes in boundaries that cause the original geographic allocation to no longer reflect the desired share allocation.[44]

There may be substantial issues with monitoring within-country production relative to overseas shipment of product that can lead a cartel to allocate domestic markets to domestic producers in the cartel. Some firms may simply be unwilling to join a cartel unless they are granted exclusivity with respect to certain customers that they have historically serviced and for whom they have made substantial relationship-specific investments. In addition, when firms join a cartel, they are naturally concerned about what will happen if the cartel fails. Maintaining geographic and customer allocations, even if coupled with a market share agreement, is a kind of postcartel insurance for member firms.

Any allocation structure that leads cartel members to engage in rent-seeking negotiations regarding members' shares of the collusive gain are disruptive to the stability and profitability of the

---

Sec. 1") (citing *United States* v. *Cadillac Overall Supply Co.*, 568 F.2d 1078, 1090 (5th Cir.), cert. denied, 437 U.S. 903, 98 S.Ct. 3088, 57 L.Ed.2d 1133 (1978)); *United States* v. *Cooperative Theaters of Ohio, Inc.*, 845 F.2d 1367, 1372 (6th Cir.1988) ("customer allocation . . . is the type of 'naked restraint' which triggers application of the per se rule of illegality"); *Mid-West Underground Storage, Inc.* v. *Porter*, 717 F.2d 493, 497–98 n. 2 (10th Cir.1983) ("[t] he essence of a market allocation violation . . . is that competitors apportion the market among themselves and cease competing in another's territory or for another's customers"); *United States* v. *Koppers Co.*, 652 F.2d 290, 293 (2d Cir.), cert. denied, 454 U.S. 1083, 102 S.Ct. 639, 70 L.Ed.2d 617 (1981)."
44. On the effects of exclusive territories on competition, see Rey and Stiglitz (1995).

cartel.[45] Overall, if any of the collusive structures has substantial deficiencies, that will lead to secret price deviations to the demise of the cartel.

In the end, as noted by Stigler (1964), a market share allocation scheme is a remarkably attractive cartel mechanism for mitigating secret price deviations, but there may be monitoring gaps or customer-specific investments that result in the use of an allocation mechanism that combines the relevant aspects of market share, customer, and geographic allocations schemes.

We reviewed the twenty-two major industrial-product cartel decisions of the EC from 2000 through 2005.[46] For each of these cartel cases we used the EC decision to classify the cartel's organization as involving one or more of a customer allocation, geographic allocation, market share agreement, or some other organization. These are shown in table 6.1.[47] Also shown in table 6.1, we indicate whether the EC decision mentions the involvement of third-party facilitator for the cartel's activities, such as a trade association or consulting/accounting firm. The write-ups of the EC decisions are idiosyncratic and do not purport to expose all information regarding a cartel's organization. So the absence of mention of third-party involvement in an EC decision does not necessarily mean that none was involved in facilitating cartel activities.

As shown in table 6.1, a market share agreement is a commonly used allocation structure among the cartels in the sample, although it is often augmented and combined with customer allocations and geographic allocations. As mentioned above, a market share agreement requires that cartel firms be able to observe the total production and/or sales of cartel members in order to confirm that their cartel shares are as specified according to the agreement. A trade association or other third-party facilitator can be valuable for providing this service to the cartel,[48]

---

45. Papers addressing features of cartel stability include Porter (1983b), Davidson (1984), Donsimoni (1985), Donsimoni, Economides, and Polemarchakis (1986), Ross (1992), Ellison (1994), Levenstein (1997), Lommerud and Sorgard (2001), Belleflamme and Bloch (2004), Diamantoudi (2005), Kuipers and Olaizola (2008), and Marshall, Marx, and Samkharadze (2011).

46. The cases reviewed include all EC decisions issued during the period 2000–2005 involving industrial products, as listed on the European Commission's "Cartels" website (http://ec.europa.eu/competition/cartels/cases/cases.html, accessed October 10, 2011), excluding cases for which no English-language decision is provided, and excluding the year-2000 decisions related to soda ash, which are at their essence monopolization cases. For a additional discussion of these and other cases, see Harrington (2006), Levenstein and Suslow (2006), and Connor (2008).

47. See also Harrington (2006, tab. 4).

48. For additional discussion of third-party facilitation, see the appendix to this chapter.

Table 6.1
Paragraph numbers associated with discussions in EC decisions indicating features of cartel organization and a role for a third-party facilitator

Case name	Customer allocation	Geographic allocation	Market share allocation	Other	Third-party facilitation
Amino acids			211	211 (output quotas)	100, 113, 122, 253
Carbonless paper			81	81 (output quotas)	83
Choline chloride	99	64	64, 99		
Citric acid			81		87, 100
Copper plumbing tubes	137	239 (home mkt)	210, 239, 350		240
Electrical and mechanical carbon and graphite products	128	131	128		82, 177
Food flavour enhancers	65, 68	172			
Graphite electrodes		50 (home mkt)	71		
Industrial and medical gases	101				105
Industrial tubes	2, 79, 106, 107		2, 79, 103, 104		2, 6, 113
Industrial bags	209, 251	209–211	209		166, 208

Table 6.1
(continued)

Case name	Customer allocation	Geographic allocation	Market share allocation	Other	Third-party facilitation
Methionine				64 (target prices)	
Methylglucamine	46, 98		43, 46		
Monochloroacetic acid	86, 125		65, 84, 124		70, 77–83
Needles		118, 122	125	119–123 (distribution and purchasing agreements)	
Organic peroxides			85		92
Plasterboard				429 (price increases)	
Rubber chemicals			66		
Sorbates				281 (output quotas)	
Specialty graphite			147		
Vitamins			2, 169		
Zinc phosphate	2, 68		2, 214		35, 69, 254

which is consistent with the prevalence in table 6.1 of support by third parties for the cartels.

6.3.2 Implementing Redistributions

Mistakes can happen, but successful collusive structures typically specify methods by which redistributions can be made to correct mistakes. The vitamins cartel addressed deviations from the market share agreement through "true-ups" by which a firm selling more than its allotted share would be required to purchase product from a firm selling less than its allotted share at the cartel's agreed-to price. In this way, firms were guaranteed to be able to sell their share at the cartel price, and any firms that reduced their price in order to sell more did not profit because they were forced to purchase that amount at the higher price fixed by the cartel.

Of course, one possible method of implementing redistributions is simply for one firm to make a cash payment to another. However, the illegality of collusion poses obvious difficulties for this approach. A variety of other more subtle mechanisms can be used to implement redistributions. In what follows, we highlight four: transactions at nonmarket prices, product swaps, sham litigation, and patents.

Transactions at Nonmarket Prices

Purchases of output by one manufacturer from another at market prices need not be the result of a collusive agreement. Production problems might leave one firm short of product for a period of time. A firm might be able to save on transportation costs by purchasing product from a manufacturer that is closer to its end customer rather than producing the output itself and then transporting it.

However, this type of transaction, when conducted at nonmarket prices represents a redistribution from one firm to another. For example, if one firm purchases a factor input from another at prices that are above market prices, then that constitutes a transfer of cash from the purchasing firm to the other. One would not expect to see transactions at nonmarket prices in the absence of an overarching explicit agreement between the firms.

Swaps of Product

In some industries, we observe that firms engage in swaps whereby firm A delivers product that it produced to firm B's customer and firm B delivers product that it produced to firm A's customer. This type of transaction can arise for noncollusive reasons if, for example, products are homogeneous, transportation costs are high, firm A's production facility is closer to firm B's customer, and firm B's production facility is closer to firm A's customer.[49] Perhaps, but if proximity to the customer represents a substantial comparative advantage, then one would generally expect competitive bidding between the producers to result in each producer winning the business of the customer closest to it.

Swaps provide a mechanism by which firms can make transfer payments to one another. It can be difficult to evaluate whether a particular product swap represents an interfirm transfer without detailed marketplace information. Swaps provide an avenue for interfirm communication about topics that specifically concern each firm's price, customers, and capacity utilization.

Sham Litigation

Firms in the same industry often have sufficient interaction that legitimate legal disputes can easily arise. With this cover, firms in an industry can create sham contractual agreements that can be used for the sole purpose of facilitating cartel transfers.

Firms can easily disguise a transfer payment by settling a contractual dispute for a cash payment. Such an exercise will be viewed as beneficial to the legal process because it avoids costly litigation that would otherwise congest the court system. Also, the settlement can be sealed to maintain privacy, which is viewed by the legal system as part of encouraging settlement. The ease with which such transfers can be conducted, their secrecy, and apparent lack of connection to anything regarding a price-fixing conspiracy make them particularly attractive from the viewpoint of a cartel.

Patents

Patent licensing, cross-licensing, and patent pools have been an ongoing source of concern for antitrust authorities because they provide ideal cover for communication and interfirm transfers by colluding firms as well as establishing artificial entry barriers and facilitating monitoring.[50]

49. Customer accounts may be acquired on a national level, implying a reasonable rationale for efficient swaps.
50. See Priest (1977). In addition, as stated congressional hearings on cartels: "In the incandescent electric lamp industry, . . . the Westinghouse Electric Co. pays the General

As stated in Priest (1977):

The Patent Act, as interpreted by the courts, has allowed persons granted or assigned patents broad authority to set licensee output, to allocate licensee territories, and even to fix minimum licensee prices. This has meant that a group of firms agreeing, in violation of the Sherman Act, either to fix prices or allocate output, could disguise its agreement by obtaining a patent on an unimportant process and executing licenses to previously competing members which incorporate the provisions of the illegal agreement. . . . The Justice Department has succeeded in Sherman Act prosecutions by demonstrating that meetings and conversations between competitors are evidence of conspiracy, but with patent licenses communication between firms over price, quality, and output is inevitable. (Priest 1977, pp. 309–10)

In addition, patents can be used to support collusive structures such as geographic allocations: "They could, for example, allocate sales territories. The Patent Act specifically authorizes a patentee or licensor to 'grant or convey an exclusive right under his [patent] . . . to the whole or any specified part of the United States.'"[51] Patent law is enforced through private attorneys general. Specifically, firms in an industry are presumed to have the incentive to challenge unworthy patents by competitors. But enforcement by industry competitors presumes that those firms are acting noncollusively. Once the firms collude, interfirm agreements about patents become a potentially powerful tool for implementing redistributions, as well as erecting entry barriers.

6.4   Enforcement Structures

Enforcement structures contribute two key elements to the collusive agreement: (1) they facilitate monitoring of compliance with the agreement and (2) they provide the threat of punishment to deter secret deviations by cartel members.

6.4.1   Monitoring

The choice of monitoring technology affects the allocation structure and can affect the incremental profitability of the cartel. Monitoring

---

Electric Co. a royalty of 1 percent on sales of lamps which do not exceed 25.4 percent of the combined lamp sales of the two concerns. It pays a royalty of 30 percent on sales made in excess of this. . . . The five other licensed assemblers are prohibited from making and selling lamps for export. They pay a royalty of 3⅓ percent on lamp sales which do not exceed a certain percentage of General Electric sales. They are required to pay an additional royalty of 20 percent on sales made in excess of their stipulated shares." (Temporary National Economic Committee 1940, p. 13341)
51. Priest (1977, p. 315).

may be done directly by the firms or through third-party organizations such as trade associations, export associations, or consulting firms.

To monitor a customer allocation, if each customer single sources, each firm need only observe that it is selling to the customers allocated to it. If a customer multiple sources, then it may be necessary to verify firms' shares of a customer's purchases. A buyer may have an incentive to allow a supplier to audit its purchases if the audit is required in order for the buyer to obtain rebates based on the share it purchases from the supplier.

With a geographic allocation, if each producer is in a separate country and information about cross-border trade is readily available, or if there are restrictions on cross-border trade, then monitoring can be straightforward.[52] If it is known which customers are in which geographic areas, and if customers single source, then each firm need only observe that it is selling to the customers in the geographic area allocated to it. Monitoring is more difficult if customers are not fixed and/or it is difficult to monitor the flow of goods across geographic boundaries.

With a market share allocation, monitoring might appear to be a daunting task. A global market share allocation requires that the cartel's total market size be assessed and communicated to cartel members so each cartel member can ascertain whether it has achieved its agreed-to market share.[53] If producers are located in the same country, and that country is a large market, then cross-border trade will not provide sufficient information to enforce a global market share allocation.

Cartel firms may be reticent to allow fellow cartel members access to their production facilities or their sales records, for audit purposes, but each firm may be willing to grant such access to a third party that works on behalf of the cartel. With a third-party auditor who has unencumbered access to all relevant information regarding each cartel firm, it may be straightforward to implement a global market share agreement, whereas in the absence of the third party, the cartel may need to allocate all home markets to the domestic producers.

52. The EC decision in *Copper plumbing tubes* at para. 622 states: "However, for certain durations and countries, control was facilitated by export statistics." The same decision at para. 144 states: "At least until 1995, monitoring was facilitated by national certification procedures. Copper plumbing tubes had to be certified in each Member State. Each Member State had its own certification label. Certification organisations . . . prohibited producers at least until 1995 to indicate different national certifications on plumbing tubes."
53. It is not always necessary for all cartel members to monitor all other cartel members. In some cases it may be sufficient to have one cartel firm take responsibility for

Cartels have often found ways to monitor members. In discussing the International Steel Cartel of the late 1930s, Hexner (1943) states:

> One should realize that violations which occurred sometimes happened many thousands of miles from the centers of cartel activities. However, more often than one might suppose, infringements of cartel regulations were reported by competing distributors within a few hours, even if they occurred in the most remote regions of the world. (Hexner 1943, p. 95)

For example, in *Amino acids*, "ADM named Ajinomoto as the office to which each lysine [amino acids] producer would provide monthly sales figures."[54] Stocking and Watkins (1991) state that in the Incandescent Lamp Cartel, "Each member was required to throw open his plants and research laboratories to the inspection of any member."[55]

In some cases, patent agreements can allow the enforcement of other aspects of a collusive agreement.[56] For example, in the Explosives Cartel, du Pont and ICI used patent agreements to enforce the suppression of rivalry:

---

monitoring. For example, Hay (1982, p. 454) describes the possibility of effective collusion with asymmetric information sharing: "For purposes of accomplishing the oligopoly tasks, the exchange of information need not be symmetrical. That is, the oligopolists may benefit as a group even if only some firms unilaterally provide information about their own activities."

A third-party facilitator is sometimes employed to assist with monitoring: "Fides is an industry-wide statistical service run by a Zurich-based accounting firm. Subscribing producers supply each month individual data on their production, sales and stock movements to the central office which collates the information from the different producers and draws up global anonymized statistics for the Western European market. From these each producer can determine its own market share but not those of competitors. The system contains confidentiality safeguards but there is nothing to prevent competitors exchanging detailed information themselves in some other forum. The official Fides totals could then be used, as was envisaged, to check the accuracy of the figures exchanged by the producers." (EC decision in *Low density polyethylene* at para. 11)

54. EC decision in *Amino acids* at para. 122. In other examples, the EC decision in *Organic peroxides* at para. 128 states, "Shortly before each quarterly meeting, one of the participants on a rotating basis would receive the date [sic] from the two other participants." In addition the EC decision in *Citric acid* at para. 85 states, "each company would report its monthly sales figures to [a Roche executive's] secretary in Basel, who would then contact the companies and provide each company's sale figures for the corresponding month. . . . since the sales of the four companies made up a significant part of total [European Citric Acid Manufacturers' Association] sales, the regular report of which provided aggregate sale figures, this could be used to identify any company that gave incorrect data."

55. In another example from *Specialty graphite*: "In addition, the frequent exchanges of shipment records among competitors [cartel members] allowed a detailed monitoring of sales and the detection of possible deviations to the cartel instructions." (EC decision in *Graphite electrodes* at para. 101)

56. See Priest (1977).

On their face, they were merely an exchange of rights to use patented or secret technology. In practice, however, they virtually eliminated all competition in explosives between the two companies throughout the world. They prohibited each company from selling its products manufactured under the cross-licensed patents or by secret processes in the other's exclusive territories, even though it might have produced them by its own patented or secret processes. Both companies remained free to sell unpatented products or products made by nonpatented or nonsecret processes in the territory of the other. However, complete cooperation in all protected lines was scarcely consistent with real competition in the unprotected ones, and in fact such competition has not developed. (Stocking and Watkins 1991, p. 440)

Trade Associations
Trade associations have a valuable pro-competitive role in many industries. They solve public good and coordination problems that individual firms would not solve, or would solve incompletely. First, every firm in an industry is interested in estimating demand for its product. But demand for the product of any given firm is highly correlated with the demand for the products of other producers in the industry. For every firm to estimate marketwide demand conditions is a duplicative activity. Instead of having each firm engage in that same activity, a trade association can do it once. This argument extends to many kinds of information collection and dissemination activities. Second, each firm may see a benefit to influencing legislation or regulations, but because each firm would only get its market share of the benefit from any influence costs it incurred, each firm underinvests in the activity relative to a trade association, which acts on behalf of all industry members and so accounts for the full industrywide benefit in its influence activities. Third, each firm may make a differentiated product where consumer demand is depressed by the lack of a uniform standard among producers. (Imagine a world where lightbulb threading was idiosyncratic to a manufacturer as opposed to being standardized.) A trade association can set industrywide standards that enhance the attractiveness of each firm's product to consumers.

Despite these important pro-competitive aspects of trade associations, they have historically been utilized by cartels to facilitate collusive conduct, primarily by either manipulating the information gathering and dissemination activities to be pro-collusive or by using the occasion of a trade association gathering to provide cover for cartel meetings.[57]

---

57. See Levenstein and Suslow (2010) on the role of trade associations for cartels. See also the supporting footnotes in chapter 2 and the appendix to this chapter.

Effective monitoring is facilitated if the cartel can enlist a trade association to, for example, collect data on cartel output and disseminate information to the cartel members. The accuracy of the information provided may be improved if the trade association audits the firms' reports.[58] For example, in *Amino acids*, "ADM stated that the way for them to communicate is through a trade association. ADM explained by way of example that ADM reported its citric acid sales every month to a trade association, and every year, Swiss accountants audited those figures."[59]

In order to verify compliance with a market share agreement, it may be sufficient for each firm to observe the total production of the cartel firms so it can assure itself that its share is as it should be. Thus, it may be possible for a cartel to monitor adequately through a trade association that only reports industry aggregates.[60] The EC decision in *Zinc phosphate* states: "Over the time period considered in this Decision, the five main European producers of zinc phosphate exchanged information and met within trade associations. These trade associations collected and compiled the sales data of each individual company and informed them in return about the size of the market."[61] If a cartel is not all-inclusive, in order for the trade association to play the same role as described above in facilitating collusion, it must report production numbers in a sufficiently disaggregated way that the cartel members can calculate the total production of the cartel firms.[62]

For half of the cartels shown in table 6.1, the authors of the EC decisions report that a third-party facilitator, such as a trade association, technical standards committee, or consulting firm, played an important

---

58. According to Clark (1983, p. 927), "In the typical case, an industry trade association is authorized to collect detailed information on the transactions executed by each member. To ensure full compliance, the association or an independent auditing firm is sometimes empowered to audit company records, and fines may be levied for failure to report sales quickly or accurately."

The EC decision in *Organic peroxides* at para. 92 describes how AC-Treuhand "organised the auditing of the data submitted by the parties" and "collected data on OP sales and provided the participants with the relevant statistics." See the appendix to this chapter.

59. EC decision in *Amino acids* at para. 100.

60. For commentary on the legality of a trade association providing such information, see the appendix to this chapter.

61. EC decision in *Zinc phosphate* at para. 35.

62. Henry (1994, p. 86) describes a DOJ Business Review Letter from 1992 that suggests approval for a trade association to report aggregate statistics for "relevant peer groups," creating room for the "legal" reporting by a trade association of aggregate statistics for a less than all-inclusive cartel.

role in the functioning of the cartel. In some of these cases, a trade association is described as playing a role by providing information to cartel members, others describe an outside firm as auditing data provided by cartel members, and others mention a trade association as providing cover for gatherings of cartel members. In all but one of these cases (*Industrial and medical gases*), the cartel organization involved a market share allocation. Viewed another way, of the sixteen cases where a market share allocation was a component of the cartel's organization, ten mention a role for a third-party facilitator such as a trade association or consulting/accounting firm.

Contractual Provisions

Most-favored customer (MFC) clauses typically require that a purchaser be given terms by a supplier that are no worse than the terms that supplier is granting to another purchaser, or any other purchaser of similar size. In this way, MFCs can deter secret price cutting because they make it more difficult for a supplier to offer a secret price cut to only one of its customers.[63]

Best-price guarantees state that a supplier will match the terms of competing suppliers. Best-price guarantees help cartel members to stay informed as to the prices being offered by co-conspirators and also to deter secret price cutting because the best-price guarantee typically gives the incumbent supplier the opportunity to match rival prices, thereby preventing a deviating cartel member from capturing additional business as a result of its offered price cut.

A fidelity rebate provides a purchaser with an end-of-period (e.g., end-of-year) rebate if the purchaser buys a sufficient share of its total purchases for the period from a given supplier. Before delivering the rebate to the purchaser, the supplier typically has the right to confirm that the conditions of the rebate have been met. This may involve auditing the purchaser's purchases from all suppliers for the period, providing the supplier with the ability to audit co-conspirators' sales to that purchaser.

When purchasers multisource, a market share agreement can be implemented on a customer-by-customer basis by having the cartel firms each offer fidelity rebates associated with their agreed-to market shares. For example, if there are three firms in the cartel, with an agreement to a 40%–40%–20% split of the market. The firms can offer fidelity rebates associated with a purchaser buying 40%, 40%, and 20%, respec-

---

63. See Cooper (1986).

tively, of its total purchases from each of the cartel firms. In this way, the purchaser has an incentive (unwittingly) to make sure the terms of the collusive market share agreement are satisfied. With audit provisions associated with the fidelity rebates, the firms can monitor compliance with their agreement.

6.4.2 Threat of Punishment

Cartels require a threat of punishment to deter secret deviations. A powerful threat available to a cartel is the threat of reversion to competitive behavior. If a cartel agreement is undermined by secret deviations, the firms can simply end the agreement and return to competitive interaction, where all firms receive their lower noncollusive profits.

The use of reversion to pre-collusive play as a punishment for deviations from collusion is explicitly mentioned in congressional testimony involving dyestuffs manufacturers. The testimony includes a letter from a foreign sales manager of a dyestuffs manufacturer, stating:

You and your contemporaries should be in a position to establish market prices based upon definite strength determination of color, which prices should be followed by you if such an understanding is reached. But, if you have any indication that a contemporary is not adhering to such prices, then immediately revert to the prices prevailing before any arrangements were established. (Senate Committee on Patents 1942, p. 2424)

The reversion to noncooperative behavior is a credible threat that can be used to deter not only deviations involving price, but also deviations involving nonprice product attributes. As stated by Ayres (1987):

Firms may also compete for consumers on the basis of several types of quality (by offering faster delivery, more reliable products, or a broader selection). A cartel could punish breaches of a cartel agreement by reverting to the competitive level of such nonprice variables. Again the size of these punishments would be limited by the notion of credibility. But as with pricing punishments, reverting to the competitive level of quality will be credible, because if all other firms are behaving competitively, no individual firm will have an incentive to deviate. (Ayres 1987, p. 306)

It may also be possible for a cartel to use targeted punishments.[64] As described by Ayres (1987, p. 321), a cartel using a geographic allocation

---

64. "The GQ-Agreement established penalties applicable to a whole group in case of nonrespect of the rules and the need to foresee 'a penalty clause for the member who spoils the agreed price level'. The EQ-Agreement only refers to penalties for individual (European) companies." (EC decision in *Gas insulated switchgear* at para. 141)

can implement a targeted punishment by sending extra sales people into the territory of the deviating firm. Ayres lists other potential targeted punishments as including exclusive dealing, territorial targets, and product exchanges, although others are available. For example, in *FTC v. Cement Institute*, the Supreme Court described a targeted punishment involving basing point pricing.[65]

Finally, in some cases a cartel may require firms to post bonds that are forfeit if the firm is caught attempting a secret deviation.[66] Stocking and Watkins (1991) describe the use of bonds in the "common fund" of the Steel Cartel (p. 183), the "guarantee deposits" of the Aluminum Alliance (p. 232), and the "indemnity funds" deposited at a Swiss corporation by the Incandescent Electric Lamp Cartel (p. 337).

6.5 Conclusion

The implementation of a cartel agreement can be understood through the framework implicitly provided by Stigler (1964). Secret deviations are the central negative force working against the ongoing profitability of a cartel. However, pricing, allocation, and enforcement structures

---

65. Ayres cites *FTC v. Cement Institute* 333 U.S. 683 at para. 714 in saying: "During the depression in the 1930's, slow business prompted some producers to deviate from the prices fixed by the delivered price system. Meetings were held by other producers; an effective plan was devised to punish the recalcitrants and bring them into line. The plan was simple but successful. Other producers made the recalcitrant's plant an involuntary base point. The base price was driven down with relatively insignificant losses to the producers who imposed the punitive basing point, but with heavy losses to the recalcitrant who had to make all its sales on this basis." (Ayres 1987, p. 321)

As described in Ayres (1987), in a "basing-point pricing system," sellers transport the good to the buyer's place of business and charge a "delivered price" that includes a charge for transportation: "Basing-point prices are calculated by determining the transportation charge as if all goods were shipped from a common base point even if the goods are shipped from a producer at a much closer location. A well-known early example is the 'Pittsburgh plus' basing-point system for steel prices, in which 'the delivered price of steel from anywhere in the United States to a point of delivery anywhere in the United States was in general the Pittsburgh price plus the railroad freight rate from Pittsburgh to the point of delivery.' Producers located between the basing point and their customers could thus charge customers 'phantom freight' for transportation costs (measured from Pittsburgh) that were not actually incurred." (Ayres 1987, p. 321, n. 129)

See also *FTC v. Cement Institute* at paras. 697–98.

66. Commenting on cartels' use of bonds, Hexner (1943, p. 102) states: "According to the EIA [continental European steel cartel] agreement, the management committee fixed rather high deposits, placed in the custody of the EIA business agency in Luxemburg, which were intended to insure the orderly fulfillment of obligations assumed with membership in the EIA and in the comptoirs closely connected with it."

often can be crafted to bring this negative force within satisfactory bounds.

There are criminal cartel cases that have arisen where managers of firms discussed pricing, and nominally reached agreements about pricing, but did not implement sufficient structures to prevent secret deviations by members. If any manager of any firm wants to initiate and participate in a successful cartel, they would do well to understand the components of collusive structures and their implementation.

Creating and running a successful cartel is, from our perspective, a remarkable accomplishment. Without access to the legal system to enforce agreements, successful cartels are able to profitably operate with ongoing stability. Given the creativity and flexibility of successful cartels in crafting solutions to problems, we expect changes to their operating environment to be greeted with quick and effective adjustments to the collusive structures.

In the next chapter, referring to Porter's Five Forces diagram, we examine cartel actions that go beyond the suppression of rivalry among cartel members and enhance cartel profits through actions that take advantage of the cartel's dominant position in the product market.

6.6 Appendix: Third-Party Facilitation

Cartels may find it useful to involve third-party facilitators.

6.6.1 AC-Treuhand

In this section, we focus on the role played by the consulting firm Fides Treuhandgesellschaft (Trust Company), later known as AC-Treuhand AG (as described in the EC decision in *Organic peroxides* at para. 20, AC-Treuhand AG is the result of a 1993 management buyout of the division offering association management within a company called Fides Trust AG). We focus on this firm because, according EC decisions, it has a long history of supporting cartels.[67]

---

67. See the EC decisions in *Wood pulp* at para. 43, *Low density polyethylene* at para. 11, *Polypropylene* at para. 66, *Cartonboard* at paras. 27–28, and *Organic peroxides* at para. 45. In addition, see the EC decision in *Monochloroacetic acid* at paras. 80–82 together with "Commission Fines Members of the Monochloroacetic Acid Cartel," *Competition Policy Newsletter*, Number 1, Spring 2005, available at http://ec.europa.eu/competition/publications/cpn/2005_1_71.pdf (accessed May 3, 2011). Also, "According to a statement from the European Commission, between 1987 and 2000, a host of chemical makers

AC-Treuhand AG describes itself as:

We are an independent consulting company offering a full spectrum of services tailored to national and international associations and interest groups. AC-Treuhand assists established organisations by performing functions which can only be carried out by a neutral body. AC-Treuhand is run by four managing partners with many years of experience in this speciality work. Trust, discretion, speed and continuity are the foundations of our business relations. Our strengths lie in our ability to accomodate [sic] conflicting interests and our understanding of different mentalities. (AC-Treuhand website, http://actreu .ch/welcome_e.html, accessed July 7, 2010)

As described in the EC decision in *Cartonboard*:

The large producer groups in effect agreed to maintain their market shares at the levels disclosed for each year by the annual production and sales figures and available in definitive form through Fides in March of the following year. Market share developments were analysed in each meeting of the [Presidents' Working Group] on the basis of the monthly Fides returns and if significant fluctuations emerged, explanations would be sought from the undertaking presumed responsible. (EC decision in *Cartonboard* at para. 37)

The EC decision in *Organic peroxides* describes the role of AC-Treuhand in the management of the cartel:

AC Treuhand: (a) organised meetings of the members of the agreement, often in Zurich; (b) produced, distributed and recollected the so called 'pink' and 'red' papers with the agreed market shares which were, because of their colour, easily distinguishable from other meeting documents and were not allowed to be taken outside the AC Treuhand premises (see details below); (c) calculated the 'pluses and minuses', i.e. the deviations from the agreed market shares, which were used for compensations; (d) reimbursed the travel expenses of the participants, in order to avoid traces of these meetings in the companies' accounts; (e) collected data on OP sales and provided the participants with the relevant statistics; (f) stored the original agreement from 1971 and other relevant documents concerning the agreement in its safe and handed them over to PC [Peroxid Chemie GmbH & Co. KG, Pullach]; (g) acted as a moderator in case of tensions between the members of the agreement and encouraged the parties to find compromises. AC Treuhand would try to stimulate the parties to work together and reach an agreement '*The*

---

including Akzo, Baerlocher, Ciba, Elementis, Elf Aquitaine, Chemtura, Reagens and even consultancy AC Treuhand participated in a price-fixing cartel for tin stabilizer and plasticizers. . . . EC's Competition Commissioner Neelie Kroes said AC Treuhand's Swiss offices were used for secret meetings because they were outside EC's jurisdiction." ("EU Chemical Giants Fined for Price-Fixing," *Purchasing*, Reed Business Information, December 17, 2009).

message from AC Treuhand was that it would get worse for the participants if they discontinued the discussions'; (h) was actively involved in reshaping the arrangement among producers in 1998 during a bilateral meeting in Amersfoort between Akzo representatives and [. . .] of AC Treuhand. During this bilateral meeting a solution aimed at meeting Atochem's demand was developed. The solution consisted of <u>a proposal of AC Treuhand</u> for the new quotas; (i) AC Treuhand advised the parties whether or not to allow other participants into the agreement; (j) instructed all participants on the legal dangers of parts of these meetings and on what measures to take to avoid detection of these arrangements' bearing on Europe; (k) participated mainly the 'summit' meetings but at least at once instance in the nineties attended also a working group meeting; (l) according to Akzo chaired at least some of the meetings, (AC Treuhand sees itself his [sic] in its reply to the SO not as chairman but as moderator); (m) was aware of the Spanish sub arrangement and was asked to calculate the deviation between agreed quotas and effective sales in Spain (n) organised the auditing of the data submitted by the parties (o) calculated the new quotas after the acquisition and integration of competitors in the agreement. (italics and underlining as in the original) (EC decision in *Organic peroxides* at paras. 91–93)

The EC decision in *Organic peroxides* continues at para. 93 to say, "During the seventies, eighties and in the early nineties AC Treuhand's predecessor company Fides performed similar tasks. The person involved since at least the eighties was the same, namely [. . .]."

6.6.2   Facilitation by Trade Associations

As described above, especially in the supporting footnotes of chapter 2 and in chapter 6.4.1, trade associations sometimes perform the role of a third-party facilitator. The material in this appendix is intended as a supplement to the discussion of trade associations provided elsewhere in the book.

Exhibit No. 2176 of the 1940 Temporary National Economic Committee (TNEC) congressional hearings on cartels is a public statement from the Department of Justice Division for Enforcement of Antitrust Laws that was released on June 27, 1939, and that states: "The Department's preliminary investigation indicates that certain trade associations not only disseminate production statistics but take steps to see that their members produce no more of the total supply than these statistics indicate has been their proportionate share."[68]

Exhibit No. 2173 of the TNEC congressional hearings on cartels gives a, ". . . list of industries involved in cases brought before the FTC and/

---

68. Temporary National Economic Committee (1940, pp. 13573–74).

or the courts over the last ten years in which the members of any industry employed a trade association or other common agency to deprive individual sellers of their freedom to determine their own output and/or the prices at which they may sell, or to exclude other sellers from the trade."[69]

In those same congressional hearings, Clair Wilcox testified that:

It would seem to me that the only way to obtain complete assurance that the merriment, diversion, and conversation of which Adam Smith speaks do not lead to the conspiracies or contrivances to raise prices, which he fears, would be to place an agent of the Federal Government in every trade association office to read all correspondence, memoranda and reports, attend all meetings, listen to all conversations, and participate in all the merriment and diversion, and issue periodic reports thereon to the Trade Commission or the Department of Justice or to some other agency of the Government. (Temporary National Economic Committee 1940, p. 13316)

On the potential legality of a trade association providing aggregated industry information, Sullivan and Harrison (1988) state:[70]

A review of the important Supreme Court cases on data dissemination indicates that the Court is inclined to approve an exchange of *past* data in summary or aggregate form which do not disclose individual transactions or customers, (1) where there is no disclosure of present or future information, (2) where there are no enforcement or coercive mechanisms that pressure the membership, (3) where the data are available to nonmembers for reasonable fees, or at least to those that have a 'commercial need to know' or would be at a competitive disadvantage without the information, and (4) where the market structure of the industry suggests that it is not highly concentrated or tending towards collusion. (Sullivan and Harrison 1988, p. 98)

The parties to the EC decision in *Organic peroxides* argued that the legality of a trade association providing aggregate statistics extends to private consulting firms hired by industry members (EC decision at footnote 49). According to Burns (1936, p. 58), "One important further consequence of providing statistics of total production at very short intervals is that each member is enabled to calculate the extent to which changes in his volume of business are paralleled by changes in the total volume, i.e., whether his share of the total is changing or not; the Department of Commerce approved of this use of the statistics."

---

69. Temporary National Economic Committee (1940, pp. 13560–62).
70. For additional commentary, see Jones (1922, p. 333) and Henry (1994).

Henry (1994, p. 503) suggests that there may even be antitrust benefits associated with using a trade association: "Employing an independent third party to undertake data collection, compilation, and dissemination can significantly decrease the antitrust risk. Third parties eliminate the need for direct contact between the information providers and, thus, reduce the risk of collusion. Moreover, third parties can aggregate the data so that particular information providers are not identifiable."

7 Beyond the Suppression of Within-cartel Rivalry

In this chapter, we consider ways in which cartels can go beyond simply suppressing within-cartel rivalry. In a coarse sense, the four perimeter forces of Porter's Five Forces are the focus of the cartel once it has successfully suppressed rivalry among members. However, Porter's Five Forces diagram can be augmented to more clearly portray these incremental sources of profit for a cartel.

7.1 Sharing Mutually Beneficial Investments

As discussed in chapter 5, and as portrayed in figure 5.1, the suppression of rivalry by cartel firms also involves the management of buyer resistance to price increases and the management of seller resistance to downward pressure on factor prices. The suppression of rivalry among cartel members as depicted in the center force, as well as the management of buyer and seller resistance as depicted in the light gray arrows from the right and left pointing at the cartel in the center box, are all part of the cartel's suppression of rivalry. The other forces in the diagram are forces that go beyond the suppression of rivalry by the cartel firms and are forces that the cartel can potentially act upon to incrementally increase profits. For example, the cartel could take actions that involve displacing, above and beyond standard competition, the noncartel firms.[1] Specifically, by acting as a dominant firm, the cartel can take actions directed at suppliers' and buyers' interaction with noncartel firms. In addition, the cartel members can take actions

---

1. Some firms win contracts in the course of normal competition, implying that others do not—in other words, normal competition displaces rival firms. If small firms are losing business above and beyond normal competitive displacement due to conduct by large firms that is intended, directly or indirectly, to excessively disadvantage smaller firms, then the large firms are engaged in an anti-competitive dominant-firm conduct.

designed to deter potential entrants and reduce the threat of substitute products. Finally, with respect to Porter's "sixth force," the government, the cartel members can make use of governmental intervention and institutions to promote cartel profits.

Once a cartel has controlled rivalry among its own members, if there is no substantial threat of deviation by those members, then the cartel begins to look beyond the control of within-cartel rivalry for incremental profits.[2] In other words, once the cartel has control of within-cartel rivalry, the cartel begins to act like a dominant firm in seeking additional profits.

Cartel investments and costly actions that increase profits beyond what members could earn through the suppression of within-cartel rivalry often provide a benefit to all firms in the industry, including firms not in the cartel. For example, if entry is encumbered or substitute products are made to appear less desirable to buyers, then all firms in the industry benefit. One firm in an oligopolistic industry acting unilaterally is unlikely to want to take on the full industrywide cost of such an investment or to implement such an action because it would only get a fraction of the benefit, presumably corresponding to its market share. A cartel may find such investments or actions to be in its interest, but this requires an agreement among cartel members as to how they will share the costs of such actions or investments. Historically, cartels have used the allocation structure for division of the collusive gain to allocate the costs of such investments or actions.[3]

2. See the empirical evidence and modeling results in Marshall, Marx, and Samkharadze (2011), which characterizes cartel concordancy in terms of a cartel's ability to address buyer resistance—a cartel that can confront buyer resistance without any substantive threat of a secret deviation by any cartel member is a concordant cartel.

3. Roche and BASF purchased a vitamin B_2 production innovation from Coors and contributed in proportion to their B_2 market shares to do so. (EC decision in *Vitamins* at paras. 287–88)

The Steel Cartel had as part of its articles of agreement a pool that was created to fund actions that would enhance cartel profits. The pool was funded by the members in proportion to their quotas. See Article XX of the International Merchant Bar Agreement, reproduced in English in Hexner (1943, app. V).

According to the EC decision in *Copper plumbing tubes* at para. 141, "Last, SANCO Club members shared costs for SANCO advertising campaigns and related activities for Benelux, France, Germany and Italy. Expenses for advertising were split between the SANCO producers on the basis of sold tonnage in the respective Member State."

As part of the Explosives Cartel, Dynamit A.G. (DAG), Du Pont, and Imperial Chemical Industries, Ltd. (ICI) paid an outside firm Westfälische-Anhaltische Sprengstoff A.G. (Coswig) that was posing a threat to the cartel to limit its operations: "To compensate Coswig for limiting its operations, DAG agreed to pay it £5,000 a year for ten years. Since

If the benefit accrues largely to a specific cartel member, then that firm can bear the cost alone. For example, if an allocation structure specifies that each firm has 100 percent market share in its home country, then any investments or actions to advance profits within a specific country, where there are no public good aspects of the action, would likely be born solely by the domestic producer.

In the remainder of this chapter, we discuss, within the Five Forces context, the profit-enhancing actions of cartels as they act like dominant firms. It is useful to use the Five Forces as an organizing principle even though some of the actions do not fall cleanly within a single force. We begin with a discussion of the distinctions between the profit-enhancing actions of cartels as they act like dominant firms versus the actions of true dominant firms.

7.2   A Dominant Firm versus a Cartel Acting as a Dominant Firm

It might seem that a dominant firm would be able to engage in any dominant-firm conduct that a cartel could engage in, plus additional ones. It seems that the cartel would be constrained by its structures in ways that do not constrain a true dominant firm. A cartel does confront incremental constraints, but a cartel can undertake dominant-firm conduct that is not available to a single large firm.

In practice, the first step in investigating a potential Section 2 violation of the Sherman Act is to determine whether there exists a single dominant firm in the industry. According to the U.S. Department of Justice: "As a practical matter, a market share of greater than 50 percent has been necessary for courts to find the existence of monopoly power. If a firm has maintained a market share in excess of two-thirds for a significant period and the firm's market share is unlikely to be eroded in the near future, the Department believes that such facts ordinarily should establish a rebuttable presumption that the firm possesses monopoly power."[4]

---

the other major cartel members, du Pont and ICI, were co-beneficiaries of this arrangement, they assumed part of DAG's indemnity obligation." (Stocking and Watkins 1991, p.447) "The parties estimated that half of the £5,000 was payable on account of Coswig's cooperation in joint South American territory. Du Pont and ICI agreed to contribute to this £2,500 in proportion to their shares in EIL [Explosives Industries, Ltd]." (Stocking and Watkins 1991, p. 447, n. 61)

4. U.S. Department of Justice, "Competition and Monopoly: Single-Firm Conduct under Section 2 of the Sherman Act," 2008, available at www.usdoj.gov/atr/public/reports/236681.htm.

A cartel functions as a clandestine operation, and there are many cartels where no single firm has a pre-cartel share of 50 percent (and obviously even more where no single firm has a two-thirds share). The implication is that if the threshold is not passed for any given firm in the cartel, then the cartel can undertake dominant-firm conduct without threat of being investigated by an enforcement authority. This same conduct would be off limits to any single firm that had a market share equal to the aggregate of the shares of all firms in the cartel.

Again, a cartel functions in a clandestine manner. Enforcement authorities do not know of the existence of the cartel, and those who buy from the cartel and those who supply the cartel are typically uncertain of its existence. The cartel is a beneficiary of this uncertainty because buyers and suppliers continue to believe that competitive processes still police the market. Noncartel firms are more likely to be aware of a cartel than buyers or suppliers. Potential entrants might be somewhere between noncartel firms and buyers/suppliers in terms of prior belief about a cartel's existence. Noncartel firms that are aware of the existence of a cartel understand that if a cartel can reach a point where it has successfully managed the suppression of rivalry among its member firms, then it will turn its attention to activities that displace the noncartel firms above and beyond normal competitive displacement. In addition, potential entrants may be concerned enough about predatory conduct by a suspected cartel to give that possibility weight in their entry deliberations.

The cartel's structures to avert secret price deviations impose constraints on the dominant-firm conduct the cartel can undertake. For example, loyalty rebates, which are sometimes associated with anticompetitive dominant-firm conduct, can create opportunities for cartel firms to offer secret price concessions to customers if cartel members cannot adequately monitor one another with regard to the size and scope of rebates. Similarly, if the terms and conditions of exclusive dealing provisions with certain buyers or suppliers offer an opportunity for secret deviations, then the cartel will need to avoid their use as well, or at least create incremental mechanisms for monitoring their implementation by each member firm.

Noncartel firms create a substantial set of monitoring issues for a cartel. When a market outcome occurs that is contrary to the profitability of the cartel, it often cannot be sure whether a noncartel firm was responsible or, instead, a cartel firm engaged in a secret deviation to its own benefit. If the noncartel firms cannot be persuaded to join the cartel, then killing them off not only benefits the cartel in terms of the elimination of a competitor, but it enhances cartel profits and cohesion by eliminating a way for cartel firms to disguise secret deviations from the cartel agreement. This is a powerful incremental incentive for anti-competitive dominant-firm conduct by a cartel that is absent for a true dominant firm.

We can tie this back to membership. Cartels often set market shares for members at their pre-cartel levels. A firm that remains outside the cartel and poaches on the cartel's elevation of prices may want to join the cartel once it reaches a certain size, but with a share of the collusive gain equal to its current market share, not its pre-cartel market share. This may pose an insurmountable issue for a cartel that has declared market shares as inalienable and nonnegotiable in order to avoid unproductive within-cartel rent-seeking squabbles. With foresight of this impasse, a cartel will have an extra incentive to eliminate noncartel firms.

7.3   Direct Actions against Noncartel Firms

From our review of cartel cases, predation by cartels generally involves a targeted effort as opposed to a price cut that affects everyone in the industry.[5] For example, a cartel might target the customers of noncartel firms for special pricing,[6] or a cartel might target a geographic territory

5. "According to Morgan, another way in which cartel members tried to ensure that the price levels which they had agreed could be maintained in practice in the marketplace was by exchanging information on and jointly acting against competitors. . . . The main strategies in this respect were: . . . To drive competitors out of business in a co-ordinated fashion or at least teach them a serious lesson not to cross the cartel." (EC decision in *Electrical and mechanical carbon and graphite products* at para. 167) The EC decision concludes at para. 173 saying: "These different actions took care of virtually all of the 'outsiders' active in the EEA market."

In response to the high prices for electric lamps resulting from the Incandescent Electric Lamp Cartel, "In 1928 the Swedish Cooperative Union (Kooperativa Förbundet), convinced that cartel prices were unreasonably high, laid plans to build a lamp factory. Phoebus promptly met this move by a substantial cut in lamp prices and by the threat of patent suits."(Stocking and Watkins 1991, p. 343)

For a theoretical model of oligopolistic predation, see Argenton (2011).

6. "A 'Sherpa' meeting was held in London on 14 January 1994 . . . . The increasing availability of Chinese production in the European market and the need for a more forceful stance by the cartel members to maintain their level of sales in the light of this were subjects of discussion at the meeting. Participants 'accepted that there would have to be a price war against the competition from China' and that they had to 'try and regain particular accounts [lost to the Chinese producers] at whatever price was necessary with the blessing of the others'. 'These customers were identified by name, and were allocated

or route (for transport services) of a noncartel firm.[7] Cartel firms might simply buy up noncartel firms to eliminate them as competitors.[8]

We also observe that cartels engage in a variety of other predatory practices that are not focused on reducing prices. For example, a cartel might engage in marketing activities designed to disadvantage noncartel firms.[9] A cartel controlling a critical factor input might cut off sup-

---

to individual participants, who were to make the necessary offers'. This catalogue of undertakings came to be known as the 'Serbia List' and was the subject of regular monitoring and discussion at subsequent 'Sherpa' meetings . . . ." (EC decision in *Citric acid* at para. 119)

7. In the International Steel Cartel, "To fight outside competition, the committee could authorize sales in any area 'at prices appreciably below normal prices.' However, if this occurred, the committee had to distribute the resultant sacrifice fairly among the several national groups." (Stocking and Watkins 1991, p. 190) *See also* Article XV of the International Merchant Bar Agreement, reproduced in English translation in Hexner (1943, app. V).

The Nitrogen Cartel compensated Belgian producers for restricting output: "The 1938 agreement also provided for an annual payment of 12*d.* to the Belgian group of producers for every 100 kg. of nitrogen which cartel members sold in their home and foreign markets to compensate the Belgian producers for restricting output under a supplementary agreement made between the DEN group and the Belgian group." (Stocking and Watkins 1991, p. 160) "These payments were made quarterly out of a common fund set up in the cartel agreement. The Chileans contributed £150,000 to the fund plus 1.5*d.* for every 100 kg. of nitrogen which they sold. The balance came from European cartel members (with the exception of the French and Italian groups) in proportion to their sales." (Stocking and Watkins 1991, p. 160, n. 68)

"A 1914 report of the House Committee on the Merchant Marine and Fisheries, known commonly as the ' Alexander Report,' found that these shipping conferences had effectively monopolized nearly every American foreign trade route, through price-fixing, allocation of markets, and pooling of revenues. They had successfully conspired to drive competitors from the market or coerce them to join the conferences, through the use of conference-subsidized ' fighting ships' that systematically undercut competitors' rates for however long it took to drive them out of business." (Statement of John M. Nannes, Deputy Assistant Attorney General, Antitrust Division, U.S. Department of Justice, Before the House Committee on the Judiciary on HR 3138, The Free Market Antitrust Immunity Reform Act of 1999, Washington, DC, March 22, 2000, p. 2, available at http:// www.justice.gov/atr/public/testimony/4377.pdf, accessed October 14, 2011) See also Scott Morton (1997).

8. As part of the International Steel Cartel, "Leading producers acquired marginal firms to stifle competition. They paid for these properties prices representing their nuisance value to the cartel, rather than values based on their independent earning power. For example, in 1930, during negotiations for renewal of the domestic cartel, members bought plants of numerous independents threatening competition at an estimated cost of 60 to 70 million marks—far more than their market value on the Berlin stock exchange." (Stocking and Watkins 1991, p. 177)

9. The Incandescent Electric Lamp Cartel had a "propaganda division," which "strove to increase the use of electric lamps, and members' lamp sales at the expense of those of non-cartel members." (Stocking and Watkins 1991, p. 335)

plies to noncartel firms.[10] A cartel might construct incentives for buyers such that the buyers essentially boycott noncartel firms.[11] In the case of an impending entrant, the cartel might buy out the noncartel firm's technological innovation.[12]

7.4   Perimeter Forces

7.4.1   Threat of Substitute Products
The profitability of elevated cartel prices can be reduced by the presence of substitute products because buyers can respond to the elevated

---

10. "A local meeting in Germany on 7 May 1992 records a discussion among cartel members on how best to act against EKL, a competitive East-German cutter that had entered aggressively into the West-German market after unification. Two strategies were agreed: First, none of the members of the cartel would supply any graphite to EKL. Secondly, EKL would be denied any market share by systematically undercutting it with all customers, so that it would not be able to sell anywhere. EKL was taken over by SGL in 1997." (EC decision in *Electrical and mechanical carbon and graphite products* at para. 157)

"According to Daiichi, BASF and Roche had another strategic incentive to raise the price of calpan and indeed of other vitamins used for animal feed. Both have a strong market position in pre-mixes by virtue of their integrated production of the vitamins used. By increasing the prices of the vitamins used in pre-mixes, they would put a price squeeze on their competitors in this downstream activity, and over time drive the smaller pre-mixers from the market." (EC decision in *Vitamins* at para. 322)

In their discussion of the Aluminum Alliance, Stocking and Watkins (1991, p. 225) state: "Whether or not one interprets Alcoa's integration and expansion program as, in part, a 'pre-emptive' buying up of bauxite deposits and hydroelectric sites and an aggressive 'buying out' of independent fabricators, other features of its development support the view that Alcoa actively tried to block independent competitive enterprise in the field. And, in the main, it succeeded. During the early stages of its integration, Alcoa's general practice was to exact from sellers of properties which it acquired covenants not to compete afterwards, directly or indirectly, with Alcoa. Similarly, it frequently required its suppliers not to deal with any other aluminum manufacturer."

11. The Second International Steel Cartel "licensed distributors in the importing countries, and required them not only to observed fixed resale prices and terms, but to handle exclusively products of cartel members. . . . Cartel members ordinarily refused to sell to unlicensed distributors." (Stocking and Watkins 1991, p. 190)

"Through tying contracts, [General Electric] forced distributors to buy all their carbon filament lamps (on which the basic patent had expired) from General Electric and associated companies if they were to obtain lamps of improved design manufactured exclusively by General Electric and its associates." (Stocking and Watkins 1991, p. 306)

In part because of patent agreements, du Pont and Röhm & Haas were at one point the only American producers of methylmethacrylate plastics. With the support of du Pont, Röhm & Haas was able to "extract from their customers a guarantee that they would not use their commercial powders in the manufacture of dentures or sell them for such use, and to cut off sales to purchasers who did not keep that promise." (Stocking and Watkins 1991, pp. 402–403)

12. See footnote 3 of this chapter.

cartel prices by switching to substitute products.[13] Cartels can take actions to encumber or block substitute products from the market.[14] The cartel actions can include marketing campaigns that advocate the cartel product as superior to the substitute or that attack the substitute product.[15] The cartel may sponsor research to "objectively" demonstrate the superiority of their product over substitutes.

Sometimes cartels take actions to expand the cartel to include the substitute products. In other cases, cartels take actions that threaten the producers of substitute products so that they do not encroach significantly on the cartel's product markets.

7.4.2   Threat of New Entrants

Entrants are lured to a product market by the possibility of above-normal profits. Cartels are aware of this and may limit the extent of their price increases in order to deter entry.[16] As we mentioned earlier, a potential entrant can be bought out by a cartel or can face predatory conduct from the cartel upon entry. A potential entrant to the production of the cartel's product can also be offered the option of purchasing the product from the cartel rather than producing it,[17] or it can be offered the option of collaboration with a cartel firm.[18]

13. "High prices for rubber resulting from collusion by rubber manufacturers spurred the development of substitutes for crude rubber." (Stocking and Watkins 1991, p. 73)
14. The antitrust case brought by RAMBUS against Hynix, Micron, Infineon, and Samsung alleges that the DRAM manufacturers conspired to exclude the competitor technology made by RAMBUS from the market. Hynix, Samsung, and Infineon had earlier pled guilty to a price fixing conspiracy in DRAM, where Micron was the amnesty applicant. ("Rambus and a Price-Fixing Tale," *Bloomberg Business Week*, October 31, 2005, available at http://www.businessweek.com/technology/content/oct2005/tc20051031_874429.htm, accessed January 18, 2011; and "Rambus Announces Developments in Patent and Antitrust Cases; Judge in Rambus Antitrust Case Rejects Defendants' Demurrer, Case to Proceed to Discovery; Micron and Hynix Patent Cases Also Move Forward," *Business Publications*, April 25, 2005, available at http://findarticles.com/p/articles/mi_m0EIN/is_2005_April_25/ai_n13650188/, accessed January 18, 2011)
15. This is advocacy of the cartel's product as a whole and not of the specific product of an individual cartel firm (e.g., the advantages of folic acid generally, not Roche's brand of folic acid specifically). Any individual firm in the cartel would likely not invest in such a campaign acting unilaterally because they would get only a small part of the benefit while incurring all the cost.
16. The 1938 agreement of the Nitrogen Cartel provided that "prices in export markets should be maintained at a level low enough to discourage the development of domestic production." (Stocking and Watkins 1991, p. 162)
17. In the Alkali Cartel, "In their 1924 compact, ICI and Alkasso agreed to sell alkali at preferential prices to a Brazilian company, Matarazzo, which was contemplating manufacture." (Stocking and Watkins 1991, p. 437)
18. In the Alkali Cartel, "In Argentina, du Pont and ICI persuaded a local paper company which had decided to manufacture its own alkalies to do so in collaboration with their local subsidiary." (Stocking and Watkins 1991, p. 437)

Entry may be encumbered if the cartel withholds necessary technology from potential entrants.[19] The withholding of technology can be facilitated by a cartel's use of patent law. Cartel members may seek and be granted process patents, where a potential entrant would need to pay for licenses and confront the possibility of being "held-up" in later negotiations as the incumbent firms in the cartel develop incremental process innovations.[20] Cartel firms may engage in cross-licensing among themselves, whereby they share technological innovations, but exclude potential entrants from full access to such innovations.[21]

Cartels can also make investments in securing government regulations that act as entry barriers. These are particularly attractive when there are grandfather clauses for incumbent firms in the industry. We discuss this in more detail in chapter 7.5 below.

7.4.3 Bargaining Power of Buyers and Suppliers

There is substantial symmetry in how the cartel can address the right and left forces in figure 1.1—the bargaining power of buyers and suppliers. Our exposition concerns buyers, although equivalent analyses can be readily applied to suppliers.[22]

The cartel must use its dominant-firm position with care so as not to reveal to buyers that competitive processes have been compromised,

---

19. A principle of the Graphite Electrodes cartel was that "there should be no transfer of technology outside the circle of producers participating in the cartel." (EC decision in *Graphite electrodes* at para. 50)

20. See Priest (1977).

21. Magnesium Cartel members Alcoa and IG "pooled all their patents and technical knowledge on magnesium production and fabrication. To exploit this common fund, they agreed to organize a joint patent-holding company, sharing equally in its ownership." (Stocking and Watkins 1991, p. 289)

As part of the Incandescent Electric Lamp Cartel, General Electric "entered into a cross-licensing patent agreement with its chief rival, Westinghouse Electric & Manufacturing Company." (Stocking and Watkins 1991, p. 305) Later, "On May 25, 1905, General Electric signed an agreement with British Thomson-Houston (in which it also owned a controlling stock interest) providing for an 'exchange of patents, information and selling rights in specified territories.' The agreement recognized North America and the colonies and protectorages of the United States as General Electric's exclusive territory, the United Kingdom as the exclusive territory of British Thomson-Houston." (Stocking and Watkins 1991, p. 322)

For the text of cross-licensing agreements between ICI and du Pont, see "Patents, Hearings before the Committee on Patents," U.S. Senate, 77th Congress, Second Session, on S. 2303 and S. 2491, Part 5, May 13 and 16, 1942, at p. 2304f.

See also Priest (1977).

22. "Together with other lamp manufacturers [General Electric] made exclusive contracts with the manufacturers of lamp-making machinery and of bulbs and tubing, binding them to sell goods exclusively to General Electric and the companies associated with it, or to sell to competing companies only at discriminatory prices." (Stocking and Watkins 1991, p. 306)

if not rendered impotent, by explicit collusion. Consider a contract with a buyer that specifies a lump-sum payment as a loyalty rebate if the buyer acquires a specific percentage of its total purchases from the firm. Of course, the percentage would be consistent with the cartel's agreement regarding the allocation of that firm's business among cartel members. Another cartel firm may have a contract with the same buyer for a different percentage, again consistent with the cartel's agreement. A third cartel firm may negotiate with the buyer to a complementary percentage.

To ensure compliance by the buyer, the cartel firms would have audit provisions in their individual contracts. The buyer could be quite happy with the lump-sum rebates, especially because there is no marginal benefit to the buyer in purchasing beyond the market share that triggers the lump-sum payment from each seller, and the shares of the buyer's annual purchases sum to 100 percent across all the cartel firms. From the perspective of dominant-firm conduct, the cartel has incented the buyer to deal exclusively with the cartel firms without ever giving the impression that competitive processes have been encumbered.

Furthermore, the cartel firms may have agreements of this nature with many buyers, all for varying percentages, where the market share of any cartel firm over all buyers equals their overall cartel market share allocation. This kind of contractual arrangement with buyers by cartel firms is an incremental testimony to the creativity of cartels in enhancing profits. The audit provision in the contracts encumbers any cartel firm from engaging in a secret deviation.

Quite remarkably, buyers often debrief bidders after a procurement regarding the details of the outcome. Sales staff of sellers are often required to file formal competitive reports regarding the information revealed from these debriefings. Under the presumption that competitive processes are policing the market, buyers may believe that providing such information to unsuccessful or partially successful bidders will result in their bidding more aggressively in future procurements. From the perspective of a cartel, this intelligence greatly facilitates the monitoring of members, and thus makes it more difficult for them to undertake secret deviations, and easier to determine which customers are buying from noncartel firms. These latter buyers can be targeted for special pricing in the future, to the detriment of the noncartel firms.[23]

---

23. See footnote 6 in this chapter.

Cartels may require that buyers deal exclusively with cartel firms.[24] In these circumstances, it appears that the buyers have no substitute product options and that noncartel firms alone cannot consistently supply such buyers. In other words, the cartel knows that it has all the bargaining power, that the buyers have no meaningful options, and that the buyers will be effectively foreclosed from supply if they resist the conspiracy.

7.5 Sixth Force of Government

Regardless of the presence or absence of a cartel, government intervention can affect industrywide profits either negatively or positively, depending on the nature of the intervention. In this section, our focus is on government intervention that is of particular value to a cartel.[25] Some such intervention is implemented as a consequence of coordinated efforts by cartel firms. Sometimes the benefits of the intervention extend to noncartel firms, but the cartel still invests effort to obtain it because the cartel is the primary beneficiary. Most government intervention that assists cartel firms falls into one of the following categories:

1. Create incremental incentives for creation of a cartel

2. Suppress within-cartel rivalry

3. Implement collusive structures

4. Directly displace noncartel firms above and beyond normal competition

5. Enhance the use of perimeter forces to displace noncartel firms above and beyond normal competition

6. Encumber entry

7. Make substitutes less desirable or ban them altogether

Government intervention in the market can be harmful to a cartel, especially when the intervention is focused on antitrust concerns and the protection of consumer surplus. However, a government may be

---

24. See footnote 11 in this chapter.
25. In some cases, antitrust exemptions are available to certain groups of firms. We do not concern ourselves with legislation targeting specific industries, such as professional sports, but rather we focus on legislation that directly or indirectly assists cartel firms in enhancing their profits.

helping cartels conduct their business when it intervenes to promote domestic industry,[26] provide domestic firms with better information,[27] increase transparency in market transactions, address externalities without harming incumbent firms, and "improve" judicial and regulatory processes. In addition, there are industries where government intervention has created entry barriers or mitigated other perimeter forces so that incumbent firms now see that the leading detriment to their profits is interfirm rivalry, implying a new focus of energy by these firms on suppressing that rivalry through collusion.

Cartels are adept at utilizing any new instrument or change in circumstance to facilitate their operation and enhance their profitability. Government intervention that is designed to help industries, under the presumption that firms are vigorously competing, will be used by a cartel to its advantage.[28] In addition, firms in an industry may advocate for certain kinds of government intervention that appear to be consistent with the pursuit of objectives that advance social surplus, when in fact this intervention is designed to facilitate cartel profits. For example, environmental regulations that substantially raise costs for new entrants but grandfather existing production facilities greatly enhance cartel profits.

There is a substantial body of U.S. law that allows U.S. firms to engage in cartel conduct provided that none of the conduct has a

26. "The important rise in prices at the beginning of the 1990s was partially responsible for a new influx of citric acid imports from China. . . . This had an important impact on the cartel's ability to maintain the agreed prices and became an increasingly serious problem, although various means of counteracting the price-depressing effect of Chinese imports were devised and implemented. Under cover of their [European Citric Acid Manufacturers' Association (ECAMA)] membership, the undertakings composing the cartel studied the possibility of causing an anti-dumping proceeding to be initiated against the Chinese importers by the European Commission. They continued to apply this type of pressure by sending representatives of Jungbunzlauer and ADM to China, on behalf of ECAMA, to inform the local manufacturers that anti-dumping proceedings would be initiated if their price-cutting practices were not terminated." (EC decision in *Citric acid* at para. 116)

27. "At least until 1995, monitoring was facilitated by national certification procedures. Copper plumbing tubes had to be certified in each Member State. Each Member State had its own certification label. Certification organisations . . . prohibited producers at least until 1995 to indicate different national certifications on plumbing tubes. This segmentation of national markets led to different price levels in different Member States. Between different Member States, margins were up to twice as high for the same copper plumbing tube." (EC decision in *Copper plumbing tubes* at para. 144)

28. As stated in Stocking and Watkins (1991, p. 344, n. 108) with respect to the incandescent electric lamp cartel, ". . . the Dutch and German Governments by means of tariffs and import quotas have aided and abetted the cartel in carrying out its restrictive programs."

negative direct or indirect impact on U.S. consumers. The appendix to this chapter reviews some of these. Export associations are a leading example. Export associations are legal entities through which U.S. firms can engage in interfirm communications and coordinate their efforts with respect to foreign markets. The set of actions that are allowed within the umbrella of an export association appear to be essentially the same as those that a cartel would want to undertake. If the firms in an industry are meeting to discuss pricing, allocation, and enforcement structures with respect to foreign markets for a product they produce and sell both domestically and overseas, it seems reasonable to believe that these firms would not undergo collective amnesia when it comes time to individually consider such issues for the United States.

7.6   Conclusion

Once a cartel is able to successfully elevate prices in the face of buyer resistance without secret deviations by members, it can then turn its attention to incrementally increasing profits through conduct that acts upon perimeter forces.[29] Remarkably, it is often the case that a cartel will be able to better take advantage of dominant-firm conduct for the enhancement of profit than a true dominant firm because a cartel's existence is disguised from both buyers and sellers as well as enforcement authorities. A true dominant firm can do many things that a cartel cannot do,[30] but that is unsurprising.

Noncartel firms create a special problem for a cartel because cartel members may be unable to determine whether a market outcome was the result of an action by a noncartel firm or arose from a secret deviation by a cartel firm. Thus, relative to a true dominant firm, a cartel has an extra incentive to eliminate smaller firms from the market. In this light, it seems reasonable that dominant-firm conduct by a cartel is more likely to be anti-competitive.

As a final point, if one observes a subset of firms in an industry engaging in dominant-firm conduct, while none of the firms is large

---

29. See Marshall, Marx, and Samkharadze (2011).
30. For example, a true dominant firm can change the allocation of production across divisions through time to maximize profits, whereas a cartel must abide by the terms of its allocation structure throughout time, which might encumber profits relative to a true dominant firm that has greater flexibility.

enough on its own to act as a dominant firm,[31] then the inference of collusion is strong. This point is further developed in part IV.

7.7 Appendix: Antitrust Exemptions

Despite U.S. government exhortations for tougher antitrust laws and enforcement,[32] the U.S. Congress has passed numerous laws that facilitate collusion, especially with regard to overseas markets. As summarized in Kihlstrom and Vives (1989):

> Some agricultural cooperatives and export associations are partially exempted from the antitrust laws. Specifically, the Capper–Volstead Act of 1922 and the Agricultural Marketing Act of 1937 apply to exempt agricultural cooperatives from the application of the antitrust laws, and the Webb–Pomerene Act of 1918 exempts export associations from these laws; see, e.g., Scherer (1980) and Madhaven et al. (1988). Thus, for agricultural cooperatives and export associations, cartel agreements involving sidepayments may, indeed, be viable and enforceable. (Kihlstrom and Vives 1989, p. 373)

We discuss two such exemptions: export trade associations and marketing orders.

7.7.1 Export Trade Associations

The Export Trading Company Act of 1982, which extends the Webb–Pomerene Act,[33] allows registered U.S. producers to function as a cartel with regard to export markets provided that there is no feedback from their collusive conduct to the U.S. market. A large number of industry groups have registered with the federal government under the Act.[34]

31. For example, consider the example offered by Kovacic et al. (2011) of vertical foreclosure conducts by a subset of firms in an industry targeted at one or a few small firms in the industry, where no single firm in the subset has sufficient market power to act unilaterally as a dominant firm.

32. See, for example, "Administration Will Strengthen Antitrust Rules," *New York Times*, May 11, 2009.

33. American participation in the International Steel Cartel was through the Steel Export Association of America, organized in 1928 under the Webb–Pomerene Act. (Stocking and Watkins 1991, p. 191, n. 48)

Similarly, American participation in the World Alkali Cartel was through the United States Alkali Export Association, Inc. (Alkasso), which was a Webb–Pomerene association formed in 1919. (Stocking and Watkins 1991, p. 433)

34. A list of current Export Trade Certificate of Review holders is available at the webpage for the Export Trading Company Act on the website of the U.S. Department of Commerce's International Trade Administration http://www.trade.gov/mas/ian/etca/tg_ian_002147.asp (accessed October 14, 2011).

For example, the U.S. Department of Commerce suggests potential partners should consider joint bidding,[35] joint selling arrangements,[36] and price fixing.[37] The application for status as an Export Trade Association requires that applicants "Describe the specific export conduct which the applicant seeks to have certified. Only the specific export conduct described in the application will be eligible for certification. For each item, the applicant should state the antitrust concern, if any, raised by that export conduct."[38] The sample application provided by the Department of Commerce, which uses a fictitious pasta manufacturer, Ninth Pennsylvania Reserve Corporation, as the example, includes the following:

1. Ninth Pennsylvania Reserve Corporation, on its own behalf or on behalf of any or all of its Members may: a. Sales Prices. Establish sale prices, minimum sale prices, target sale prices and/or minimum target sale prices, and other terms of sale in export markets; b. Marketing and Distribution. Conduct marketing and distribution of Products in export markets. c. Promotion. Conduct promotion of Products; d. Quantities. Agree on quantities of Products to be sold, provided each Member shall be required to dedicate only such quantity or quantities as each such Member shall independently determine. e. Market and Customer Allocation. Allocate geographic areas or countries in the Export

35. "U.S. firms can increase sales and profits through joint bidding. As a group, the joint venture can respond to foreign orders requiring quantities beyond the productive capacity of the individual member firms, and it can accomplish sales while frustrating a foreign buyer's ability to play U.S. sellers off against one another." (Webpage for Export Trading Company Affairs describing the Export Trade Certificate of Review Program on the website of the U.S. Department of Commerce's International Trade Administration, http://trade.gov/mas/ian/etca/tg_ian_002154.asp, accessed October 14, 2011)
36. "Any number of joint venture partners may join together and submit a single bid on a particular project or tender. The partners can use the same overseas representative, agree to sell separate products as a unit, prepare joint catalogs, and allocate among participating partners the sales which result from joint bidding or selling arrangements." (Webpage for Export Trading Company Affairs describing the Export Trade Certificate of Review Program on the website of the U.S. Department of Commerce's International Trade Administration, http://trade.gov/mas/ian/etca/tg_ian_002154.asp, accessed October 14, 2011)
37. "Two or more joint venture partners might agree to establish uniform minimum export prices for particular products in order to avoid price rivalry with each other. For some joint ventures, higher profits might be secured through joint negotiations on prices and on terms of sale with foreign buyers." (Webpage for Export Trading Company Affairs describing the Export Trade Certificate of Review Program on the website of the U.S. Department of Commerce's International Trade Administration, http://trade.gov/mas/ian/etca/tg_ian_002154.asp, accessed October 14, 2011)
38. Item 10 of the Sample Application for an Export Trade Certificate of Review on the website of the U.S. Department of Commerce International Trade Administration, http://trade.gov/mas/ian/build/groups/public/@tg_ian/documents/webcontent/tg_ian_002211.pdf, accessed October 7, 2011.

Markets and/or customers in the Export Markets among Members; f. <u>Refusals to Deal</u>. Refuse to quote prices for Products, or to market or sell Products, to or for any customers in the Export Markets, or any countries or geographical areas in the Export Markets; g. <u>Exclusive and Nonexclusive Export Intermediaries</u>. Enter into exclusive and nonexclusive agreements appointing one or more Export Intermediaries for the sale of Products with price, quantity, territorial and/or customer restrictions as provided above;

2. Ninth Pennsylvania Reserve Corporation and its Members may exchange and discuss the following information: a. Information about sale and marketing efforts for the Export Markets, activities and opportunities for sales of Products in the Export Markets, selling strategies for the Export Markets, sales for the Export Markets, contract and spot pricing in the Export Markets, projected demands in the Export Markets for Products, customary terms of sale in the Export Markets, prices and availability of Products from competitors for sale in the Export Markets, and specifications for Products by customers in the Export Markets; b. Information about the price, quality, quantity, source, and delivery dates of Products available from the Members to export; c. Information about terms and conditions of contracts for sale in the Export Markets to be considered and/or bid on by Ninth Pennsylvania Reserve Corporation and its Members; d. Information about joint bidding or selling arrangements for the Export Markets and allocations of sales resulting from such arrangements among the Members; e. Information about expenses specific to exporting to and within the Export Markets, including without limitation, transportation, trans- or intermodal shipments, insurance, inland freights to port, port storage, commissions, export sales, documentation, financing, customs, duties, and taxes; f. Information about U.S. and foreign legislation and regulations, including federal marketing order programs, affecting sales for the Export Markets; g. Information about Ninth Pennsylvania Reserve Corporation's or its Members' export operations, including without limitation, sales and distribution networks established by Ninth Pennsylvania Reserve Corporation or its Members in the Export Markets, and prior export sales by Members (including export price information); and h. Information about export customer credit terms and credit history.

3. Ninth Pennsylvania Reserve Corporation and its Members may meet to engage in the activities described in paragraphs 1 and 2 above. (Response to Item 10 of the Sample Application for an Export Trade Certificate of Review on the website of the U.S. Department of Commerce International Trade Administration, http://trade.gov/mas/ian/build/groups/public/@tg_ian/documents/webcontent/tg_ian_002211.pdf, accessed October 7, 2011)

There is a remarkable breadth of allowable interfirm anti-competitive communications and legally enforceable agreements that are possible under this Act. It is difficult to imagine how U.S. firms could engage in an export trade association meeting, having detailed discussions about pricing in foreign markets, quantity restrictions, the use of common agents, redistributions, and mechanisms for ongoing interfirm communication, and not have this spill over in any way to aspects of the U.S. domestic market.

7.7.2 Federal Marketing Orders

As described on the USDA website, under a Federal Marketing Order, groups of growers and handlers for agricultural products (dairy products, fruits, vegetables, and specialty crops)[39] can "elect to operate under self-imposed rules to enhance the marketability of their commodity."[40]

Federal marketing orders are locally administered by committees made up of growers and/or handlers, and often a member of the public. Marketing order regulations, initiated by industry and enforced by USDA, bind the entire industry in the geographical area regulated if approved by producers and the Secretary of Agriculture. Marketing orders and agreements (1) maintain the high quality of produce that is on the market; (2) standardize packages and containers; (3) regulate the flow of product to market; (4) establish reserve pools for storable commodities; and (5) authorize production research, marketing research and development, and advertising. (Webpage for "Marketing Orders and Agreements" on the website of the U.S. Department of Agriculture http://www.ams.usda.gov/AMSv1.0/FVMarketingOrderLandingPage, accessed October 14, 2011)

In 2009, as part of a Federal Marketing Order in tart cherries, tart-cherry farmers were told to leave up to 40 percent of their crop unharvested:

The tart-cherry industry operates under a government-sanctioned plan called a federal marketing order that dates to 1933. It allows farmers and processors to legally regulate supply to keep prices stable. . . . This year, the industry board, a 18-member panel of growers and processors determined that there were more than enough cherries in the fields to satisfy demand and to replenish the reserves. So the board limited how much processors can put on the market in the U.S. That leaves farmers with cherries they can't sell and are left to rot. ("Bumper Cherry Crop Turns Sour," *Wall Street Journal*, August 22–23, 2009)

---

39. Webpage for "Marketing Orders and Agreements" on the website of the U.S. Department of Agriculture, http://www.ams.usda.gov/AMSv1.0/ (accessed October 14, 2011).
40. Webpage for "Industry Marketing and Promotion" discussing "Marketing Orders and Agreements, and Generic Promotion" on the website of the U.S. Department of Agriculture, http://www.ams.usda.gov/AMSv1.0/ams.fetchTemplateData.do?template=TemplateA&page=FVOrdersandPromotion (accessed October 14, 2011).

III Economics of Bidding Rings

In this part of the book, we focus on bidding rings at auctions and procurements. Much of the economic analysis of auctions applies to procurements and vice versa. In an auction, bidders have values associated with owning the object, and they bid to maximize their expected surplus, which is the difference between their value for the object and how much they have to pay if they win, times the probability that they win. In a procurement, bidders have costs for providing the object being procured, and they bid to maximize their expected surplus, which is the difference between the amount they would be paid if they win and their cost, times the probability that they win. The often tight relation between auctions and procurements means that the issues faced by bidding rings are similar regardless of whether the ring operates at an auction or procurement. Thus, we do not present separate analyses for auctions versus procurements.

In chapter 8, we discuss the gains to the suppression of competition by bidders. In chapter 9, we discuss the structures required to successfully implement the suppression of rivalry, providing examples based on real cases. In chapter 10, we consider how the design of an auction or procurement affects the structures required for a ring to successfully operate.

8   Suppression of Interbidder Rivalry by Rings

Before delving into the suppression of interbidder rivalry, we offer an introduction regarding the important role that competition plays with regard to information revelation and price discovery for market participants.

8.1 Role of Auctions and Procurements in Price Discovery

Auctions and procurements are used throughout market-based economies and account for a large volume of economic transactions. In particular, the public sector is heavily reliant on auctions and procurements. The mere weight of transaction from auctions and procurements mandates an analysis of bidding rings.[1] In addition, to implement a price-fixing agreement, a cartel will, with rare exception, need to discuss and agree upon bids to be submitted at procurements, or at least provide their sales forces with incentives to maintain the elevated prices that were agreed to by those running the cartel.

In contrast to a cartel, bidding rings are narrowly focused on the suppression of competitive bidding at auctions or procurements. Although the firms involved in a bidding ring may have more far-ranging collusive arrangements, a bidding ring's agreement pertains

---

1. The U.S. Department of Justice gives special attention to bid rigging, as distinct from price fixing. See, for example, Department of Justice publications: "Price Fixing and Bid Rigging—They Happen: What They Are and What to Look For: An Antitrust Primer for Procurement Professionals" (available at http://courses.cit.cornell.edu/econ352jpw/readme/pfbrprimer.pdf, accessed April 30, 2010), "Price Fixing, Bid Rigging, and Market Allocation Schemes: What They Are and What to Look For: An Antitrust Primer" (available at http://www.justice.gov/atr/public/guidelines/211578.pdf, accessed April 30, 2010), and "Preventing and Detecting Bid Rigging, Price Fixing, and Market Allocation in Post-disaster Rebuilding Projects: An Antitrust Primer for Agents and Procurement Officials" (available at http://www.justice.gov/atr/public/guidelines/disaster_primer.pdf, accessed June 24, 2010).

only to bidding at auctions or procurements and the consequent division of the collusive gain obtained from that bidding. Members of a bidding ring may compete with one another in other aspects of their business. For example, firms that function as a ring at factor input auctions may compete in their product market. Unlike the industrial cartels of part II, the collusion described in this part is narrowly targeted at the suppression of interbidder rivalry at an auction or procurement.

Auctions and procurements play an important role in the price discovery process, especially for relatively uninformed sellers and buyers, respectively. To illustrate this, we provide the following example.

Suppose that a firm wants to buy some file cabinets. If it is just one file cabinet, then perhaps it can be purchased at a major office products store. Perhaps the firm has already solicited discounts from major office products suppliers and the firm can order from a catalog with the standard discount applied. The firm may learn of a bankruptcy auction of another firm and attend to bid on the file cabinets offered for sale. Alternatively, if the firm wants a large number of file cabinets, it might solicit bids from a number of primary manufacturers of file cabinets. In other words, there are many ways to purchase file cabinets, and it is only when a small number of file cabinet are being purchased as an unusual one-time acquisition that the firm would pay a posted price that was not established through a buyer-specific competitive process.

The experience of most individuals is different from the sales and purchasing methods of firms. The typical individual consumer confronts posted prices for most everyday transactions and invokes competition by "shopping around" to find the lowest posted price. The vast majority of consumers would not go to an auction to buy everyday kitchen items or conduct a procurement to acquire toothpaste. However, firms typically want to simultaneously consider multiple offers by potential sellers when purchasing and to simultaneously consider multiple offers from potential buyers when selling.

Economics textbooks typically do not delve into auctions and procurements because they emphasize markets that can be characterized as perfectly competitive, such as major agricultural commodities like wheat, corn, or pork bellies. Even though the equilibrium price emerges from a double auction, little is typically offered to understand the underpinnings of the price-determination process beyond the graphical demonstration of the intersection of supply and demand.

To see what the simultaneous consideration of offers accomplishes, return to the example of a firm purchasing file cabinets. Suppose a firm wants to acquire 2,000 file cabinets of a particular size and capacity. Suppose there are numerous vendors that make such file cabinets. The firm is not going to send an employee to the local office products store to buy 2,000 file cabinets. The division manager of the firm may only have a loose idea about the best deal they could get for that many file cabinets.

The firm's manager can check online to see that major stationers charge around $125 per file cabinet for such units, so that is an upper bound on what they will need to pay. The lowest price that they may be able to pay is unknown to them. Perhaps the cabinets will cost $100 per unit when bought in such volume, but perhaps they could be acquired for as little as $50 per unit.

A manager could invest resources in developing expertise about the production of file cabinets so as to better understand the range of prices they might pay, but this is costly, especially if such a purchase occurs infrequently. The manager could make inquiries of a major manufacturer of file cabinets. After gathering information from one such supplier, the manager could just buy from them, or the manager could follow up with a discussion with another supplier. Once the second supplier's quote is in hand, the manager still faces questions of whether to play the two suppliers off each other or perhaps contact a third supplier. The manager also decides whether to reveal to the suppliers that they are facing competition.

The manager wants to get the best value possible in procuring the 2,000 file cabinets, but how can that be done given the manager's ignorance about the production costs and demand conditions for file cabinets? The producers of filing cabinets know their own production costs, have information about the production costs of their rivals in the business, and understand current demand conditions.

The best way for the manager to get the producers of file cabinets to reveal their information in a way that translates into the best deal for the purchase of 2,000 file cabinets is to use competitive processes. Specifically, the manager can invite a large number of file cabinet producers to submit their best offers for providing 2,000 files cabinets, letting each producer know that a large number of their rivals have also been invited to submit best offers. The manager can specify that these best offers need to be received by a certain time/date. The manager can rank these offers and award the contract to the producer that offers the best value relative to all other offers that were submitted.

As the producers of file cabinets prepare their best offers for submission, each knows its cost of production and has a reasonably good idea about the costs of its rivals. Each producer considers its own cost, its beliefs about its rivals' costs, as well as the number of rivals that have been invited to participate, to determine what offer is best in terms of the profits it can expect to obtain. The more producers that have been invited to participate, the more intense will be the rivalry and the lower will be the price that the firm will need to pay for the file cabinets.

The manager uses a procurement, where the best offers of informed bidders are simultaneously considered, to overcome his or her relative ignorance about the market for file cabinets. The producers solve the problem for the manager through their own rivalry. The rivalry, which is essential for the procurement to do what the manager wants it to do, is contrary to the joint interests of the file cabinet producers. If the file cabinet producers can see that, and act upon that observation to reduce their own rivalry, they can increase their joint profits, and this can translate into an increase in their individual profits if they can find a way to share the benefits to reduced rivalry.

The simultaneous consideration of offers by informed bidders, who know that they must prevail against similarly informed rivals in head-to-head competition in order to obtain any payoff, is a powerful policing force whether being used by a seller with respect to many buyers or by a buyer with respect to many sellers. The intensity of the rivalry among bidders encumbers the profits of the bidders. This is consistent with the center force of Porter's Five Forces. Collusion by the bidders increases payoffs by suppressing that rivalry.

8.2   Suppression of Rivalry at an Auction

In this chapter, we discuss the gains to the suppression of competition by bidders at two different auctions, an ascending-bid auction and a sealed-bid auction.[2]

2. Seminal papers on auction theory include Vickrey (1961, 1962), Riley and Samuelson (1981), Myerson (1981), and Milgrom and Weber (1982). See also the auction theory textbook by Krishna (2009). As we noted in the preface, we focus on the independent private values framework. With regard to procurements, we focus on homogeneous products where the only relevant dimension of the bid is the price. Procurements where bidding is multidimensional are commonplace, especially when the bid solicitation describes a function rather than a product (i.e. computation rather than computer equipment). The mapping of multidimensional bids into a single score can create additional opportunities for collusive conduct (see Marshall, Meurer, and Richard 1994).

In general, an auction is the simultaneous consideration of offers from potential buyers by a seller.[3] At an ascending-bid auction, a seller solicits increasingly higher bids from a group of bidders until only one bidder is remaining, who is awarded the item for the amount of its last bid. At a sealed-bid auction, the seller collects sealed bids from bidders until some prespecified deadline. The winner is the highest bidder, and that bidder pays the amount of its bid to the seller.[4]

Consider a seller who has one item for sale,[5] and suppose that the seller is the owner of the item.[6] It would be typical for the owner to advertise the sale, with the intent of attracting more bidders. All else equal, more bidders would increase the price paid for the item. In order to focus on rivalry, we assume that a fixed number of bidders participate in the auction.

Initially, to understand the suppression of rivalry by bidders at an auction, we ignore seller resistance and assume that the seller simply

3. In contrast, the standard procedure for selling real estate typically involves offers being considered sequentially and without recall.
4. Additional details of the auction game include: *Players*: The number and identities of all potential and actual bidders are common knowledge. *Information*: Bidder values are privately known by each bidder. Each bidder knows the distribution from which every other bidder draws its value. If a given bidder learned another bidder's value, it would not influence its own value, although it might affect some aspect of its strategic behavior at the auction. For simplicity, it is assumed that the seller has a value of zero. *Strategies*: Each bidder submits one bid to maximize its expected payoff. A bidder cannot withdraw its bid. *Payoffs*: A bidder's payoff is equal to zero if it does not win and is equal to its value minus the price paid if it does win. The seller maximizes its expected revenue from the auction. Bidders and the seller are risk neutral. There are no costs to the bidders to bid or costs to the seller to sell. A winning bidder is obligated to pay for the item according to the auction rules.
5. Often auctioneers sell multiple items to an assembled group of bidders. For simplicity, we assume one item. The analysis of one item applies to a multiple-item auction if there are no interconnections between the items being sold. If buyers view the multiple items as substitutes or complements, then those interconnections must be considered, but the central issues described below remain.
For theoretical work on collusion at single-object auctions, see Fehl and Güth (1978), Robinson (1985), Graham and Marshall (1987), Mailath and Zemsky (1991), McAfee and McMillan (1992), Deltas (2002), Lopomo, Marshall, and Marx (2005), Chen and Tauman (2006), Dequiedt (2007), Tan and Yilankaya (2007), and Marshall and Marx (2007). On collusion in repeated single-unit auctions, see Feinstein, Block, and Nold (1985), Fudenberg, Levine, and Maskin (1994), Aoyagi (2003), Skrzypacz and Hopenhayn (2004), and Blume and Heidhues (2008). On collusion in repeated multiple-unit auctions, see Fabra (2003) and Dechenaux and Kovenock (2007). For theoretical work on collusion at multiple-object auctions, see Brusco and Lopomo (2002), Levin (2004), and Albano, Germano, and Lovo (2006).
6. Auctioneers are typically employed by sellers on a commission basis. Also, auctioneering is a skill. But the consideration of this skill is not essential to the central point of this section, so we assume the item is being sold by the owner.

collects bids, ranks bids, determines a winner, and collects a payment from the winner. In the vernacular of game theory, the seller is not a player, at least not initially. We return to seller resistance to low prices in chapters 9 and 10.

We denote the number of bidders as n, where n is some number 1, 2, 3, ... We assume that the number n is known to everyone, including the seller and all the bidders. The number of bidders can be an important measure of the amount of rivalry.

We assume each bidder has a value for the item. A bidder's value is the bidder's maximal willingness to pay for the item. Each bidder knows its own value and does not know the value of any other bidder, although each bidder has a reasonable idea about the values of the other bidders.

We capture the idea that each bidder has a belief about the values of the other bidders, without knowing their exact values, by assuming that each bidder's value is obtained as a random draw from a probability distribution and that these probability distributions are known to all the bidders. Thus, all the bidders know that bidder 1's value was obtained as a random draw from a particular distribution, but all bidders except bidder 1 do not know the amount of bidder 1's draw.

For example, it might be known that all bidders draw their values from the uniform distribution on the interval from 0 to 100. If we focus on integer values, this would be akin to each bidder drawing a ball from an urn containing 101 balls, where each ball had a number 0, 1, 2, . . ., 100 written on it (with the balls replaced into the urn before each draw).

We assume that bidders' values for the item are personal in the sense that if a bidder were to find out another bidder's value for the item, it would have no impact on the bidder's own value for the item.[7] This assumption simplifies our analysis, but it is not always appropriate. For example, in some settings, if a bidder with a value of $100,000 were to find out that another bidder had a value of $100, the first bidder might reconsider its value and revise it downward, inferring that it did not correctly understand some aspect of the item being sold. Nevertheless, we assume that a bidder's value is not influenced by any other bidder's value.

7. On collusion at auctions with affiliated values, see Lyk-Jensen (1996, 1997a, b). On collusion at auctions with affiliated and common values, see Hendricks, Porter, and Tan (2008). On collusion at auctions with externalities, see Caillaud and Jéhiel (1998) and Maasland and Onderstal (2007).

We assume that the seller does not know any of the individual values but knows the distributions from which each bidder draws its value. If the seller knew the highest value of the bidders and the bidder with that value, then a strategic seller could just make a take-it-or-leave-it offer to that bidder at a price slightly below the bidder's value.

With this background we can now address the analysis of rivalry in ascending-bid and sealed-bid auctions.

8.2.1 Ascending-Bid Auctions

Most people are familiar with an ascending-bid auction. One can imagine an auctioneer standing before a group of assembled bidders and soliciting ever higher bids until there is only one bidder remaining. That bidder wins and pays the auctioneer the amount of the last bid.

In practice, ascending-bid auctions typically have minimum bid increments, but this detail will cloud some of our analysis, so we assume continuous bidding. One can imagine a dollar-incremented thermometer-like device, visible to all assembled bidders, that indicates the current high bid. Each bidder raises a hand to be active as a bidder. Whenever more than one hand is raised, the thermometer rises continuously. At the moment only one bidder has a hand raised, the thermometer pauses. Others can come back in and the thermometer will continue to rise. But, if after a brief pause no one else raises a hand, the item is awarded to the last remaining bidder who had a hand raised for the price shown on the thermometer.

Noncollusive Bidding

Bidders at an ascending-bid auction determine when they should have their hands in the air and when they should no longer raise their hands—a bidder will want to raise a hand until the thermometer reaches its value and then the bidder will want to lower it. To see why this is optimal, consider some alternatives.

Consider a bidder that follows the strategy of keeping a hand in the air until the price reaches 90 percent of its value and then lowers it, never raising it again. If the bidder wins the item, it means the auction ended before the bidder reached the point of lowering its hand. So the strategy of lowering the hand early did not matter. If the bidder loses the item, but the price paid by the winner exceeds the bidder's value, then the bidder would have lost even if the bidder kept a hand up until the price reached its value. Again, the strategy of lowering the hand early did not matter.

However, if the bidder loses the item and the price paid is less than the bidder's value, then the bidder might have won the item for a price less than the bidder's value by committing to keep a hand raised until the price reached its value. In that case, the bidder would have secured a payoff from winning equal to the difference between the bidder's value and the price paid.

Comparing the two bidding strategies, the bidder's payoff is either unaffected or greater when the bidder keeps a hand up until the price reaches its value. This logic applies to any percentage of the bidder's value that is less than 100 percent. Thus, a bidder would never want to lower its hand before the price reaches its value.

Now consider a strategy of keeping a hand in the air until the price reaches 110 percent of a bidder's value. If the bidder loses to a higher bid, then the bidder would have lost anyway by dropping out of the bidding at its value, so there is no change in payoff relative to bidding only up to its value. If the bidder wins at a price below its value, the bidder would have won anyway, so again there is no change in the payoff between the two scenarios. However, if the bidder wins at a price in excess of its value, the bidder earns a negative payoff that could have been avoided by bidding only up to its value. By this logic, each bidder strictly prefers to commit to keep its hand in the air up to its value rather than 110 percent of its value, and this logic extends to all percentages above 100 percent.

Putting these arguments together, each bidder maximizes its surplus from the auction by keeping its hand in the air up to, but not past, its value. This result applies to each bidder individually regardless of what other bidders are doing—even if the other bidders are not behaving this way, a bidder still finds it individually optimal to bid up to, but not past, its value. Thus, for ascending-bid auctions, all bidders keep their hands in the air until their values are reached and then they lower their hands.[8]

The rivalry at an ascending-bid auction is apparent from the hands in the air. Anytime two or more bidders have their hands in the air, the

8. The strategy of a bidder remaining active until its value is reached may not be optimal when there are multiple units for sale. For example, if multiple identical units are offered sequentially, a bidder may choose not to remain active up to its value for the initial units offered, allowing other high-valuing bidders to win those, in the hope of winning a later unit at a lower price. The characterization of bidding behavior is also different if the item for sale has some underlying unknown value for which each bidder obtains some signal.

thermometer rises. Each bidder makes the unilateral decision to keep a hand in the air until its value is reached. The bidder who is the last one with a hand in the air prevails. Survival of the fittest translates into survival of the bidder with the highest value.

The payment the seller receives depends on where the thermometer stops. The thermometer stops when only one hand remains in the air. This happens when the thermometer reaches the second-highest value among the bidders. Therefore, the seller receives a payment for the item equal to the second-highest value.

The seller relies on the ascending-bid auction to police the market. The seller did not know much about the bidders' values, but through the use of an ascending-bid auction, the seller was able to use the rivalry to identify and collect the second-highest value from among all of the bidders.

The winning bidder receives a payoff from participation in the auction equal to the difference between that bidder's value (the highest value) and the second-highest value, where the second-highest value is the price paid.

As the number of bidders increases, the expected value of the second-highest value increases, so the expected revenue to the seller increases. In addition, as the number of bidders increases, the expected difference between the highest and second-highest values decreases, so the expected payoff to the winner decreases.

Rivalry among bidders reduces the bidders' payoffs from participation in the auction. Returning to the center force of Porter's Five Forces, bidders can potentially increase their aggregate payoff if they can mitigate rivalry among themselves.

Collusive Bidding

At the ascending-bid auction, rivalry among bidders is expressed by bidders keeping their hands in the air up to their values. The suppression of this rivalry is the suppression of hands in the air.

Consider two bidders who have a discussion before the auction. For now, assume that they reveal their values to one another.[9] The two bidders reach a simple agreement about the suppression of their own rivalry. Specifically, the higher valuing bidder of the two will keep a hand in the air up to its value, while the other bidder will never raise

9. See Graham and Marshall (1987) and Marshall and Marx (2007) for the details of how this would occur.

a hand.[10] If the cartel wins the item, then the collusive gain would be divided in some way.[11]

At this point it will be useful to introduce some notation. Let v_1 be the highest value from among all the bidders, v_2 the second highest, and so on. Thus the values of the n bidders are $v_1 \geq v_2 \geq \ldots \geq v_n$.

If the highest value from among the two colluding bidders is less than v_1, then there is no gain from the suppression of rivalry by the two bidders. The bidder with value v_1 will win the auction. For the two to gain from suppressing their rivalry, it is necessary that one of the two bidders has the value v_1. It is necessary but not sufficient. If one of the bidders in the ring has value v_1 but the other has a value less than v_2, then there still will not be a gain from the suppression of the rivalry of the two bidders because, although the ring bidder with value v_1 will win, the price paid will be v_2. Therefore, in order for the two bidders to gain from the suppression of their rivalry, they must have the two highest values. Then they will win the item for the price v_3, which is lower than the noncooperative price of v_2.

Now suppose that there are $k < n$ bidders who meet, reveal their values to one another, and reach a similar agreement regarding the suppression of the rivalry. The highest valuing of the k ring members will keep a hand raised until its value while the other $k - 1$ will never raise their hands.[12] Similar to what was just described for the two-bidder case, for the k ring members to gain from suppressing their rivalry, the two bidders with the highest and second-highest values must be among them. Assuming that the ring contains the bidder with the highest value, the ring will win and pay an amount equal to the highest value from the bidders outside the ring. For example, if there are 10 bidders in the ring ($k = 10$) and the top 5 values from among all the bidders are held by ring members, but not the sixth highest value, then the suppression of rivalry will result in the ring paying the sixth-highest value for the item.

10. Alternatively, the colluding bidders could agree that if either one has a hand raised, then the other will not raise a hand, and that if one of the colluding bidders wins, then the two will meet after the auction to determine ultimate ownership of the item. We describe post-auction allocation mechanisms in chapter 9.
11. The division of the collusive gain is also a topic that will also be discussed in the next chapter. For now, we want to focus on the gain from the suppression of rivalry between the bidders.
12. As was the case for $k = 2$, the agreement can be that if any one of the k has a hand raised, then none of the other $k - 1$ raises a hand. If the other ring members drop their hands, a ring member is free to enter, but only one of the ring members may have a hand in the air at any time.

8.2.2   Sealed-Bid Auctions

Most people are also familiar with a standard sealed-bid auction where the bidder submitting the highest bid wins and pays the amount of its bid to the seller. Bidders are assumed to bid so as to maximize their expected payoff from winning. Thus, each bidder chooses a bid to make the payoff from winning, weighted by the probability of winning, as large as possible. Each bidder solves the same problem. These solutions are internally coherent (and form a Nash equilibrium) if, for any given bidding strategy by all the other bidders, a given bidder does not want to change its bidding strategy, and this is true for all bidders.[13]

Noncollusive Bidding

Unlike an ascending-bid auction, no bidder will bid its value at a sealed-bid auction. Any bidder doing so earns a zero payoff. (Each bidder can earn a zero payoff by staying home.) To have a chance of earning a positive payoff, each bidder bids less than its value.

Rivalry affects the probability that a particular bid will win. The larger is the number of bidders at the auction, the smaller is the chance of winning with any given bid. Intuitively, as the number of bidders increases, a bidder increases its bid to respond optimally to the increased rivalry.

For example, one can show that if bids are drawn from the uniform distribution between zero and 100, then the equilibrium bid submitted by a bidder with value x is $b(x) = [(n - 1)/n]x$, where n is the number of bidders at the auction. If there are two bidders ($n = 2$), each bidder submits a bid equal to one-half of its value. If there are three bidders ($n = 3$), each bidder submits a bid equal to two-thirds of its value. If there are 100 bidders ($n = 100$), each bidder submits a bid equal to 99 percent of its value.

As the number of bidders increases, for any given set of values, the bids of all bidders increase. Each bidder evaluates the following trade-off: increasing one's bid increases the probability of winning, but it also decreases one's payoff in the event the bid wins. The optimal evalua-

13. Let $b_i(x_i)$ denote the bid of bidder i with value x_i. If all bidders draw their values from the same distribution $F(\cdot)$, we can assume that each bidder uses a symmetric bid strategy, so we can drop the subscript on b. The equilibrium bid function b is such that for all values x, a bidder with value x maximizes his or her expected payoff conditional on all other bidders using the bid function b by submitting a bid of $b(x)$. For each bidder, the bid function provides a best response to what the other bidders are doing. This is a Bayesian Nash equilibrium.

tion of that trade-off, accounting for all other bidders, produces the optimal bid function.[14]

The ascending-bid and sealed-bid auctions may seem quite different in terms of the description of bidder behavior, but the auctions produce similar noncollusive outcomes. Suppose that there are four bidders who draw their values from the uniform distribution between zero and 100. On average, their values will be 20, 40, 60, and 80. For those values, the ascending-bid auction would be won by the bidder with value 80 for a price of 60. For a sealed-bid auction, the bidder with value 80 would win for a price of $3(80)/4 = 60$ which is again the second-highest value. This is a general result. The price paid at an ascending-bid auction is the second-highest value and, when all bidders draw their values from the same distribution, the expected price paid at a sealed-bid auction is the expected second-highest value. Therefore, when all bidders draw their values from the same distribution, regardless of the auction scheme, rivalry among bidders produces the same expected outcome for the seller.

Collusive Bidding

Consider two bidders having a discussion before a sealed-bid auction with the intent to suppress their rivalry. As with the ascending-bid auction, the other bidders are assumed to continue to act noncollusively. If the two engaging in the conversation were to learn each other's value, then the one with the highest value could bid at the main auction while the other did not bid. (Alternatively, the other bidder could submit any intentionally losing bid, i.e., a bid known to be less than the bid submitted by the bidder with highest value.) We assume that the collusive behavior of the two bidders is common knowledge among all bidders. Is there a gain from this suppression of rivalry by the two bidders?

We begin by looking at the colluding bidder with the highest value, who we refer to as the ring bidder. Let n denote the total number of bidders. Instead of facing $n - 1$ other bidders, as the ring bidder would under noncooperative bidding, the ring bidder faces only $n - 2$ other bidders. The noncollusive bid by the ring bidder reflects the optimal trade-off between the probability of winning and the payoff from winning. If the ring bidder submits that same noncollusive bid in the collusive environment, the payoff from winning is the same, but the

---

14. On the existence and uniqueness of equilibrium bid functions at sealed-bid auctions, see Maskin and Riley (1996a, b, 2000a, b), Lebrun (1996), and Athey (2001).

probability of winning would be higher because the ring bidder is competing against $n - 2$ others instead of $n - 1$ others. This means that the noncollusive bid is not optimal for the collusive environment. For example, if the ring bidder decreases its bid to produce the same probability of winning as when the ring bidder acted noncollusively, that will automatically increase the ring bidder's payoff should that bidder win. This increases the ring bidder's expected payoff. This shows that in the collusive environment, the ring bidder will bid less than its optimal noncollusive bid.

Now consider the outside bidders. Each confronts the other outside bidders plus one ring bidder whose value can be viewed as the highest value from the two colluding bidders. The noncolluding bidders take into account that the ring bidder will bid less aggressively than when acting noncollusively. This causes the noncolluding bidders to decrease their bids relative to purely noncollusive bidding. There is a unique equilibrium of this game.[15] The equilibrium bid functions are different from those for noncollusive bidding and provide the colluding bidders with an increase in their expected payoff as a result of the suppression of their rivalry.

Suppression of rivalry means that the bidder with the smaller value does not bid meaningfully at the auction. This is the analogue to suppressing hands that would have been raised with noncollusive bidding at an ascending-bid auction.

As with an ascending-bid auction, at a sealed-bid auction, the two-bidder cartel needs to include the bidder with highest value in order to realize a gain. But, due to the nature of the bidding at a sealed-bid auction, it can happen that a cartel that includes the bidder with highest value does not win the item. In addition, the cartel need not contain the bidder with the second-highest value to realize a collusive gain. The difference between the sealed-bid and ascending-bid auctions stems from the payment rule and consequent implication for bidding strategies.

8.2.3 Summary
Colluding bidders suppress their rivalry through the elimination of meaningful bids by all colluding bidders except for the ring bidder with the highest value. All other details and logistics of bidder collusion flow from this foundational principle of the ring.

15. See, for example, Lebrun (1999, 2006), Bajari (2001), and Maskin and Riley (2000a, b).

When bidders act noncollusively, the seller receives the second-highest value at an ascending-bid auction and, on average, with symmetric bidders,[16] the seller receives the second-highest value at a sealed-bid auction. However, the equivalence between the two auction formats typically does not continue to hold when bidders act to suppress rivalry.

At an ascending-bid auction, when a subset of bidders collude, the highest-valuing collusive bidder keeps a hand in the air up to its value. This is what the bidder would have done had it been acting noncollusively. The implication is that if a noncolluding bidder wins, then that noncolluding bidder pays what it would have paid for the item if there had been no collusion. Therefore, if a ring wins, and there are gains to their collusion, then the ring captures all of those gains; however, if the ring loses, there are no gains from the collusion for nonring bidders. The collusion is self-contained in this sense.

At a sealed-bid auction, when a subset of bidders colludes, the highest-valuing collusive bidder submits a bid that is strictly less than what that bidder would have submitted acting noncollusively in order to potentially realize a gain from the collusion. The noncolluding bidders, even accounting for all bidders' mutual best responses to one another, will sometimes win when they would not have won with all bidders acting noncollusively. Specifically, the extra bid shading by the highest-valuing colluding bidder opens the possibility that the ring does not capture all the gains to its collusive conduct. The noncolluding bidders are beneficiaries, in expected terms, from the collusion. See appendix A for a numerical illustration of this phenomenon. The leakage of some of the collusive gain to the outside bidders, which is absent at the ascending-bid auction, means that typically the incentives for suppression of rivalry through collusion are weaker at the sealed-bid auction than at the ascending-bid auction.[17]

8.3   Ring Composition

The suppression of rivalry is profitable, but in order to suppress rivalry the ring has a number of problems to solve, starting with the most fundamental issues of membership and participation. As shown in

16. By symmetric bidders, we mean that bidders draw their valuations from the same distribution.
17. For theoretical support, see, for example, Waehrer (1999), Kovacic et al. (2006), and Marshall and Marx (2007).

chapter 5, for the case of cartels, there may be cases where not all bidders wish to join a ring or where a ring does not wish to extend membership to all bidders.

We address three questions related to ring composition.

1. Membership: Do ring bidders want to extend invitations to nonring bidders to join the ring?

2. Participation: Do nonring bidders want to join the ring if extended an invitation?

3. Membership sequence: Does the order with which bidders join the ring affect their membership decisions, participation decisions, and the payoffs that ring members receive?

As shown in the discussion below, the allocation rule for division of the collusive gain is an essential foundation for the ring in discussing membership, participation, and the sequence of membership/participation decisions.

8.3.1 Membership and Participation

It might seem that all ring members want those currently not in the ring to join, and that all nonring bidders would want to join the ring. This is generally correct for ascending-bid auctions, but not necessarily for sealed-bid auctions.

Ascending-Bid Auctions

At an ascending-bid auction, there is no leakage to nonring bidders, so bidders have no incentive to remain outside the ring. Nonring bidders prefer to participate regardless of the magnitude of the share of the collusive gain allocated to them by the ring. In addition, at an ascending-bid auction, the ring is always able to find a payment to new ring members that shares the collusive gain in a way such that the ring wants to include the new member. At an ascending-bid auction, when bidders are symmetric, the ring prefers to invite all to join and each bidder wants to join.[18]

One caveat is that if a post-auction knockout is being used for division of the collusive gain, then ring bidders may not want to endure

---

18. Rings at ascending-bid auctions are not typically all-inclusive. The illegality of the activity may be one reason. Also, in other informational environments certain "types" of bidders may be concerned about surplus extraction by fellow ring members. See chapter 3 regarding brokers not being in dealer rings.

the overbidding and consequent surplus extraction that an additional bidder would engage in at the knockout. Another caveat is that ring bidders may prefer to take actions to eliminate a nonring bidder rather than incorporate it into the ring. Rather than granting the nonring bidder a share of the collusive gain, the ring bidders may prefer to engage in predatory behavior directed at the nonring bidder, along the lines of the dominant-firm conduct for cartels discussed in chapter 7.

Sealed-Bid Auctions

At a sealed-bid auction, the leakage of the collusive gain to nonring bidders can affect ring membership and participation. The leakage is an external benefit to nonring bidders that is absent in an ascending-bid auction. Even though the ring's per-capita collusive gain may increase with the addition of one more ring member, implying that another nonring bidder would be invited to join, leakage of the collusive gain from the ring to the nonring bidders means that the payoff to a nonring bidder from staying outside the ring may exceed its share of the collusive gain from participating in the ring, depending on the offer made to a nonring bidder by the ring.

For example, suppose that there are three bidders and that two of the bidders typically draw high values, while the third bidder almost never draws a high value and usually draws a value that is quite low. Noncooperative bidding would be characterized by bidder 3 winning rarely, while bidders 1 and 2 would fiercely compete given their similarity.

Suppose that bidder 3's bidding is so weak relative to bidders 1 and 2 that its probability of winning with noncooperative bidding is less than 0.1 percent. Now suppose that bidders 1 and 2 form a ring. Their only competition is bidder 3. Suppose that bidders 1 and 2 offer bidder 3 a share of 0.1 percent of the collusive gain if it joins, allowing them to form an all-inclusive ring. Bidder 3 has to evaluate that offer against remaining outside the ring and bidding optimally against the ring. Compared to how bidders 1 and 2 bid noncooperatively, once bidders 1 and 2 form a ring, their bids will be greatly depressed because bidder 3 is such a weak opponent. But bidder 3 will be able to take advantage of this depressed bidding by bidders 1 and 2 to increase its probability of winning and increase its expected payoff well above noncooperative levels, and perhaps also above its small share of the collusive gain if it joins the ring. We provide a numerical example of this equilibrium phenomenon in appendix B.

This example applies to the situation where there are a large number of equal-sized bidders. In that case, a single bidder left out of a cartel consisting of, say, 100 other bidders might prefer to not join the ring. However, if there were only a smaller number of equal-sized bidders, then a nonring bidder might find ring participation to be profitable. With a smaller number of equal-sized bidders, an individual bidder is more likely to prefer to join a ring consisting of the other bidders.[19]

8.3.2 Membership Sequence

If the ring contains all but one of the total bidders, then the last bidder to join a ring provides a large incremental benefit because the inclusion of that bidder suppresses all competition. However, if the last bidder to join is rewarded disproportionately for joining, then each ring bidder will want to be the last to join.

Consider an ascending-bid auction with 100 bidders who draw their values from the same distribution. If 2 of the 100 bidders form a ring, with the remaining 98 acting noncollusively, the collusive gain for those two will be quite small. However, if a ring of size 99 already exists, then the payoff to the ring from inclusion of the one-hundredth bidder is quite large. If the one-hundredth bidder receives a payment for participation in the ring that is close to its contribution from being the last to join the ring, then the ring has an immediate instability. Namely, each ring bidder will want to be the last to join, but the ring does not earn enough collusive payoff to make such payments to all ring participants. Because of this, rings often adopt an ex ante rule for the payment received by a ring participant.

In our example with 100 ex ante identical bidders, the collusive gain would be equally divided among the ring participants. That gain, per ring member, would increase with the size of the ring. But the ring will

---

19. In the U.S. Department of Justice and Federal Trade Commission Horizontal Merger Guidelines (http://www.ftc.gov/os/2010/04/100420hmg.pdf) (hereafter "Guidelines"), emphasis is placed on the role of "maverick" firms, where a "maverick" is implicitly defined as "a firm that has often resisted otherwise prevailing industry norms to cooperate on price setting or other terms of competition." (Guidelines, sec. 2.1.5) But, contrary to the implication from the Guidelines, a "maverick" can be an endogenous characteristic of a bidder, not an innate trait. A firm may find it desirable not to join a ring today, but find it profitable to do so at a future date. The payoff to participation is the key determinant of a firm's participation decision, not an immutable characteristic of a firm. Our results show that as the number of firms increases, there will eventually be firms who prefer to not participate in the ring. This provides a formal basis for the argument that collusion becomes more difficult as the number of bidders grow as described in Baker (2002).

reject any attempt by a nonring bidder to hold-up the ring for a larger payment simply because of the sequence with which the bidder is considered for ring membership.

When bidders are not ex ante identical, the problem becomes more difficult, but it is one that rings have solved. In that case, the collusive mechanism can be designed to pay collusive bidders the average of their marginal contribution to joining the ring. (See chapter 9 for details.) The ring will not use an equal division rule when bidders differ ex ante. Rings will pay "strong" bidders more than "weak" bidders by an amount that appropriately measures the difference between "strong" and "weak."[20]

It is essential for the ring to determine the allocation prior to the auction because otherwise the ring will find itself confronting conflicting claims by members for shares of the collusive gain. Solving the problem before the auction, and declaring the solution to be inalienable and nonnegotiable, prohibits costly ex post rent seeking by ring members.

8.4   Effects of Auction Format and Ring Size*

To illustrate differences between ascending-bid and sealed-bid auctions and the effects of ring size, we present an example for an auction with five bidders, each of which draws its private value independently from the uniform distribution on the interval [0, 1].

If the bidders behave noncooperatively, the expected auction price under either an ascending-bid or sealed-bid format is $4/6$. To see the intuition for this, note that if the five values were evenly spaced on the interval [0, 1], they would be located at $1/6$, $2/6$, $3/6$, $4/6$, and $5/6$. Thus, the second-highest value would be $4/6$. This is the amount that would be paid in expected terms at an ascending-bid auction.

At a sealed-bid auction, one can show that the noncooperative bids when there are five bidders drawing values from the uniform distribution on [0, 1] involve each bidder submitting a bid that is four-fifths of its value. Thus, the expected high bid would be $4/5 \times 5/6 = 4/6$. The expected surplus to a bidder under noncooperative bidding is the expected difference between the highest and second-highest value, $1/6$, times the probability that a bidder has the highest value, which is $1/5$, that is, $1/6 \times 1/5 = 1/30 = 0.033$. The expected surplus to a bidder in

---

20. See Graham, Marshall, and Richard (1990).

an all-inclusive ring is the expected value of the highest value, 5/6, times the probability that a bidder has the highest value, which is 1/5, that is, $5/6 \times 1/5 = 1/6 = 0.167$.

As shown in table 8.1, the seller's expected revenue decreases as more bidders join a ring because the diminished competition results in a lower expected auction price. Similarly, the expected surplus to ring members increases as more bidders join the ring. The expected surplus to outside bidders at an ascending-bid auction is not affected by the size of the ring. Those outside bidders only win if they have the highest value, and they pay the second-highest value overall, regardless of whether the second-highest-valuing bidder is in the ring or not. However, at a sealed-bid auction, the expected surplus of the outside bidders increases as the size of the ring increases. At a sealed-bid auction, outside bidders benefit from the lower bids that are submitted by the members of a larger ring. In this sense some of the benefits to collusive bidders at a sealed-bid auction spill over to the bidders outside the ring, and the benefits to the outside bidders increase in the size of the ring. This is the phenomenon we refer to as "leakage."

Focusing on the comparison between the two auction formats, table 8.1 shows that for the environment we consider, a less than all-inclusive ring (2, 3, or 4 bidders in our example) hurts the auctioneer more in an ascending-bid auction than in a sealed-bid auction. The table shows that for these auction formats and for the environment we consider, the collusive gain to ring members in a less than all-inclusive ring is more at an ascending-bid auction than at a sealed-bid auction. Thus, this example illustrates that the incentives for collusion at an ascending-bid auction can be higher than at a sealed-bid auction.[21]

Table 8.1 also shows that, in contrast to an ascending-bid auction, at a sealed-bid auction, the outside bidders benefit from collusion, although the expected surplus to a bidder from being outside a ring of size $k - 1$ is always less than the expected surplus to a bidder from being inside a ring of size k. This shows that, in this example, bidders always want to join the ring. As shown in appendix B of this chapter, this is not always the case at a sealed-bid auction. The fact that the expected surplus to the ring members is increasing in the size of the ring in this example implies that the ring in this example always wants additional bidders to join.

21. This is not a general result; see Maskin and Riley (2000a).

Table 8.1
Comparison of ascending-bid and sealed-bid auctions with varying numbers of ring members

Number of bidders in the ring	Expected auction price		Expected surplus to ring members		Expected surplus to outside bidders	
	Ascending bid	First price	Ascending bid	First price	Ascending bid	First price
1	0.667	0.667	0.033	0.033	0.033	0.033
2	0.650	0.651	0.042	0.035	0.033	0.037
3	0.600	0.609	0.056	0.041	0.033	0.049
4	0.467	0.506	0.083	0.057	0.033	0.086
5	0.000	0.000	0.167	0.167	0.033	0.086

Note: Values are assumed to be drawn from the uniform distribution on [0,1], and the reserve price is assumed to be zero. All ascending-bid calculations and first-price calculations for 1 bidder in the ring are analytic. Other first-price calculations are from Marshall et al. (1994, tab. III), which are computed by Monte Carlo using 100,000 draws.

8.5   Conclusion

As was the case with cartels, a ring will need to put structures in place in order to achieve the potential payoffs to collusion identified in this chapter. Auction design affects the incentives for collusion. In the next chapter, we discuss the implementation of bidder collusion, and in the following chapter, we discuss how auction design can deter or facilitate collusion.

8.6   Appendix A: Numerical Example of Leakage at a Sealed-Bid Auction*

At sealed-bid auctions, there is leakage of potential collusive surplus to the outside bidders. The outside bidders benefit from the presence of a ring because colluding bidders submit lower bids than would a noncooperative bidder who had the same value as the highest value from among the ring members.

As an illustration of this, figure 8.1, which is taken from Marshall et al. (1994, fig. 2), considers the case of five bidders, each drawing a value from the uniform distribution on [0, 1]. The figure shows the equilibrium bid functions for a ring of four bidders competing against a single outside bidder. As shown in the figure, the ring's bid

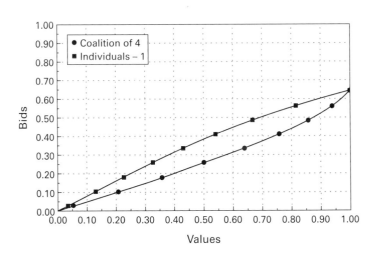

Figure 8.1
First-price equilibrium bid functions for a ring of four bidders competing against a single outside bidder, with values drawn from the uniform distribution on [0, 1]. Source: Marshall et al. (1994, fig. 2).

function is below that of the outside bidder. For example, if the highest value among the four ring members is, say, 0.5, then the ring will submit a lower bid than the outside bidder would have submitted if it had drawn a value of 0.5.

As shown in figure 8.1, the outside bidder will bid approximately 0.40 if it has a value of approximately 0.54 (this can be read off the figure by starting on the vertical axis at 0.40, reading across to the bid function indicated by squares, and reading down to the horizontal axis), and the ring will bid approximately 0.40 if the highest value among the four ring members is approximately 0.76. Thus, if the outside bidder has a value of 0.54, and the highest value from among the four ring members is between 0.54 and 0.76, the outside bidder will win the auction even though the ring has a higher value for the object. This would not have happened under noncooperative bidding—with all bidders drawing values from the same distribution, the highest-valuing bidder wins in equilibrium. At a sealed-bid auction, the ring suppresses its bids in a way that allows an outside bidder to win the auction in cases when it would not have won under noncooperative bidding. This is one way collusion by the four ring members generates a benefit to the outside bidder.[22]

8.7   Appendix B: Numerical Example of Membership and Participation at a Sealed-Bid Auction*

Analysis of the payoffs from collusion can provide insights as to which rings would have an incentive to form.

To focus on the issues of ring membership and participation, in this appendix we consider an example with 101 bidders all drawing values from the uniform distribution on [0, 1]. Table 8.2 shows the expected auction prices and expected surpluses to the bidders. As shown in the figure, the expected payoff to ring members is increasing in the number of bidders in the ring.

As shown in table 8.2, at an ascending-bid auction, starting from the case of 99 bidders in the ring and 2 out, each of the outside bidders would like to join because their surplus would increase from 0.0001 to 0.0049. Then, starting from the case of 100 bidders in the ring and 1 out, the last bidder prefers to join to obtain the surplus of 0.0098.

---

22. The other comes from the simple reduction in bids by the cartel relative to noncollusive conduct.

Table 8.2
Comparison of ascending-bid and sealed-bid auctions with varying numbers of ring members and 101 total bidders

Number of bidders in the ring	Expected auction price		Expected surplus to ring members		Expected surplus to outside bidders	
	Ascending bid	First price	Ascending bid	First price	Ascending bid	First price
99	0.6665	0.7787	0.0033	0.0015	0.0001	0.0159
100	0.4999	0.6578	0.0049	0.0025	0.0001	0.0412
101	0.0000	0.0000	0.0098	0.0098		

Source: Marshall et al. (1994, tab. V).
Note: Values are assumed to be drawn from the uniform distribution on [0, 1], and the reserve price is assumed to be zero. All ascending-bid calculations and first-price calculations for 1 bidder in the ring are analytic. Other first-price calculations are from Marshall et al. (1994, tab. III), which are computed by Monte Carlo using 100,000 draws.

The analysis for the sealed-bid auction is different. When there is a ring of 99 bidders, each outside bidder has expected surplus of 0.0159, but the payoff from being a member of a 100-bidder ring is only 0.0025, so the outside bidders do not want to join. Similarly, when there is a ring of 100 bidders, each outside bidder has an expected surplus of 0.0412, which is larger than the payoff of 0.0098 from being part of a 101-bidder ring.

This implies that at a sealed-bid auction, even if there is just one bidder outside the ring, and so adding that bidder would make the ring all-inclusive and drop the expected price from 0.6578 to zero, that outside bidder prefers not to join. Although the addition of that last bidder creates sufficient incremental surplus for the ring so that the ring could profitably compensate the outside bidder sufficiently in order to induce it to join, this will not happen if the ring structures itself so that no bidder has the right to "hold up" the ring and demand a differential payment (or disproportionate payment given the bidders ex ante types). This unwillingness of the last bidder to join the ring suggests that the difficulties in organizing a large ring go beyond the simple "dinner party" effects; that is, the larger is the number of people, the more difficult it is to coordinate logistics.[23] It can be difficult to organize a large ring because as ring size increases, outside bidders may increasingly have an incentive to remain outside the ring.

This example shows how leakage at a sealed-bid auction can create a situation where a ring would like additional bidders to join the ring, but the outside bidders prefer not to join. Thus, the available payoffs to bidders both inside and outside the ring can affect the membership of rings that emerge in practice.

---

23. See Baker (2002), which argues that economists have relied on "dinner party stories" without any formal analysis to support the notion that collusion becomes more difficult as the number of firms increases. On the relation between the number of firms and the competitiveness of a market, see Chamberlin (1933), Bain (1951), Stigler (1964), Dolbear et al. (1968), Selten (1973), Kwoka (1979) Werden and Baumann (1986), Bresnahan and Reiss (1991), and Huck, Normann, Oechssler (2004), and Kovacic et al. (2007).

9 Implementation of Collusion by Rings

The previous chapter shows what a bidding ring potentially can achieve through the suppression of rivalry. In order to achieve those gains from collusion, a bidding ring must overcome certain hurdles. The Stiglerian collusive structures described in figure 6.1 apply to rings as well as cartels.

9.1 Rings versus Cartels

Rings use pricing structures, allocation structures, and enforcement structures to increase their collusive profit and deter secret deviations. We identify and discuss some of the unique features of rings with specific cases including cast-iron pipe, wholesale stamps, antiques, used industrial machinery, and real estate.

The examples we consider cover three key auction environments: a sealed-bid auction, an ascending-bid auction with limited observability of bidder identities at the auction, and an ascending-bid auction with full observability of bidder identities at the auction. Just as the collusive structures used by a cartel must recognize and adapt to the environment in which the firms operate, the collusive structures used by rings must be tailored to the auction environment.

Some auction environments place a greater burden on the ring, for example, by often requiring more effort on the part of the ring to effectively monitor compliance with mandated bidding behavior. In the next chapter, we focus on ways in which auction designers can take advantage of these effects to deter collusion at their auctions.

9.2 Ring Secret Deviations

A member of a bidding ring engages in a secret deviation if that ring member, or the member's agent, submits a clandestine bid at the main auction that is contrary to the recommendation of the ring and that cannot be traced to the deviant member without substantial cost. In contrast, if a ring member wins an item at the main auction but, contrary to ring rules, refuses to bring the item they won to the ring's post-auction knockout, then this is a *public* deviation from ring rules that the ring can punish immediately and directly, usually by expelling the member from the ring.

Secret deviations are a major concern at sealed-bid auctions and a lesser concern at ascending-bid auctions. This should be unsurprising in light of the previous chapter. The highest-valuing ring member at an ascending-bid auction can always remain active up to its value when confronting nonring bidding opposition. Because this conduct is not different from what the highest-valuing ring bidder would do acting noncollusively, there is no room for secret deviations at an ascending-bid auction. However, for a sealed-bid auction, the highest-valuing ring member reduces its bid below its noncooperative bid in order to potentially realize a collusive gain, opening the door for potential profitable secret deviations by fellow ring members.

9.3   Ring Pricing Structures and Seller Resistance

Rings suppress competitive bidding in an attempt to lower auction prices and raise procurement prices. There is no typical analogue to price discrimination or quantity restrictions within the narrow scope of a ring's business. Typically there is no analogue to price announcements for a ring. There is also no analogue to a sales force that needs to have its incentives changed to be consistent with those of the ring because ring bidding is rarely delegated to those who are uninformed about the ring.

A ring at an auction will often confront seller resistance. Substantial seller resistance can take the form of auction designs that encumber collusion. We develop this topic further in the next chapter. In addition, a seller can take actions within the context of a given auction to resist depressed prices. These include actions such as raising the reserve price during the course of the auction as a result of bids being excessively depressed as well as awarding the item to nonring bidders at low prices (to encourage their ongoing participation and let ring bidders know that they run the risk of not winning items that they value highly).[1]

---

1. These actions are referred to as "lift lining" and "quick knock," respectively. See Graham, Marshall, and Richard (1996) and Marshall and Meurer (2001, 2004). See also Thomas (2005).

9.4   Ring Allocation Structures

Allocation structures for a ring parallel those for a cartel. The allocation structure for a ring specifies the division of the collusive gain among ring members. The key difference comes from the narrowness of the ring's focus. A ring typically squares up all side payments among members after each auction, whereas a cartel typically engages in an ongoing monitoring of quantity to assure compliance and then at year end, and only if needed, trues-up allocations among cartel members.

Just as a cartel might allocate different collusive shares to members based on pre-collusive market shares, a ring typically allocates shares of the collusive gain based on the ex ante (pre-auction) strength of each bidder. In the cases discussed in this chapter, we illustrate how cartels have adopted allocation structures that address differences in the relative contribution of ring members to the collusive gain.[2]

9.5   Ring Enforcement Structures

While cartels typically monitor both price and quantity, a ring is usually just concerned with price, but monitoring is done for the same enforcement reasons. As with cartels, reversion to noncollusive play is the standard threat to avert secret deviations. Targeted punishment can be used as well. These usually entail the expulsion of the deviator from the ring.

In a sealed-bid auction, ring members who have been asked to suppress their bids must be monitored to ensure that they do not submit "real" bids at the auction in competition with the ring member selected to represent the ring. For example, in the cast-iron pipe ring described in chapter 9.6.1, the ring was able to monitor all bids submitted, including amounts and identities of the bidders.[3] Alterna-

---

2. In some auction and procurement environments, especially in the public sector, disadvantaged or losing bidders can protest the decisions of the awarding authority before an administrative court or authority. Bid protests are a form of private attorneys general enforcement of competition law. As with patent law, the use of a private attorney general relies on the firms acting competitively. If firms are acting collusively, then the settlement process associated with a bid protest can provide a legal means for exchanging side payments among members of a bidding ring. Furthermore, the anticipation of the settlement phase will often support the submission of fully collusive bids. See Marshall, Meurer, and Richard (1994).

3. "A very large proportion of the orders which are placed for cast-iron pipe are placed after advertising for bids and receiving proposals which are opened in the presence of, and read to the bidders. . . ." (*U.S.* v. *Addyston Pipe and Steel Co. et al.*, 85 Fed. 271, Transcript of Record, p. 189, hereafter *Addyston Pipe* Transcript of Record)

tively, the ring may submit all of its bids through a single designated member.[4]

In an ascending-bid auction where ring members report their values prior to the auction, bids can be controlled by using a third-party bidding agent to submit bids as in the wholesale stamp ring described in chapter 9.6.2. In ascending-bid auctions where the ring uses the rule of not bidding against each other, it monitors the identity of the current high bidder throughout the auction.

In some ascending-bid auctions, the identity of the current high bidder is revealed only as a bidder number. In this case, prior to the auction, each ring member communicates its bidder number to the others, and then at the auction, ring members follow the rule of not bidding if the current high bidder is a recognized ring bidder number, and otherwise bidding as long as the current price is below their value for the object. With this bidding rule for the ring members, no ring member has an incentive to try to disguise itself by not revealing its bidder number to the other ring members.

9.6   Ring Mechanisms for Standard Auction Types

To illustrate the collusive structures used by rings at auctions of different types, we discuss the structures used by rings operating in cast-iron pipe, collectable stamps, antiques, machinery, and real estate.

The cast-iron pipe ring described in chapter 9.6.1 operated at sealed-bid procurements.[5] This example allows us to discuss ring behavior in a procurement context. The issues at a procurement for a homogeneous product are analogous to those at an auction, but with the auctioneer being a buyer instead of a seller. The stamp dealers ring described in chapter 9.6.2 operated at ascending-bid auctions using a mechanism that did not rely on being able to observe the identities of the bidders during the running of the auction. The ring developed its bidding strategy prior to the auction and sent an agent to bid on its behalf. The rings of dealers in antiques, machinery, and real estate described in chapter 9.6.3 operated at ascending-bid auction using mechanisms that

---

4. For example, the selected ring member might take control of submitting the bids for the ring members as in *U.S. v. Brinkley & Son* (1986), where Brinkley turned in the bid form for at least one of his competitors. (*U.S. v. W.F. Brinkley & Son Construction Company, Inc.*, 783 F.2d 1157 (4th Cir. 1986))

5. *U.S. v. Addyston Pipe and Steel Co. et al.*, 85 Fed. 271. Our descriptions are based in part on the *Addyston Pipe* Transcript of Record.

relied on their being able to observe the identity of the current high bidder at the auction and the identity of and price paid by the winner.

As these examples illustrate, there are some differences in the collusive structures required to support ring behavior depending on the auction type.

9.6.1 Sealed Bid—Cast-iron Pipe

Some time before the end of 1894, major U.S. cast-iron pipe manufacturers Addyston Pipe & Steel, Dennis Long & Co., Howard-Harrison Iron Co., Anniston Pipe & Foundry Co., South Pittsburg Pipe Works, and Chattanooga Foundry and Pipe Works formed a cartel, the Southern Associated Pipe Works.

The cartel divided the market for cast-iron pipes into different territories, including "pay territories," "free territories," and "reserved cities." After May 27, 1895, for (sealed-bid) procurements held in pay territories, the cartel members operated a bidding ring whose structure we describe in stylized form below.[6]

The ring members met prior to procurements to determine which of the ring members would be permitted to bid. To determine which ring member would bid at the procurement, the ring held a knockout in which each ring member submitted a bid, the high bidder was selected to bid at the procurement, and the amount of that ring member's bid was distributed among all the ring members.[7] Losing ring members were prevented from bidding at the auction, while the selected ring member bid against any outside bidders.

To facilitate the knockout, the members of the cast-iron pipe ring set up a "representative board" to whom all enquiries for pipe were referred.[8] A central office for the representative board, which consisted of each cartel member's representative, was set up at Cincinnati. The board would take bids from the "respective shops for the privilege of handling the order."[9]

In this environment, the value to a ring member associated with winning the knockout is the value to that ring member associated with being the lone ring member to attend the procurement. The higher is

6. This model and the associated equilibrium bidding strategies are developed by McAfee and McMillan (1992). As they show, with symmetric bidders, the ring mechanism allows a cartel to suppress all ring competition.
7. The distributions varied among members depending on their production capacities.
8. *Addyston Pipe* Transcript of Record, p. 83.
9. *Addyston Pipe* Transcript of Record, pp. 83 and 361.

a ring member's value for the contract, the greater is the value to that ring member from attending the procurement. If the ring members are symmetric with one another, the highest-valuing ring member will win the knockout and be sent to the procurement to bid against any outside bidders.[10]

In the cast-iron pipe ring, to reduce buyer resistance and disguise the ring's activities, ring members not selected to win the object were told to submit deliberately losing bids.[11]

Once at the procurement, the selected ring member faced competition only from outside bidders and not from the other ring members. Because of this, the selected ring member's optimal bid at the procurement was greater than it would have been in the absence of the ring. With reduced competition at the procurement, the selected ring member's bid was higher. In the event that the selected ring member won the procurement, it received the amount of this bid from the procurer. The reduction in competition led to a higher bid by the selected ring member, which produced a collusive gain when that ring member won.

For example, Howard-Harrison won a procurement auction in St. Louis by bidding $24, while Addyston and Dennis Long protected it with bids of $24.37 and $24.57, respectively. The gains from the auction pool were evident from the fact that the Chattanooga foundry could have provided the pipes to St. Louis at $17 or $18 and still made a profit.[12]

9.6.2   Ascending Bid *without* Information on Identities of Bidders—Wholesale Stamp Dealers

In the 1990s, a bidding ring of eleven wholesale stamp dealers operated at ascending-bid auctions for collectable stamps, primarily in New York auction houses.[13]

The ring's pricing structure can be described in stylized terms as follows.[14] Ring members reported values to a ring center, and then the

---

10. If the ring does not select the highest-valuing ring member, then the gain to collusion is not maximized because this mechanism has no provision for reallocating the object to a different ring member after the auction.

11. "[T]he party securing the order shall have the protection of all the other shops." (*Addyston Pipe* Transcript of Record, p. 83)

12. *Addyston Pipe* Transcript of Record, p. 362.

13. See Asker (2010). The case from which the data are taken is *NY et al.* v. *Feldman et al.*, No. 01-cv-6691 (S.D.N.Y.).

14. For a description of the implementation of this ring in collectable stamps, see chapter 3, footnote 15.

Table 9.1
Payments to ring members

Ring member	Transfer payment
1	$-\dfrac{r_k - p}{2} - \dfrac{r_{k-1} - r_k}{2} - \cdots - \dfrac{r_2 - r_3}{2}$
2	$\dfrac{r_k - p}{2}\dfrac{1}{k-1} + \dfrac{r_{k-1} - r_k}{2}\dfrac{1}{k-2} + \cdots + \dfrac{r_2 - r_3}{2}$
$\vdots$	$\vdots$
k	$\dfrac{r_k - p}{2}\dfrac{1}{k-1}$
$k + 1, \ldots, n$	0

ring center bid at the auction on behalf of the highest-valuing ring member, while the other ring members suppressed their bids. After the auction, if the selected ring member won the object, that ring member made payments to other ring members, where those payments depended on the reports made by each ring member prior to the auction and the price paid at the auction.

Side payments were calculated as follows:[15] ring reports were ranked

$$r_1 > r_2 > \ldots > r_k > p > r_{k+1} > \ldots > r_n,$$

where p is the actual price paid at the auction. Ring members $k+1, \ldots, n$, who submitted reports below the price p paid at the auction, received nothing. Ring member k's report exceeded p by amount $r_k - p$. Half of this amount was awarded to the winner, ring member 1, and the other half was divided equally among the $k - 1$ losing ring members with reports above p. Ring member $k - 1$'s report exceeded k's report by $r_{k-1} - r_k$. Half of this amount was awarded to the winner, ring member 1, and the other half was divided equally among the $k - 2$ losing ring members with reports above r_k. This process continued, so that the payments to the ring members were as shown in table 9.1.

The calculation of side payments can be summarized as follows:

Thus, the side payments involve ring members sharing each increment between bids, provided that their bids are above the target auction price. Half the increment is kept by the winner of the knockout, and the balance is shared equally between those bidders who bid equal to or more than the 'incremental'

15. See Asker (2010). The mechanism used by the ring is a variant of the mechanism described by Graham, Marshall, and Richard (1990).

bid. The side payments were aggregated and settled on a quarterly basis. (Asker 2010, p. 728)

This mechanism distributed the collusive gain in a way that respects differences in the ring members' contributions to the collusive gain. Ring members with higher values received larger payments. As noted by Asker (2010) and as pointed out in Graham, Marshall, and Richard (1990), there will be an incentive to overreport to inflate payoffs from the knockout. This issue is recognized by rings as part of the cost of doing business in much the same way that cartels accept some degree of misrepresentation of sales and production quantities by members.

9.6.3   Ascending Bid *with* Information on Bidder Identities— Antiques, Machinery, and Real Estate

The collusive structures used by the rings described above involve ring members submitting reports or bids to a ring center prior to the auction and then letting the bidding behavior at the auction (appropriately monitored) determine the allocation of the object. In the sealed-bid example above, the allocation of the collusive gain is based only on the pre-auction reports. In the ascending-bid example, the allocation of the collusion gain depends on reports made prior to the auction as well as the auction outcome, including the identity of the winner and the price paid.

As we describe in chapter 3, some ascending-bid auction environments allow ring members to observe the identity of the current high bidder at each point in the auction. In these environments, it is possible for rings to operate without communication prior to each auction. They can instead operate under the rule that no ring member will raise the bid if the current high bidder is another ring member. Then after the auction, any objects won by ring members are brought together to determine their allocation among ring members and the appropriate distribution of the collusive gain.

In *U.S. v. Seville, U.S. v. Ronald Pook*, and *District of Columbia v. George Basiliko*, all of which involve collusion at ascending-bid auctions, the collusive mechanism used by the cartel involved no communication prior to the auction, except possibly to establish the identity of the cartel members or, in the case of *District of Columbia v. George Basiliko*, to designate a cartel member who would bid on behalf of the cartel. As stated in the 1988 decision in *U.S. v. Ronald Pook*:

When a dealer pool was in operation at a public auction of consigned antiques, those dealers who wished to participate in the pool would agree not to bid against the other members of the pool. If a pool member succeeded in purchasing an item at the public auction, pool members interested in that item could bid on it by secret ballot at a subsequent private auction ("knock out") . . . . The pool member bidding the highest at the private auction claimed the item by paying each pool member bidding a share of the difference between the public auction price and the successful private bid. The amount paid to each pool member ("pool split") was calculated according to the amount the pool member bid in the knock out. (*U.S. v. Ronald Pook*, p. 1)

A similar mechanism was used by the industrial machinery cartel of *U.S.* v. *Seville Industrial Machinery* in the period after 1970,[16] and by the real estate cartel of *District of Columbia* v. *George Basiliko.*

The decision in *District of Columbia* v. *George Basiliko* states that:

T]he defendants and the co-conspirators discussed and agreed . . . not to compete with one another to win the bid; selected a designated bidder to act for the conspirators . . . ; discussed and agreed on specific payoffs that conspirators present would receive for not bidding, or discussed and agreed to hold a private, secret auction among themselves after the designated bidder won the public real estate auction . . . ; in many instances, held a secret auction in which the conspirators bid solely among themselves to acquire the property for a price higher than the price paid by the designated bidder at the public real estate auction and agreed to divide the difference between the public real estate auction price and the secret auction price by making payoffs among the conspirators; arranged by contract or other means for the secret auction winner to take title or ownership of the property; and made the payoffs that they had agreed to make. (*District of Columbia* v. *George Basiliko*, p. 6)

In these examples, during the ascending-bid auction, the identity of the current high bidder is observed by all bidders. In particular, it is not possible for a ring member to be the current high bidder and have that fact not be observed by all the other ring members. In this case, the only pre-auction communication required is whatever is necessary for the ring to establish its membership. It must be known to all ring members who the other ring members are.

Given this auction environment, the ring can operate under a rule that no ring member will raise the bid if another ring member is the current high bidder. Any ring member winning the object pays the

16. See *U.S.* v. *Seville Industrial Machinery*. Prior to 1970, members of the industrial machinery cartel were given an opportunity to make vague indications of interest prior to the auction, and then only the cartel organizer submitted bids at the auction based on his subjective estimate of the likely high value for the object from among the ring members. This mechanism was clearly inefficient.

auctioneer and then takes the object to a knockout, which is a procedure for allocating the object among the ring members and determining
the allocation of the collusive gain. The threat that a ring member
would be excluded from future participation in the ring prevents a ring
member from winning the object and then refusing to take it to the
knockout.

The antique and machinery rings used nested knockout procedures
as we describe in chapter 3.4.2. Simply put, individual ring members
make different contributions to the collusive gain, and those incremental contributions are reflected in the differential payments awarded by
these knockout procedures.

9.7 Efficiency of Allocations

In all the cases described in this chapter, the ring organized itself so
that the object was likely to be allocated to the ring member with the
highest value.[17] This efficient allocation within the ring is important
to maximize the gain from suppressing rivalry. In certain theoretical
auction environments, it is straightforward to design ring mechanisms
that are fully efficient in the sense that they suppress all ring competition and allocate the object to the highest-valuing bidder, regardless
of whether that bidder is in the ring or not.[18] That is, the mechanism
allocates the object to the highest-valuing ring member if and only
if the highest-valuing ring member is the highest-valuing bidder
overall.[19]

However, achieving the fully efficient outcome requires conditions
that one would not typically expect to hold in reality. For example, if
the ring is all inclusive and the ring members all draw their values from
the same distribution, which is common knowledge among the ring
members, then the mechanism of the cast-iron pipe ring is efficient at
a sealed-bid auction. If the ring members do not draw their values from
the same distribution, then bidding strategies in the pre-auction are not
symmetric, and so the highest-valuing ring member does not necessarily win. If there are outside bidders, even if they are initially symmetric
with the ring bidders, once the ring is represented only by the highest-

17. With asymmetries among ring members, the object may sometimes be allocated to
a ring member that does not have the highest value.
18. On the efficiency of collusion at auctions, see, for example, Aoyagi (2007).
19. See Mailath and Zemsky (1991) and Marshall and Marx (2007) for descriptions of
fully efficient mechanisms based on pre-auction communication.

valuing ring member, asymmetry is created.[20] The asymmetry between the highest-valuing ring bidder and the outside bidders means that the sealed-bid auction is not efficient (the highest-valuing bidder does not necessarily win). Thus, in practice, one would expect some inefficiency associated with ring pricing structures.

In the ascending-bid mechanisms described above, ring members can have an incentive to behave in a way that can lead the ring to win the object when an outside bidder actually has the highest value. In the mechanism of the wholesale stamp dealers, ring members' reports affect the payments they receive if some other ring member wins the object. Thus, they have an incentive to report amounts somewhat higher than their values. This leads the ring to bid at the auction as if the highest ring value is higher than it actually is. If a post-auction knockout is used, the knockout can be designed so that it efficiently allocates any objects won among ring members, but in that case ring members have an incentive to bid somewhat more than their values at the auction because they may be able to receive a payment from the knockout.[21]

9.8   Conclusion

The structures required to support collusion differ depending on the auction environment. For an ascending-bid auction with information on bidder identities, the requirements for enforcement structures are minimal. The ring can bid in such a way that profitable deviations are not possible. Most of the emphasis for a ring in this environment is on the allocation structure, which provides a mechanism for determining which ring member receives the object and what payments should be made to and from each ring member.

For an ascending-bid auction without information on bidder identities, the ring implements more elaborate structures to enforce the desired bidding behavior, for example by using a third-party bidding agent to submit bids at the auction. Nevertheless, in this case the emphasis remains on the allocation mechanism.

For a sealed-bid auction, enforcement plays a greater role. Bids must be monitored to prevent secret deviations by ring members. In the

---

20. In theory, there is the possibility that the distribution of the highest value from the ring will be the same as the distribution from which the outside bidders draw their values, but this is not of practical interest.
21. See Lopomo, Marshall, and Marx (2005).

absence of auction procedures that facilitate this monitoring, such as requirements that all bids be publicly revealed, enforcement is a substantial challenge. For a sealed-bid auction, the allocation structure may be simplified if the ring's bids result in the highest-valuing ring member winning the auction, although some mechanism for sharing the gains from collusion is still required.

This chapter and the previous one highlight the vulnerability of certain auction mechanisms to collusion by bidders. Overall, pricing and enforcement structures are more difficult for a ring to implement in sealed-bid than ascending-bid auctions, while allocation structures are somewhat equivalent. But this statement is contingent on the specific auction designs for the sealed-bid and ascending-bid auctions that we have considered in this chapter. In the next chapter, we examine the auctioneer's design problem in more detail and discuss what auction design choices can be made to improve an auction's robustness to collusion.

10   Effects of Auction Design on Rings

As shown in chapter 8, the profitability of a bidding ring is affected by whether the auction format is ascending bid or sealed bid. As shown in chapter 9, the collusive structures required to support a bidding ring vary according to the auction format and other details such as whether bidder identities are observable during an ascending-bid auction. These results suggest that an auctioneer can potentially deter collusion by making certain choices about auction design.[1] In this chapter, we discuss how auction design affects the profitability of collusion or costliness of the collusive structures required to support collusion.[2]

The robustness of an auction to collusion can have a large impact on auction revenue.[3] Most other design issues are focused on relatively small margins around the second-highest value. In contrast, by inhibiting collusion, the designer can be confident that the second-highest

---

1. On the problem of identifying and testing for bid rigging, see, for example, Hendricks and Porter (1989), Porter and Zona (1993, 1999), Baldwin, Marshall, and Richard (1997), Pesendorfer (2000), Bajari (2001), Bajari and Summers (2002), Bajari and Ye (2003), Banerji and Meenakshi (2004), and Ishii (2009). For related theoretical results, see LaCasse (1995).
2. See Kovacic et al. (2006) on the design of anticollusion measures for auctions and procurements. See also Pavlov (2008). On the design of multiple-object auctions to deter collusion, see Ausubel and Milgrom (2002) and Ausubel and Cramton (2004).
3. In a theoretical model, Che and Kim (2006) show that any auction mechanism can be converted into one that is collusion proof in the sense that no ring can profit by manipulating the bids of the ring members. The main results in Che and Kim (2006) assume independent types and an all-inclusive ring. When types are correlated, to get results the authors must make additional assumptions, including a finite type space. When the ring is not all inclusive, Che and Kim show that any mechanism that has a noncooperative equilibrium in dominant strategies satisfying ex post individually rational can be made collusion proof. See also Che and Kim (2009). Che and Kim's (2006) collusion-proofing algorithm has the feel of the auctioneer selling the object to the ring (as a whole) at the expected noncooperative price. We provide an example to illustrate the use of the Che and Kim algorithm in the appendix A, but we do not pursue it further here because, as described in the appendix A, the algorithm has limited practical applicability.

value (or something relatively close to it) is what the seller receives as opposed to, say, the fifth, six, or tenth-highest value, which might be the outcome from effective collusion.

As with chapters 8 and 9, we focus our attention on two standard auction formats—ascending-bid and sealed-bid. The choice between these two formats has implications for collusion, and within each format, design parameters affect the auction's susceptibility to collusion.

10.1   Auction Transparency

The amount of information provided by the auctioneer to bidders before the start of the auction, during the auction, and at the conclusion of the auction affects the ability of bidders to collude because it affects the ability of the ring to monitor compliance by ring members to the collusive agreement. As a general rule, the more information the auctioneer conveys about bidder identities, the bids submitted, and auction outcomes, the easier it is for a ring to be effective in its work of suppressing rivalry among members. This point follows directly from the Stiglerian enforcement structure. In what follows, we show that increased transparency in auction design can transform an auction from being robust to collusion to being susceptible to collusion.

Thus, it would seem natural that auctions would be designed to be largely nontransparent in that the auctioneer conveys as little as possible to bidders about their rivals. However, the Federal Acquisition Regulations and other government rules regarding auction and procurement processes mandate transparency.

The delegation of buying and selling authority to employees who do not have high-powered incentives to obtain high auction prices or low procurement prices can create some classic agency problems. Specifically, the employees with the delegated authority to run the auctions or procurements may want to unnecessarily restrict the number of bidders to ease their burden of running the competitive process. Additionally the employees may unjustly skew awards to specific bidders with whom they have personal familiarity or, worse, from whom they are receiving compensation for doing so.[4]

With regard to auctions and procurements in the public sector, elected officials have reacted to the possibility of shirking or malfeasance by government employees by implementing rules requiring that

4. See Compte, Lambert-Mogiliansky, and Verdier (2005).

nothing be hidden from public view.[5] The set of bidders is publicly announced before the bidding begins, and in the case of a sealed-bid auction or procurement, bids and bidder identities are made available at the end of the auction. These transparency measures that are implemented to correct agency problems create increased opportunities for bidder collusion. It would make sense for a bidder coalition to lobby in support of greater transparency, nominally to put all bidders on a level playing field and avert bid-taker shirking and malfeasance, but where the true motivation of the ring is to increase their collusive payoff.

Technological innovations in the implementation of competitive processes, including automated bidding procedures, can alleviate many of the agency concerns that have driven the requirements for increased transparency. For example, the U.S. Federal Communications Commission's (FCC's) spectrum license auctions are a competitive process where even the perception of bid-taker agency problems have been nearly eliminated through automation. For competitive process that can be automated, mandates of transparency facilitate collusion without a countervailing benefit.

Although auction automation eliminates or substantially mitigates issues of bid-taker cheating, if the auction design is pro-collusive, then the fact that the auction is automated will do little to thwart collusion, especially if the design conveys much information to bidders about their rivals, or if the design permits bidders to do that through their actions.

As an example, in the early development of the FCC's spectrum licenses auctions, bidders were allowed to raise the current high bid by the bid increment of their choice.[6] With bids in the millions of dollars, the final digits of the bids were, in a sense, available for bidders to use to encode communication. Bidders took little time to realize that the last three digits offered the opportunity for anticompetitive signaling.[7] In response, the more recent FCC auction designs allow the current

5. See Marshall, Meurer, and Richard (1994).

6. For discussions of FCC auctions, including the susceptibility of some FCC auctions to collusion, see McMillan (1994), McAfee and McMillan (1996), Weber (1997), Klemperer (1998, 2000, 2002), Cramton and Schwartz (2000, 2002), Kwasnica and Sherstyuk (2001), Brusco and Lopomo (2002), and Milgrom (2004). For an analysis of inefficiencies induced by FCC auction design choices, see Bajari and Fox (2007). On strategic jump bidding, see Avery (1998).

7. As described in Weber (1997), this kind of signaling occurred at the FCC's PCS A & B Block Spectrum Auction (FCC Auction 4).

high bid to be raised by only one fixed increment in each round, limiting the ability of bidders to communicate through bids. In addition, more recent FCC auction designs do not reveal information to bidders about the identities of rivals submitting competing bids while the auction is in progress (the bidding history is revealed after the auction is over).

Even in the private sector, it is commonplace to observe auction or procurement designs that unnecessarily create opportunities for a ring to enhance monitoring of members. For example, in a procurement setting, it is often the case that the incumbent supplier is given a right of last refusal. In other words, before the close of the procurement, the incumbent is notified of the leading bid and offered the opportunity to meet the bid to retain the business. Notifying an incumbent of the bids of others before the procurement ends provides the incumbent with a way to monitor the bidding behavior of potential co-conspirators and react in real time to deviations from agreed collusive bidding. It deters deviations by ring members and so is pro-collusive.

10.1.1 "Shill" Bidders

A "shill" bidder acts as an incentiveless agent of a "real" bidder, but other bidders may not be able to recognize a shill as such. Namely, other bidders put positive probability on the shill being a real bidder. Shill bidders exist in real auctions,[8] but they are also a convenient expositional device for us in that monitoring issues within specific auction designs are easily discussed and understood when posed in terms of the possibility of shill bidders. If ring members at a sealed-bid auction have the ability to submit bids under disguised names through shill bidders,[9] it is more difficult for the ring to police the bids submitted by its members. In particular, ring members who have been instructed by the ring to submit losing bids may have an incentive to try to win the item under a disguised name, thereby avoiding penalties for cheating.

Because of the potentially destabilizing effect of shill bidders on bidding rings, particularly at a sealed-bid auction, the auctioneer may

---

8. See the appendix to chapter 12.
9. In some settings, it is not realistic that bidders could disguise identities—for example, a Department of Defense procurement for a missile system for which only two suppliers have the production capability. In addition, restrictions on the ability of a procurement winner to subcontract production can limit the ability of bidders to use agents to bid on their behalf.

have an incentive to facilitate the use of shill bidders. For example, the auctioneer might keep private the identities of the bidders, perhaps referring only to bidder numbers. Also, the auctioneer can allow a bidder to submit more than one bid under different bidder numbers, or under different identities.

10.1.2 Registration

It is common for auctioneers to require bidders to register prior to an auction, perhaps assigning a bidder one or more bidder IDs to be used in the bidding process.[10]

Consider two possible registration regimes: *nontransparent* registration, where the auctioneer does not reveal the set of assigned bidder IDs nor any information linking bidder IDs with their underlying identities; and *transparent* registration, where the auctioneer announces the set of all assigned bidder IDs and their underlying identities. We assume that any information revealed by the auctioneer is accurate, although the auctioneer may choose not to reveal certain information. Under transparent registration, bidders know which auction participant is associated with every bidder ID. Thus, if one registrant has more than one bidder ID, that is revealed to all the bidders. With transparent registration, a shill bidder will be revealed as such to all bidders before submission of bids. Under nontransparent registration, bidders do not even know the set of assigned bidder IDs prior to the auction. In this case, shill bidders may exist and be unknown as such to all but the bidder employing the shill.

Under transparent registration, a ring can use a pricing and allocation structure that requires ring members to report their values and then instructs the highest-reporting ring member to bid up to its value at the auction, with other ring members suppressing their bids. If a ring member wins the object (something that can be observed under transparent registration), then that ring member makes a payment to the ring equal to the difference between the second-highest report among the ring members and the price paid at the auction, when that difference is positive.[11] With these structures in place, no ring member has an incentive to cheat.

10. See Marshall and Marx (2009).
11. This mechanism is described in Graham and Marshall (1987). The mechanism assumes ex ante budget balance so that the payment by a ring member winning the object to the ring is shared among ring members using fixed payments that balance the ring's budget in expectation.

Under nontransparent registration, a ring may not be able to suppress rivalry among members. In that case, the ring only observes the bidder ID of the winner and cannot necessarily be sure whether that bidder ID corresponds to a ring member or not. Nevertheless, one can show that at an ascending-bid auction where bidder identities are revealed continuously throughout the auction, even if ring members can register additional 'shill' identities, this need not disrupt the ring. The ring can use a pricing structure that requires the highest-valuing ring member to reveal its bidder ID to the other ring members (not required under transparent registration), instructing the less than highest-valuing ring members to bid (if the price is less than their values) if the highest-valuing ring member is not the high bidder and the auctioneer is about to close the auction. The highest-valuing ring member is instructed to bid promptly whenever it is not the current high bidder and the price is less than its value. Ring members bid up to their values as long as they perceive competition from bidder IDs not claimed by the ring, and this deters deviations based on disguised identities. The pricing structure defeats attempts by the highest-valuing ring bidder to use an alternative bidder ID to win the object and thereby avoid having to bring the object to a post-auction knockout or make transfer payments to other ring members because it ensures that a ring member deviating in this way cannot win the auction at a price below what it would have paid through noncooperative bidding.

In contrast, at an ascending-bid auction where bidder identities are not revealed during the bidding at the auction, nontransparent registration is disruptive. To see this, note that the ring must require a payment from a ring member that wins the auction, or else ring members would have an incentive to falsely claim that their value was highest so that the bids of the other ring members would be suppressed. This deviation would increase the deviating ring member's payoff whenever its value was greater than those of the outside bidders, but not the highest in the ring. But, if the ring requires a payment from a ring member only if it wins the auction, then a ring member can profitably deviate by taking an action so the ring views it as having the highest value and also registering a bidder ID that it does not reveal to the ring. The deviating ring member can use that bidder ID to bid its value at the auction.

To summarize, if the auction is an ascending-bid auction where the auctioneer does not reveal bidder identities during the course of the auction and the registration is nontransparent, a ring cannot suppress all competition among ring members by using an allocation structure that requires payments only from ring members that win the object. However, regardless of the information revealed during the course of the auction, the ring can suppress competition if registration is transparent.

These results show that even among particular types of ascending-bid auctions, the profitability of collusion can be reduced by altering other design parameters, such as the transparency of the bidder registration process.

10.1.3   Information on the Object Being Sold

There are auction environments in which bidders have considerable expertise relevant to the evaluation of the item or project. For example, antique dealers have expertise in assessing the authenticity of a period piece or timber mills have expertise in assessing the quality of standing timber in a particular drainage area. In such cases, bidders have an extra incentive to collude because competitive bidding would transfer the rents from their expertise to the auctioneer.

An auctioneer can mitigate this incentive through the appropriate choice of an information revelation policy. If the seller reveals information that reduces winner's curse then that will lead to more aggressive bidding, especially by less well-informed bidders, which might typically be the nonring bidders. However, if the seller has information that is coarser than the bidders it can be in the interest of the seller to not reveal that information if collusion by bidders is a possibility. Intuitively, if an auctioneer has a signal of low value but colluding bidders know the item is high value, the auctioneer is potentially diminishing its payoff by revealing its signal.[12]

10.2   Frequency of Auctions

Some bidding rings make transfer payments among themselves after the auctions at which they collude, or perhaps keep records of amounts owed and only infrequently make payments to clear the accounts. Such behavior is made easier if the bidding ring knows there will be a regular stream of auctions in which they can participate. When there are auctions at regular intervals, a bidding ring can more easily imple-

---

12. See Samkharadze (2011).

ment a bid rotation scheme and use enforcement structures that involve the punishment of ring members at future auctions if they deviate.[13] If the value of the items being sold at any individual auction is small, then ring members may have little incentive to disobey the instructions of the ring because the gains to doing so are small relative to the threat of future punishment.

For these reasons, an auctioneer concerned about collusion may prefer to hold fewer auctions, each with a larger number of items being sold. Or the auctioneer may prefer to create higher valued items by bundling a number of lower-valued items. An auctioneer may prefer not to announce a fixed schedule for future auctions, instead bringing objects up for sale at irregular intervals. Longer time intervals between auctions may encourage ring members to defect from the ring because the potential for retaliation by the other ring members is pushed farther into the future.

10.3   Record of Bidding

The design of an ascending-bid auction warrants yet additional attention because the record of bids is naturally less informative than at a sealed-bid auction. At a sealed-bid auction, typically all participating bidders submit bids, and the auctioneer should have a written (or electronic) record of all of these bids. As noted by the U.S. Department of Justice,[14] having fewer than the normal number of competitors submit bids suggests the possibility of collusion, so colluding bidders at a sealed-bid auction can be expected to arrange for ring members that are not designated as the winning bidder to submit complementary bids to disguise the presence of the ring.

Losing bids at a sealed-bid auction can contain information of relevance for inferring collusion.[15] Although a bidding ring always attempts to suppress bids, for collusion to be effective at a sealed-bid auction, a ring must prevent its own ring members from cheating on the collusive agreement. The incentive for ring members to cheat is mitigated if bidders elevate their bids somewhat, but to enforce these elevated bids, the ring may need to have a ring bidder submit a bid that is just underneath the highest ring bidder's bid. This implies that sequential bids

---

13. See Aoyagi (2003).
14. See the U.S. Department of Justice primers listed in chapter 8, footnote 1.
15. See Porter and Zona (1993).

may be very close to one another, even when they are losing bids. Bids of this nature may be an indication of collusion.[16] Thus, the paper trail available to an auctioneer at a sealed-bid auction may facilitate the prosecution of collusion.

At an ascending-bid auction such a paper trail typically does not exist. First, the bids themselves may be submitted orally, and so there may be no formal record of submitted bids. Second, depending on the auction format, many bidders may not submit bids at all, even in a noncollusive environment. So the observation that only a small number of bidders actually submitted bids may not be suggestive of collusive activity the way it is at a sealed-bid auction. Third, one may not even be able to identify who all the participants are at an ascending-bid auction because one may only know about those who actually submitted bids. These issues mean it is typically more difficult to develop evidence of collusion from the bids submitted at an ascending-bid auction than at a sealed-bid auction.

10.4   Conclusion

As discussed in this chapter, an understanding of the role of rivalry at auctions and the collusive structures that rings can apply to suppress rivalry can inform the design of collusion countermeasures in auctions. Among other steps, auctioneers can take the following measures to deter collusion:

1. Use a sealed-bid auction rather than an ascending-bid auction.

2. Limit the amount of information provided to bidders regarding their rivals including the identities of bidders, the auction outcomes, and the bids of their competitors.

3. In the absence of compelling reasons, do not grant the right of last refusal to an incumbent supplier.

4. Allow bidders to submit multiple bids, with some under disguised identities.

5. Regarding the revelation of the auctioneer's information about the item being sold, select a policy that accounts for potential collusion.

6. Hold auctions at long, irregular time intervals.

---

16. See Marshall and Marx (2007).

10.5   Appendix: Collusion-Proof Mechanisms*

In this appendix, we provide an example to illustrate the use of the Che and Kim (2006) algorithm for constructing a collusion-proof mechanism. As noted above, the algorithm has limited practical applicability. In particular:

1. The mechanism requires all bidders to make payments to the auctioneer, not only the bidder winning the object. This is potentially problematic if bidders cannot verify that the mechanism was implemented correctly, that is, if the auctioneer can cheat by demanding higher-than-required payments from the bidders.

2. The auctioneer knows the number of bidders and the set of types of the bidders and the identities and types of two of the bidders in the ring.[17]

3. The ring submits a bid for every ring member, despite possible incentives for the ring to suppress some bids.

Consider a single-object, second-price auction with four bidders and independent private values drawn from $U[0, 1]$. Assume no reserve price.

Converting a second-price auction into the notation of the paper, we have $n = 4$, $v = 0$ (auctioneer has zero value for the object), the allocation is

$$q_i^*(\theta) = \begin{cases} 1, & \text{if } \theta_i > \max_{j \neq i} \theta_j, \\ 0, & \text{otherwise.} \end{cases}$$

(We ignore ties, but you could give the object to the lower numbered bidder in the event of a tie at the maximum value and adjust the payments accordingly.) The payments by the bidders are

$$t_i^*(\theta) = \begin{cases} \max_{j \neq i} \theta_j, & \text{if } \theta_i > \max_{j \neq i} \theta_j, \\ 0, & \text{otherwise.} \end{cases}$$

---

17. Che and Kim's (2006) game requires that bidders agree to participate in the mechanism prior to the ring-formation game. In addition, which bidders will have the opportunity to form a ring (only one ring is allowed to form) is fixed prior to bidders' agreeing whether to participate in the mechanism. As shown in Che and Kim (2009), under certain conditions, similar results hold when bidders first decide whether to collude and then decide whether to participate in the auctioneer's mechanism.

Che and Kim specify a "collusion-proof" mechanism based on the second-price auction that has $\hat{q} = q^*$ (allocation rule is the same) and payment rule $\hat{t}$, where

$$\hat{t}_i(\theta') = E_{\theta_{-i}}\left[t_i^*(\theta_i', \theta_{-i})\right] - \frac{1}{3}\sum_{j \neq i} E_{\theta_{-j}}\left[t_j^*(\theta_j', \theta_{-j})\right] + \frac{1}{3}\sum_{j \neq i} E_{\theta}\left[t_j^*(\theta)\right].$$

So in this example,

$$\hat{t}_1(\theta') = \int_0^{\theta_1'} 3x^3 dx - \frac{1}{3}\left(\int_0^{\theta_2'} 3x^3 dx + \int_0^{\theta_3'} 3x^3 dx + \int_0^{\theta_4'} 3x^3 dx\right)$$
$$+ \frac{1}{4}\int_0^1 \int_0^y 12x^3 dx dy$$
$$= \frac{3}{4}(\theta_1')^4 - \frac{1}{4}\left[(\theta_2')^4 + (\theta_3')^4 + (\theta_4')^4\right] + \frac{3}{20}.$$

Note that

$$E_{\theta_{-1}}(\hat{t}_1(\theta_1', \theta_{-1})) = \frac{3}{4}(\theta_1')^4 - \frac{1}{4}\left(\frac{1}{5} + \frac{1}{5} + \frac{1}{5}\right) + \frac{3}{20}$$
$$= \frac{3}{4}(\theta_1')^4$$

and

$$E_{\theta_{-1}}\left[t_1^*(\theta_1', \theta_{-1})\right] = \int_0^{\theta_1'} 3x^3 dx = \frac{3}{4}(\theta_1')^4,$$

so bidders' expected payments are the same under the new mechanism as in the second-price auction under noncooperative behavior.

In this new mechanism, the bidder with the highest report wins the object and each bidder makes a payment, where i's payment is $\hat{t}_i(r)$. To see that incentive compatibility is satisfied in the new mechanism, note that player i's expected payoff given report r_i and assuming truthful reporting by the other players is

$$\theta_i \Pr\left(\max_{j \neq i}\theta_j < r_i\right) - E_{\theta_{-i}}\left[\hat{t}_i(r_i, \theta_{-i})\right] = \theta_i r_i^3 - \frac{3}{4}(r_i)^4,$$

which is maximized at $\theta_i = r_i$, so incentive compatibility is satisfied.

Suppose all four bidders get together to try to collude. The collusive mechanism considered does not allow one bidder not to participate—each bidder continues to submit some message. But if they did try to collude by having the highest-valuing bidder submit its value and the other bidders submit zero, then their total payments would be, assuming $\theta_1 > \theta_2, \theta_3, \theta_4$,

$$\sum_{i=1}^{4} \hat{t}_i(\theta_1, 0, 0, 0) = \frac{3}{5}.$$

For any possible reports, the payments of the two bidders sum to 3/5. Under noncooperative play their total expected payments are also 3/5, so no collusive mechanism is profitable.

It is interesting that in contrast to a second-price or sealed-bid auction, in the collusion-proof mechanism, a bidder's payment is decreasing in its rival's report.

IV   Detection of Collusion Using Economic Evidence

In chapters 11 and 12, we discuss the use of economic evidence to infer collusion. This issue is central to (1) purchasers concerned about potential collusion by suppliers, (2) sellers concerned about potential collusion among purchasers, (3) parent corporations that are concerned about potential collusion by their division managers, and (4) enforcement authorities that are charged to safeguard consumer surplus. In the absence of a "smoking gun," such as recordings of actual cartel/ring meetings or a paper trail of direct conspiratorial communications, these market participants and enforcement authorities only have economic evidence to rely upon to infer the existence of a cartel or ring. In chapter 11, we address detection with respect to cartels, and in chapter 12, we focus on rings.

Chapter 13 is not concerned with detection, but instead with its close cousin, the anticipation of coordinated behavior among the remaining firms in an industry after a merger. We argue in chapter 13 that enforcement authorities can enhance their analysis of potential post-merger coordination in an industry by extending standard analyses that are typically done to examine unilateral effects of a merger.

11   Plus Factors

Plus factors are the body of economic circumstantial evidence of collusion, above and beyond the parallel movement of prices by firms in an industry.[1] Plus factors are the economic criteria that can assist with the diagnosis of collusion.[2] When a plus factor delivers a strong inference of collusion, we refer to that plus factor as a super-plus factor.[3]

11.1   Organizing Plus Factors within a Taxonomy of Cartel Structures

We begin by reviewing the structures used by cartels and the observable conduct within these structures that can generate plus factors. In part I, we described nine broad baskets for the conduct of an explicit cartel (see chapter 4.3).[4] We can now use the collusive structures developed in parts II to more clearly articulate this taxonomy.

Cartel conduct that is associated with collusive *pricing structures* includes:

1. *Price elevation*: Raise prices above what they would have been without the conspiracy.

2. *Quantity restriction*: Reduce total industrywide quantity below what it would have been without the conspiracy.

3. *Steps to reduce buyer resistance*: Take steps to reduce resistance by buyers to price increases.

4. *Internal incentive shifts*: Change within-firm incentives so as to inhibit interfirm competition and foster higher prices.

1. ABA Section of Antitrust Law (2007, pp 11–16).
2. See Kovacic et al. (2011) and Harrington (2008).
3. See Kovacic et al. (2011).
4. These are drawn in part from Kovacic et al. (2011).

Cartel conduct that is associated with collusive *allocation structures* includes:

5. *Allocation of collusive gain*: Allocate the collusive gain among members.

6. *Redistributions*: Redistribute gains and losses among members so as to maintain compliance with the agreement.

Cartel conduct that is associated with collusive *enforcement structures* includes:

7. *Communication and monitoring*: Monitor compliance with the agreement and communicate regularly regarding all relevant features of the conspiracy that require discipline, especially production, sales, and market shares.[5]

8. *Enforcement and punishment*: Stand ready to abandon collusive conduct if some cartel members continually engage in substantial noncompliant conduct.

In addition, a cartel that has used collusive structures to successfully suppress rivalry within the cartel may consider incremental actions designed to act on the other forces affecting industry profits. This additional conduct includes:

9. *Dominant-firm conduct*: Once interfirm rivalry has been suppressed successfully, seek additional profits through activities such as dominant-firm conduct.

In chapters 11.2 through 11.5, we discuss in more detail examples of plus factors associated with the cartel conducts listed above. Then in chapter 11.6, we discuss how the mathematics of conditional probabilities can be used to help one think more clearly about, and potentially quantify, the inferences that can be drawn from plus factors. In chapter 11.7, we summarize the super-plus factors identified in chapters 11.2 through 11.5. In chapter 11.8, we briefly discuss cartel and ring reactions to detection based on super-plus factors.

11.2   Plus Factors Related to Pricing Structures

We highlight several plus factors and super-plus factors related to pricing structures, and we discuss how plus factors that may be indi-

---

5. Kuhn (2001) characterizes types of communication likely to facilitate collusion.

vidually weak can potentially be viewed in combination to provide a strong inference of collusion.

11.2.1   Price Elevation

Effective collusion by sellers elevates the price that buyers pay relative to noncollusive conduct. If one could account for all material factors that influence price when sellers are not explicitly colluding, then the elevation of price beyond that level would lead to the inference that the sellers were colluding. There is a strong inference of collusion if, for example, a reliable predictive econometric model that accounts for all material noncollusive effects on price, estimated using benchmark data where the conduct was presumed noncollusive,[6] produces predictions of prices that are not consistent with the path of actual prices in the period or region of potential collusion, at a specified confidence level.

If such measurement were readily available, it would be of great value to public enforcement authorities investigating potential collusion, procurers who suspect potential collusion by certain sellers, as well as corporate managers concerned that division managers may be exposing the corporation to antitrust liabilities through collusion with their counterparts at other firms.[7]

Empirical Model*

In what follows, we describe one approach to modeling and estimating a but-for price. The presentation below assumes a familiarity with basic econometrics. A parent corporation can typically require divisions to provide transaction-level data, along with all data relevant to the underpinnings of pricing, such as factor costs and demand conditions; thus, for a parent corporation, there are fewer barriers to the implementation of the methodology described below than for buyers or public enforcement authorities.

In order to calculate whether prices are elevated relative to noncollusive conduct, one estimates what the price would have been had there not been a cartel.[8] This is often referred to as the but-for price— but-for the existence of a cartel, what would the price have been?

---

6. The noncollusive benchmark is a period during which firms would be assumed to take into account their mutual interdependence. Thus, changes relative to this benchmark period would be attributed to explicit collusion.
7. On the use of empirical techniques to detect collusion as applied to citric acid and lysine, see Bolotova, Connor, and Miller (2008).
8. See White, Marshall, and Kennedy (2006).

Figure 1.1 contains two calculations of but-for prices for vitamin A acetate 650 feed grade. If the concern is cartel detection, then there would typically not be a plea agreement. This implies the need to search for a noncollusive benchmark, which adds a layer of difficulty to an already demanding problem.

Price variation can arise from many sources. In an attempt to isolate the effect of collusion on price, as one option, we can construct a model that reliably predicts price variation during circumstances where we can be reasonably assured conduct is noncollusive. If the model predicts price movements in this benchmark accurately, then it can be used to predict what prices would have been during the period of collusion. However, this requires an assumption about a period of time, a geographic location, or a product space that is noncollusive and thus can be used as a reliable benchmark. For now, we assume the existence of both a known benchmark time period and a conjectured collusive time period, where each is of reasonable length.

Undergraduate textbooks in econometrics, which form the basis for many conceptual understandings in econometrics, rely to a great extent on the teaching device of an experiment. For example, we might be asked to envision 1,000 one-acre plots that are planted in corn—500 plots receive a treatment of fertilizer, while the others do not. The 1,000 plots are spread across several counties within a state. Temperature, rainfall, soil fertility, hours of sunlight, and humidity all have some degree of variation between the plots. All of these can be measured. Regression analysis can be used to control for these exogenous factors in calculating the marginal effect of the fertilizer application on crop yield.

To apply this teaching device to cartel detection, instead of 1,000 one-acre plots of corn, assume that we have many periods of time in which the product price can be observed. Instead of crop yields, we have price realizations. Instead of temperature, rainfall, soil fertility, hours of sunlight, and humidity, we have factor input prices, demand shifters, inventories, capacity utilizations, exchange rates, and other variables potentially relevant to pricing. Instead of the treatment of fertilizer to some acres, we have a conjectured "treatment" of collusion for a specific period of time.

However, in general, economic environments are not controlled experiments. There are not 1,000 separate island economies, where 500 of the economies receive a cartel treatment and 500 do not. The reality of economic life is that the world is nonexperimental. Thus, the challenge of detecting a cartel is not a trivial extension of a standard experimental teaching device.

There are no strategic players in the crop experiment, but a cartel is a major strategic player. In an experimental setting, we think nothing of using rainfall to explain crop yields, or controlling for rainfall to understand the impact of fertilizer on crop yields. Rainfall is exogenous. The experimenter cannot change rainfall, and the mere production of crops does not change rainfall. But, there are many factors influencing a product's price that may be affected by the presence of a cartel, or even strategically manipulated by a cartel.

For example, the cartel may actively monitor and change inventory levels and/or capacity utilization as part of its conduct. The inclusion of these variables in the model, where the estimation is conducted over both the benchmark and collusive time periods, is inappropriate because we cannot determine the price but-for the cartel when that determination is based on variables that the cartel directly influences.

Consider inventory levels. Suppose that during the benchmark period, high inventories lead to vigorous competition and that this has a depressing effect on price. In addition, suppose that as prices increase a cartel has leading members agree to build up large inventories as both a threat against smaller cartel members that may deviate and as a threat against potential new entrants. An inventory variable cannot be included in a model to accurately determine the price but-for the cartel when that variable is being altered strategically by the cartel.

This point is important for both estimation and prediction. First, if estimation is conducted over both the benchmark and conjectured collusive period, and inventories are included as a regressor in the model, then the estimated impact of inventories will capture a confluence of the aforementioned effects, where one effect dominates in the benchmark period and another in the conjectured cartel period, despite the fact that the single variable is treated identically by the estimation between the two. Second, even if the estimation is conducted only over the benchmark period, when one uses those estimates to predict but-for prices over the conjectured cartel period, the inventory variable will be poisoned by the strategic use of inventories by the cartel. Specifically, inventories will have a different effect on price during the conjectured cartel period versus either before or after the conjectured cartel period.

Advertising expenditures may be another such variable. If firms were advertising solely to steal market share from one another during the benchmark period, but during the conjectured cartel period they jointly agreed to advertise to expand demand for their product as a whole, then advertising expenditures cannot be included in an estimation designed to obtain an accurate and reliable but-for price.

It might appear that the prices of factor inputs would be immune from this critique, but this requires thought as well. If the conjectured cartel can use its bargaining power against factor input suppliers to influence the price they pay, then that factor input price is under the influence of the conjectured cartel and cannot be used to produce an accurate and reliable but-for price.

It is the responsibility of the econometrician to understand the industry and product market well enough to know what is and is not a variable that could potentially be under the direct influence of and/ or manipulation by the conjectured cartel.

There is an additional issue with a variable such as a factor input price. Suppose that the factor input is a true commodity in the sense that the conjectured cartel is too small relative to the world market for the cartel to have any impact on the factor input's price or availability. The reaction of firms in a noncollusive oligopoly to changes in a factor input price can be entirely different from that of a cartel. Oligopoly pricing may be more sensitive to movements in the factor price than cartel pricing. If possible, one should avoid using data from both the conjectured cartel period and the benchmark period to estimate the effect of variables on price movements.

Within the experimental methodology, factor input prices are typically interacted with the cartel treatment variable, thereby allowing for different effects of factor input prices in the benchmark period versus the conjectured cartel period. For many applications, a preferable methodology is to use the benchmark period, where it is assumed that the conduct is noncollusive, to estimate parameters, and then use these estimates to predict price movements during the conjectured cartel period.

Another issue concerns the use of variables such as exchange rates. Suppose that exchange rates were included because the record indicated that price increases by the colluding sellers were often justified by pointing to changes in exchange rates. However, it may be that the cartel launches price increases when exchange rates change in order to use those changes as "cover," when exchange rates have no real impact on prices in the industry. If this is the case, and exchange rates are included in a model where estimation is conducted over both the benchmark and conjectured cartel period, then the variable may be found to be important, even though it has no real effect and should have no role in the determination of a but-for price.

Time series variables that have no true underlying economic relationship may appear to be important in the experimental approach for spurious reasons. For example, many economic variables move through time in similar ways because of underlying economic conditions or general growth of the economy. A regression analysis may identify such variables as important for fit, but these variables may have nothing to do with price changes for the product of interest. Appropriate treatment of such variables is needed in the analysis so as to account for their true informational content regarding changes in price.

Some important information may not be available. Omission of important information is always a source of concern. For example, suppose that some freight rates are an important cost and that they are set by long-term contract. Suppose that these prices are unavailable. Then proxies for this important cost should be sought. In this case, there may be a price index available for freight rates that could be used as a candidate regressor.

The objective is to obtain an accurate and reliable estimate of the but-for price during the conjectured cartel period. The model that is estimated over the benchmark period is used to predict but-for prices over the conjectured cartel period.[9]

To ensure that the model produces accurate and reliable predictions, the predictive accuracy of the model is evaluated for the benchmark period. Envision that a candidate set of variables have been selected that can potentially explain price movements, and that these variables are not subject to potential strategic manipulation by the cartel. This could be a long list of variables.

There is only so much data available, and thus only so much information available to evaluate a model. Variables are included based upon their contribution to the predictive accuracy of the model in the benchmark period. Over the benchmark period, blocks of time are withheld ("hold-out periods") from the estimation of a model. That model is estimated and used to determine how well the model predicts during the hold-out periods. This is done systematically for all the potential models and for a large number of time periods within the benchmark. The best model is the one that predicts best within sample.[10]

---

9. See Shao (1993), Racine (2000), Bernheim (2002), Inoue and Kilian (2006), and Giacomini and White (2006).
10. See Racine (2000).

The best model contains a specific subset of the candidate variables. When estimated in the benchmark period, that model is then used to predict the price for the conjectured cartel period. That is the but-for price.

Coefficient estimates in the predictive model should not be used to assess the model's reliability or accuracy. The coefficients in a predictive model do not have this kind of structural interpretation. The coefficients are just weights on variables, where those weights are such that they jointly produce the best prediction of the but-for price.

A strict structural interpretation of coefficients is rooted in an ideal experimental world. For example, suppose that we are trying to predict the price of a vitamin product. It is well known that oil is an important factor input. One would expect an increase in the price of oil to cause an increase in the price of the vitamin product, all else held constant. Suppose that the best predictive model produces a "coefficient" on the price of oil that is negative. This does not mean that the model is flawed. The price of oil was selected for inclusion in the model and the coefficient was selected as the best weight for the purposes of prediction. A coefficient in a predictive model should not be viewed as capturing a ceteris paribus marginal effect.

Returning to figure 1.1, one can see a large difference between the actual and but-for price during the plea-era period. The difference between the actual and but-for price can be used to determine the harm from a cartel and also used to detect cartel conduct. Specifically, when a significant difference between actual and but-for prices starts to emerge, as is evident in vitamin A acetate 650 feed grade by at least 1992, the inference of collusion is strong.

11.2.2 Quantity Restriction

Effective collusion reduces the total industrywide quantity below what it would have been in the absense of collusion. For example, the output restrictions of the OPEC cartel are widely publicized. To the extent that agreements among OPEC countries reduce the output of oil below what it otherwise would be, they increase the market clearing price for oil above what it would have been without the constraints.

As discussed in chapter 6, a class action complaint indicates that the United Potato Growers of America Inc., under the expectation of being covered by the Capper–Volstead Act, allegedly implemented a quantity reduction scheme that involved commitments by members to reduce potato acreage, to be monitored by satellite surveillance and ground inspections.

11.2.3 Steps to Reduce Buyer Resistance

As part of the pricing structure in the vitamins cartel, the cartel organized attempts to reduce buyer resistance by publicly announcing price increases, with the announcements reported in leading trade journals. Comparing vitamins price announcements during the admitted cartel period to those in the period prior to 1985, when explicit collusion was less likely, we can characterize collusive price announcements for a range of vitamin products produced by participants in the vitamins cartel as follows:[11]

1. *Collusive price announcements are made relatively more frequently than noncollusive price announcements.* The frequent use of price announcements by cartels reflects the importance of their role as part of a cartel pricing structure.

2. *Collusive price announcements occur at somewhat regular intervals.* The regularity of cartel price announcements reflects the regularity of the cartel meeting schedule. For example, each semi-annual cartel meeting might be followed by a new price announcement, giving a semi-annual structure to the price announcements.[12]

3. *Collusive price announcements are gradual in the sense of involving relatively modest individual price increases.* The gradualism of price increases directly addresses buyer resistance. As described above, cartel members in *Electrical and mechanical carbon and graphite products* faced buyer resistance because of the size of the price increase they announced. In addition, as noted by Harrington (2006), gradual price increases may reduce the probability of detection.

4. *Collusive price announcements are typically "joint announcements," with one firm leading and then others matching with identical announcements soon thereafter.* The use of joint announcements also directly addresses buyer resistance. If buyers observe that all the firms in an industry, or at least an important subset of firms in an industry, have announced identical price increases, then they will be less likely to expect aggressive price negotiations with the firms to be worthwhile. Price announcements by the vitamins cartel typically involved delays between the announcements of cartel members of seven or fewer days (the relevant trade journals are weekly publications).[13] The EC decision in *Vitamins*

---

11. Price announcement behavior is specific to a product/market/industry, so these characterizations do not necessarily apply beyond the products considered in Marshall, Marx, and Raiff (2008).

12. See Marshall, Marx, and Raiff (2008).

13. See Marshall, Marx, and Raiff (2008).

states that, "The parties normally agreed that one producer should first 'announce' the increase, either in a trade journal or in direct communication with major customers. Once the price increase was announced by one cartel member, the others would generally follow suit. In this way the concerted price increases could be passed off, if challenged, as the result of price leadership in an oligopolistic market."[14]

5. *Collusive price announcements may be led by a firm other than the market leader.* Noncollusive price announcements will typically be led by the market leader because smaller firms will fear being undercut by larger firms, while a larger firm will have less concern about a smaller firm operating under its price umbrella.[15] Empirically, in the vitamins industry prior to 1985, firms other than the market leader for a vitamin product, typically Roche, rarely led joint announcements, but after 1985, firms other than Roche frequently led joint announcements.[16]

6. *Collusive price announcements typically have long lead times before the new price becomes effective.* Publicly announced prices are sometimes effective immediately and sometime effective at some future date. When announced prices have a future effective date, suppliers may choose to withdraw or alter their announced prices. Lead times for the effective dates of public price announcements allow the cartel to monitor acceptance of the price increase and retract an announced increase that is being heavily resisted by buyers before incurring disruptions in cartel market shares. Approximately 50 percent of the price announcements made by the vitamins cartel were made well prior to the effective dates for the price increases; however, in an earlier benchmark period where explicit collusion was unlikely, only 5 percent of price announcements were made prior to the effective dates for the price increases.[17]

In *Wall Products* v. *National Gypsum*,[18] the colluding firms announced pricing policies that were all to become effective on the same future date.[19] Because of the role that the pre-announcement of price increases can play in supporting a collusive agreement, competition authorities

14. EC decision in *Vitamins* at paras. 203–204.
15. See Marshall, Marx, and Raiff (2008).
16. For example, in vitamin A acetate 650 feed grade shown in figure 11.1, starting in late 1989, the first six announcements are joint announcements led by first Roche, then BASF, then Rhone Poulenc, then BASF, then Roche, then BASF.
17. See Marshall, Marx, and Raiff (2008).
18. *Wall Products Co.* v. *National Gypsum Co.* 326 F. Supp. 295, 316 (N.D. Cal. 1971).
19. This is as reported by Clark (1983).

have in certain cases prohibited the announcement of prices prior to their effective date. Such a prohibition was imposed on an association of sugar refiners in 1934,[20] but the Supreme Court reversed that portion of the district court order.[21] More recently, a prohibition on advance price announcements was included in the 1967 consent agreement in *U.S. v. Pennsalt Chem. Corp.*[22] In addition in *Ethyl Corp.*,[23] the U.S. Federal Trade Commission found advance announcement of price changes to have an anti-competitive effect.

To show price announcements in action, we present the price announcement and transaction price data for the vitamins cartel.[24] Data on price announcements come from an exhaustive review of two weekly trade journals, *Feedstuffs* and the *Chemical Marketing Reporter*, for the years 1970 to 2001. This is a complete set of the public price announcements in the United States during this time period for a sample of vitamin products.[25] In figure 11.1 we show the price announcements for vitamin A acetate 650 feed grade, and in appendix A of this chapter, we show the price announcements for Calpan (B5) SD feed grade (figure 11.4), Calpan (B5) USP (figure 11.5), and vitamin E acetate oil USP (figure 11.6).[26]

Figure 11.1 shows the price announcements and prices for vitamin A acetate 650 feed grade. The actual average transaction prices are traced by the thick line, and the announced prices are indicated by filled or open circles, squares, and triangles representing different types of announcements. A joint announcement is defined as one in which one or more cartel members announce the same price within ninety days. Joint announcements are indicated by filled shapes. Single announcements are those not followed by another announcement of the same price and are indicated by open shapes. The shape itself indicates the firm making a single announcement or leading a joint announcement, as stated in the legend. The figure also indicates with vertical bars for each announcement (using the right vertical axis) the

20. *U.S. v. Sugar Inst.*, 15 F. Supp. 817, 830, 908 (S.D.N.Y. 1934).

21. *Sugar Inst. v. U.S.*, 297 U.S. 553, 603 (1936).

22. *U.S. v. Pennsalt Chem. Corp.*, 1967 Trade Cas. (CCH) P71, 982, at 83,475 (E.D. Pa. 1967).

23. In re Ethyl Corp., 3 Trade Reg. Rep. (CCH) at 22,546 (F.T.C. Mar. 22, 1983).

24. Although the vitamins cartel was international in breadth, our empirical analysis relies only on public price announcement data for the U.S.

25. See Marshall, Marx, and Raiff (2008).

26. Data on prices were reverse engineered from the graphs in Bernheim (2002). Section 12 of Bernheim (2002) provides the monthly weighted average unit price in dollars per kilogram from 1980 to 2002, the dates of the plea-period, and the identities of the cartel firms.

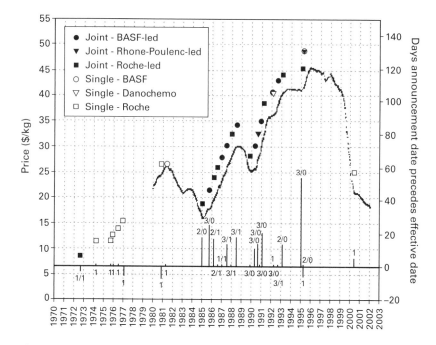

Figure 11.1
Price announcements and prices for vitamin A acetate 650 feed grade

number of days between the announcement date and the effective date for the price increase. In some cases, the announcement was made after the effective date, so the number of days between is negative. Finally, above the bars indicating the days until the effective date are two numbers, first, the number of cartel members included in the joint announcement and, second (after a "/"), the number of noncartel members included in the joint announcement. For vitamin A acetate 650 feed grade, there were three cartel members: Roche, BASF, and Rhone-Poulenc,[27] so the first number is at most three.

The plea period for vitamin A acetate 650 feed grade was January 1990 to February 1999, although Bernheim (2002) places the start of the conspiracy in January 1985.[28] As can be seen in figure 11.1, January 1985 corresponds to a distinct change in the price announcement behavior and is the beginning of a multi-year run-up in price. Prior to 1985, there are relatively few price announcements, and almost all price announce-

27. See figure 1.1.
28. See Bernheim (2002, p. iii).

ments are single announcements—namely, an announcement by one firm that is not followed by another announcement by another firm at the same price. Also, prior to 1985, announcements tend to be made shortly before or after the effective date for the price change, but after January 1985 announcements tend to be made well in advance of the effective date for the price change. This behavior continues during the conspiracy period. After February 1999, when the conspiracy was identified by antitrust authorities, joint price announcements ceased and the price fell dramatically.

Despite the fact that manufacturers may offer discounts off of their announced price, figure 11.1 suggests that cartel price announcements and actual prices move together.[29]

As shown in figure 11.1, the firms tend to announce price increases, not price declines. The announced prices after January 1985 show a steady rate of increase and lead the actual prices. The prices being announced at any point in time tend to be a similar distance above the current price, except at price peaks after 1985, when the cartel firms continue to announce increasing prices as the transaction prices flatten out or turn down. The figure shows evidence of resistance to further price increases at the price peaks in 1988 and again in 1994.

In the appendix to this chapter, we provide the price announcement graphs for an additional feed grade vitamin and two human vitamins. The characteristics of these figures are remarkably similar to those of figure 11.1.

29. As another example, in the EC decision in *Cartonboard* the announced prices and actual prices were characterized by the EC as follows: "If the purpose of the economic study was simply to show that the cartel was ineffective, it does not fulfil this objective either. The Commission never alleged that the actual prices charged went up by the full amount of the proposed increase to all customers on the first day the new prices became effective and it would be unrealistic to expect that they would (see recitals 101 and 102). The various graphs in the economic study commissioned by the producers (and on which they rely to support the argument that there was no causal connection between 'announced' and 'actual' prices) in fact show a close linear relationship between the two sets of data, both in absolute domestic currencies and converted to ecu in real terms (see recital 21). The net price increases achieved closely tracked the price announcements, albeit with some time lag. The author of the report himself acknowledged during the oral hearing that this was the case for 1988 and 1989. It is only to be expected that when account is taken of individual arrangements, discounts and concessions on timing—and sometimes general customer resistance—the actual net increases achieved should be somewhat lower than those announced. The use of 'average' increases also tends to obscure the fact that in many cases the producers succeeded in making the customer pay the full amount of the announced increase." (EC decision in *Cartonboard* at para. 115).

11.2.4 Internal Incentive Shifts

If a division manager opts to join a cartel, there are internal features of the operation of the division that he or she will need to change. Specifically, as noted in chapter 5, sales staff cannot be incented to strive for increased market share but, instead, it will be necessary for the division manager to change the incentives for the sales force to "price before volume."[30] In other words, the sales staff will be required to implement the coordinated price increases of the cartel and not engage in the disruptive activity of stealing customer accounts from rivals. The mandate of "price before volume," or any of the numerous variants, cannot survive in a marketplace where rivals are incenting their sales forces to pursue increased market shares. A firm unilaterally advocating "price before volume" is a sitting duck as rivals undercut its price. It is a sensible change to internal incentives if a large number of other firms simultaneously adopt the change. In an industry in which firms make relatively homogeneous products, a change in the within-firm incentives for a sales force that abruptly shifts from the pursuit of market share to the enforcement of pricing discipline is a super-plus factor.

11.2.5 Economic Evidence in Combination

In some cases, one might observe a constellation of economic evidence, where each individual component is not compelling, that in aggregate constitutes a super-plus factor. For example, there might be conduct that would be consistent with unilateral actions by firms in the face of depressed market demand and separate conduct that would be consistent with unilateral actions by firms in the face of rising demand. However, the simultaneous observation of both types of conduct might be inconsistent with unilateral conduct and lead to the strong inference of collusion.

Suppose that the largest producers are all restricting production. This could happen as a consequence of a negative demand shock. Separately, suppose that prices are relatively high. In isolation, there may be many noncollusive reasons for high prices, such as a positive demand shock. Separately, suppose that profits are relatively high for each of the producers. In isolation, this could also arise for noncollusive reasons, such as a positive demand shock. However, the concurrent occurrence of high profits, high prices, and production restrictions

---

30. See chapter 2.5.

being implemented by major producers is highly unlikely without collusion. Specifically, if prices and profits are relatively high, then the unilateral response of a producer should be to sell as much as possible to earn the increased profit margin on incremental units. A restriction in production across several firms when the opportunity cost of doing so is extraordinarily high leads to the strong inference of collusion.

When prices are increasing, a buyer is going to invest incremental resources in resisting those increases. Resistance will involve eliciting "special" deals from some suppliers to sell additional volumes to buyers at relatively lower prices. For suppliers to react to such offers from buyers by implementing supply restrictions is contrary to unilateral competitive forces.

As discussed in chapter 11.3, "fixed relative market shares" is a plus factor but, alone, not super plus. There are many noncollusive reasons that market shares may be relatively stable in an industry. But suppose that the firms in the industry undertake many other actions in proportion to their relative market shares. For example, suppose that firms restrict supply in proportion to market share, and that they are doing so at a time when demand is relatively robust. As another example, suppose that a new technology that might compete with current suppliers is bought by a consortium of suppliers where their payments are in proportion to their market shares. These incremental conducts, in addition to the relative fixity of production market shares, constitute a super-plus factor.

11.3   Plus Factors Related to Allocation Structures

We highlight two plus factors related to allocation structures: the stability of market shares, which might be associated with a cartel's use of a market share allocation, and the observation of interfirm transfers.

11.3.1   Allocation of Collusive Gain

As discussed in chapter 6.3, many cartels use a market share agreement as a basis for their allocation structure. An implication of a market share agreement is that market shares should remain stable, something that may be observable to those outside the cartel.

Figure 11.2 portrays the worldwide market shares for all producers of vitamin C from 1980 to 1998, where we have grouped the producers into three categories: noncartel firms, cartel firms, and Chinese firms. It is clear from the figure that the Chinese producers made large inroads

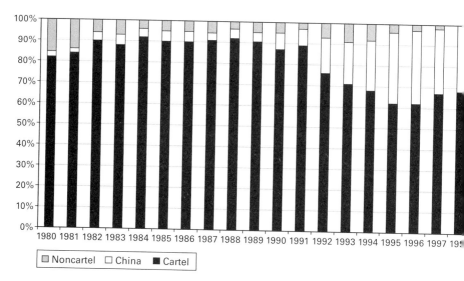

Figure 11.2
Overall market shares for vitamin C. Source: Bernheim (2002, fig. 8-7).

into the vitamin C market in the early 1980s, suggesting that customer loyalty is not a major factor for this product. It would be difficult to surmise a cartel in vitamin C with a quick visual inspection of this figure.

Figure 11.2 stands in sharp contrast to figure 11.3—the latter depicts the within-cartel market shares for the vitamin C producers. Figure 11.3 shows remarkable market share stability over a prolonged period, especially 1990 to 1994, which is the period where the cartel firms admitted to their participation in a cartel. So, despite the substantial inroads by the Chinese producers into the vitamin C market and a consequent diminishing market share for cartel firms as a whole, the cartel firms were able to maintain the allocation and enforcement structures required to adhere to a within-cartel market share agreement.[31]

In this case, stability of market shares for a subset of firms in the face of substantial entry is a plus factor. But market share stability alone is typically not a super-plus factor because it can arise through unilateral conduct. The same is true for geographic and customer stability. However, market share, geographic, and/or customer stability in conjunction with excess capacity in the industry and prices and profits that

31. See the EC decision in *Vitamins* at para. 394.

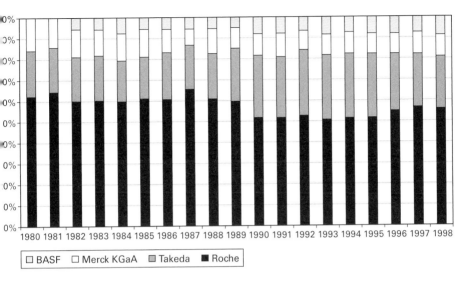

Figure 11.3
Cartel market shares for vitamin C. Source: Calculated based on Bernheim (2002, fig. 8-7).

are relatively high and increasing constitute a constellation of factors that are jointly a super-plus factor.

11.3.2 Redistributions

Cartels may need to engage in redistributions to keep the allocation of the collusive gain among co-conspirators consistent with their agreement.[32] For example, a market share agreement may require that some cartel firms buy product from other cartel firms at cartel prices so that the market share agreement is not violated.[33] Interfirm transfers within a broad class of settings are inconsistent with unilateral conduct and, additionally, not part of tacit collusion by definition. Such transfers are a super-plus factor.

Consider an oligopoly where firms are making a commodity product, and consider the interproducer purchase and/or sale of output by the firms. Such purchases and sales have a quantity and price associated with them. If two firms in an oligopoly that make identical products have excess capacity to make such products, engage in transactions for that product at nonmarket prices, then those transactions are inconsistent with unilateral conduct. Such transactions and transfers cannot be

---

32. See chapter 2.6.
33. See chapter 2, footnote 48.

part of tacit collusion by definition.[34] These types of transaction are a super-plus factor.

Not all interfirm transactions are interfirm transfers. Consider transactions at market prices. Suppose that two firms in an oligopoly make identical products and each has excess capacity to make such products. Suppose that these two firms engage in transactions for the product at market prices. The firms may offer an efficiency justification for such transactions. For example, perhaps firm A has a customer near firm B's location, and conversely, so to avoid costly shipping the firms provide their product to the other's customer. This conduct facilitates explicit collusion, and if the value/weight ratio of the product is high, such a justification lacks credibility, especially when viewed in conjunction with some consequence of the transaction that has no grounding in unilateral self-interested conduct. That is, if the transaction leads to the same market shares this year for some group of firms as had existed in previous years, then such transactions are a super-plus factor.

Again, the details of such interfirm transfers are often observable by the parent corporation, unlike buyers who may not be able to observe them without litigation-based discovery and/or actions to acquire such evidence by public enforcement authorities from dawn raids (European Commission) or civil investigative directives (U.S. Department of Justice).

11.4   Plus Factors Related to Enforcement Structures

11.4.1   Communication and Monitoring

It is natural for firms in an industry to attempt to learn about the status, intent, and actions of their rivals. Such information can enhance profits. For example, knowing that a rival is functioning near full capacity can enhance the expected profitability for a seller from upcoming buyers' procurements. The flip side of this argument is that a firm should want to guard against its own firm-specific information getting into the hands of rivals. However, a critical component of the operation of a cartel is monitoring the status and conduct of member firms. Thus, firms in a cartel will exchange information with one another in order

---

34. Tacit collusion requires the absence of communication and transfers. If one firm buys a large volume of the product from a "competitor" at the price of $1 per pound when the market price at that time is $10 per pound, then the seller has transferred $9 times the number of pounds sold to the buyer.

to monitor compliance with the cartel agreement. Specifically, a firm will provide firm-specific information to other cartel members that it would almost never provide when acting noncollusively.

For example, firms in a cartel using a market share agreement may ensure compliance by reporting to one another their production and sales data, with some means by which fellow cartel members can be assured of the accuracy of these reports.[35]

If a firm possesses information about a rival that it could have learned from good market surveillance, then we do not have a super-plus factor. However, if a firm knows something about rivals that is important for monitoring compliance with the collusive agreement, and that information would not be unearthed through reasonable market surveillance, or have been of no interest to a rival if the firms were acting noncollusively, then the knowledge and conveyance of such information constitutes a super-plus factor.

Standard market surveillance might reveal which firms have won recent contracts. After the award decision, buyers may even provide information to losing bidders about winning bids. However, many buyers will not provide such information, and therefore it will not be possible to aggregate and construct accurate firm-specific sale and production numbers from just this kind of market surveillance. If a firm knows the sales and production numbers of individual "competitors," then this constitutes a super-plus factor. Although any firm would want to know this information, no firm would want to convey this information to "competitors" unilaterally.

Standard market surveillance will not unearth interfirm transactions between other "competitors." Firm A would not know the details of a transaction between firms B and C unless B and/or C conveyed this information to A. Firm B and/or C would convey such information to A if the transaction was part of the maintenance of a collusive agreement for the cartel consisting of firms A, B, and C. If firms B and C were simply engaged in a noncollusive interfirm transaction, there would be no reason for either to convey the existence or details of the transaction to A.

Information exchange as a super-plus factor is not about the assessment of individual firm guilt but, instead, about the inference of collusion among a set of firms. If firm A knows something about firm B that firm B would not unilaterally reveal, and unilateral information gather-

35. See, for example, chapter 2, footnote 24.

ing efforts by A would almost surely not produce the information, then this is a super-plus factor. Firm A will argue that if information drops in its lap, it is entitled to retain it and use it, and that it cannot be responsible for firm B's confidentiality standards, but this argument is irrelevant. If firm A knows something about firm B that firm B would almost surely never convey to A in a world where the firms were acting noncollusively, then we have a super-plus factor with respect to the inference of collusion between firms A and B.

Unlike buyers that need litigation discovery, dawn raids, or civil investigative directives to uncover such activities, the parent corporation will typically have access to this type of information through information demands of the division managers.

11.4.2 Enforcement and Punishment

Cartels must stand ready to address secret deviations. If secret deviations are unearthed and any attempts to remedy problems, perhaps through redistributions, fail, then the cartel must respond. As noted in chapter 2 (footnote 57), historically some cartels have had members post bonds as a guarantee against deviations. Evidence of such bond posting is a super-plus factor. Although the posting of bonds can be explicit, as in the cases of the steel, aluminum, and incandescent electric lamp cartels,[36] it can also be more subtle.

For example, aspects of licensing agreements for patents can provide opportunities for cartel firms to exact punishments on one another.[37] Co-ownership of certain assets can also provide such a mechanism. For the case of colluding used machinery dealers as described in Marshall and Meurer (2004, p. 109, n. 99), "A given dealer typically had several machines in inventory that were co-owned with many different dealers. The warehousing dealer had substantial latitude in determining the final transaction price for the machine. The true final transaction prices were not verifiable. This provided dealers with an additional mechanism for punishing deviant ring bidders."

11.5 Plus Factors Related to Dominant-Firm Conduct

Once a cartel has successfully suppressed within-cartel rivalry, it has an incentive to dampen other forces that might depress the profits of firms within the cartel. When there is no dominant firm in an industry

---

36. See chapter 2, footnote 57.
37. See Priest (1977).

and we observe dominant-firm conduct, it may be possible to infer that firms in the industry are explicitly colluding.

We begin by defining a dominant firm. "A dominant firm is a seller that is able to exercise substantial market power (or, equivalently, monopoly power) unilaterally, without the need for collusive arrangements." (Schmalensee 1985, p. 3)

It follows from this definition that if collusive arrangements are needed for the exercise of substantial market power, then none of the firms in the collusive arrangement is dominant. U.S. enforcement agencies (DoJ and FTC) have offered the assessment that no single firm can act as a dominant firm in an industry with less than a 50 percent market share.[38] It follows that if we observe dominant-firm conduct undertaken by a number of firms in an industry that in aggregate have more than 50 percent of the market, but where no firm has a market share exceeding 50 percent, then it is highly likely that a subset of the firms are acting as a cartel.[39]

This super-plus factor has the advantage that dominant-firm conduct is readily observable by third parties without litigation discovery, dawn raids, or civil investigative directives. No distinction between pro-competitive and anti-competitive dominant-firm conduct is needed to draw the inference of the existence of a cartel when no firm has a market share in excess of 50 percent.

However, caution should be taken if a conduct is observed to be undertaken by only one firm because some dominant firm conducts, such as tying, may occur unilaterally.

11.6 Differentiating Plus Factors*

To the extent that the conduct described above is observed, it may be viewed as a plus factor supporting the inference of collusive behavior. Kovacic et al. (2011) offer a way to assess the strength of plus factors. We review the basics of that approach in this section.

38. "The Department is not aware of any court that has found a defendant to possess monopoly power when its market share was less than 50 percent. As a practical matter, a share greater than 50 percent has been necessary for courts to find the existence of monopoly power." (Barnett and Wellford 2008, pp. 5–6).
39. Posner (2001) identifies certain dominant-firm conduct by firms in an oligopolistic industry as a plus factor. Heeb et al. (2009) note that cartels often engage in dominant-firm conduct. Marshall, Marx, and Samkharadze (2011) note that once cartels have successfully suppressed interfirm rivalry, they move on to seek incremental profits through dominant-firm conduct.

An observed economic conduct is a plus factor, and can be used as an indicator of collusion, if the probability of there being a cartel conditional on observing the plus factor is greater than the unconditional probability of a cartel.

To more clearly state ideas, it is convenient to introduce some mathematical notation. The probability of a cartel conditional on observing a plus factor can be written as $\Pr[C \mid F]$, where the vertical bar is standard notation read as "given," so the expression is read "probability of C given F," with C denoting the event that there is collusion and F denoting the presence of a plus factor.

We can write the probability of a cartel given a plus factor, $\Pr[C \mid F]$, as depending on other probabilities. In particular, we can write this probability as depending on the probability of observing a plus factor conditional on whether there is or is not a cartel, $\Pr[F \mid C]$ and $\Pr[F \mid \text{not} C]$, and on the unconditional probability of a cartel:[40]

$$\Pr[C \mid F] = \frac{\Pr[F \mid C] \cdot \Pr[C]}{\Pr[F \mid C] \cdot \Pr[C] + \Pr[F \mid \text{not } C] \cdot \Pr[\text{not } C]}. \tag{11.1}$$

This formula is useful because it tells us that when the probability of a specific plus factor given no cartel, $\Pr[F \mid \text{not } C]$, is close to zero, then the probability of a cartel given that plus factor is near one.[41] To see this in equation (11.1), note that when $\Pr[F \mid \text{not } C]$ is very close to zero, then the numerator and denominator on the right side of the equation are essentially the same, and so the ratio is very close to 1. The implication is that if we can identify a plus factor that is unlikely to appear when there is no cartel, then the observation of that plus factor indicates that there is a cartel with high probability. We refer to plus factors with this characteristic as super-plus factors. Using the notation, if $\Pr[F \mid \text{not } C]$ is near zero, then $\Pr[C \mid F]$ is near one, and so F is a super-plus factor.

For some plus factors, the probability of collusion conditional on observing the plus factor may not be much greater than the uncondi-

---

40. The formula is often referred to as Bayes' Theorem.
41. As an illustration, suppose that cancer type X produces a marker that shows up in blood tests. The presence of cancer is analogous to the presence of collusion, and the marker is analogous to a plus factor. If the blood marker is almost never observed when a person does not have cancer, that is, the probability of the marker conditional on no cancer is close to zero, then the probability of a person having cancer, conditional on observing the blood marker, is close to one.

tional probability of collusion. In this case, the observation of the plus factor does not increase the assessed probability of there being collusion by much. For example, the observation of relatively fixed production market shares in the linerboard industry would not by itself be much of a plus factor given the nature of linerboard production (see chapter 6.2.6). However, plus factors that do not individually do much to increase the assessed probability of collusion may, when considered as part of a group of plus factors, lead to the conclusion that the probability of collusion is high.

The strength of a plus factor can be quantified by the ratio of the probabilities of observing the plus factor conditional on collusion and no collusion:[42]

$$S = \frac{\Pr[F \,|\, C]}{\Pr[F \,|\, \text{not } C]}.$$

Conceptually, the strength of a plus factor, S, provides a way to rank plus factors, and it can be extended to apply to groupings of plus factors as well.[43]

11.7 Super-Plus Factors for Cartels

As described in chapter 11.6, plus factors can be differentiated in terms of their strength. Plus factors or combinations of plus factors that deliver a strong inference of collusion are super-plus factors. Below we summarize the super-plus factors identified in chapters 11.2 through 11.5. Thus, we provide a partial listing of super-plus factors for cartels:

1. *Transaction prices above predicted levels*: A reliable predictive econometric model that accounts for all material noncollusive effects on

---

42. See Kovacic et al. (2011). To see why S measures the strength of a plus factor, note that if we let O denote the baseline odds against a cartel,

$$O = \frac{\Pr[\text{not } C]}{\Pr[C]},$$

then one can show that

$$\Pr[C \,|\, F] = \frac{1}{1 + O/S}.$$

Thus, an increase in S results in an increase in $\Pr[C \,|\, F]$.

43. See Kovacic et al. (2011) for further development of plus factor strength.

price, estimated using benchmark data where conduct was presumed noncollusive, produces predictions of prices that are not consistent with the path of actual prices in the period or region of potential collusion, at a specified confidence level.[44]

2. *Communication and information sharing:* A firm or subset of firms has extensive knowledge of the details of another firm's transactions, production, sales, and/or inventories where the latter firm would be competitively disadvantaged by conveying that information unilaterally.

3. *Interfirm transfers:* Firms engage in interfirm transactions that are transfers of resources and are largely void of productive noncollusive motivations.

4. *Within-firm incentives:* In an industry where the product made by different firms is largely homogeneous, there is a discrete change in the within-firm incentives of the sales force, across a subset of firms during a given period, that shifts from the pursuit of market share to maintenance of elevated prices (e.g., a shift to "price before volume").

5. *Dominant-firm conduct by nondominant firms:* A subset of firms, with an aggregate market share large enough to have dominant-firm market power, jointly engage in a dominant-firm conduct when no single firm has the market power to act unilaterally as a dominant firm by engaging in that dominant-firm conduct.

6. *Economic evidence in combination:* When prices and profits are relatively high and increasing:

a. a subset of firms restricts production, or

b. among a subset of producers, market shares, customer incumbency, or geographic dominance is stable when the firms have excess capacity.

11.8 Response to Detection Based on Super-Plus Factors

If collusive firms view super-plus factors as something that will be used by courts to draw a strong inference of explicit collusion, then

---

44. The higher is the degree of confidence, the stronger is the plus factor. Suppose that the confidence level is 95%. Then the probability of observing the actual price path exiting the confidence bounds (outcome F) in the absence of collusion is 5% ($\Pr(F \mid \text{not } C) = 0.05$). For example, with this confidence level, and with $\Pr(F \mid C) = 0.99$ and baseline odds against collusion of 2 (i.e., $\Pr(C) = 0.33$), we obtain $\Pr(C \mid F) = 0.908$, surpassing a potential criminal liability threshold of 90%.

colluding firms will try to avoid creating super-plus factors.[45] However, avoiding super-plus factors can greatly encumber the profitability and stability of a cartel and may even deter the conspiratorial conduct.

For example, if interfirm transfers are considered super-plus factors by antitrust enforcement authorities, then colluding firms have an incentive to avoid making interfirm transfers or to take additional steps to disguise them. However, avoiding transfers can increase the monitoring burden for a cartel. For example, a market share cartel would need to ensure there were no year-end deviations from the designated cartel market shares.

As another example, if market share stability, in conjunction with other factors, is viewed as a super-plus factor, then colluding firms will have an incentive to artificially manufacture market share volatility. However, this could be destabilizing to a cartel, especially one naturally rooted in a market share agreement.

11.9   Appendix: Additional Price Announcement Graphs

1.9.1   Calpan (B5) SD Feed Grade Price Announcements

Figure 11.4 shows the prices and price announcements for Calpan (B5) SD feed grade. The plea period for this vitamin was January 1991 to February 1999, with Bernheim (2002) dating the start of the conspiracy at January 1985.[46] The cartel firms were Roche, BASF, and Daiichi.[47]

11.9.2   Calpan (B5) USP Price Announcements

Figure 11.5 shows the prices and price announcements for Calpan (B5) USP. The plea period for this vitamin was January 1991 to February 1999, with Bernheim (2002) dating the start of the conspiracy at January 1985.[48] The cartel firms were Roche, BASF, and Daiichi.[49]

---

45. See Kovacic et al. (2011). See Harrington (2003, 2004a) on potential effects of antitrust laws on cartel behavior. See also Cyrenne (1999).
46. See Bernheim (2002, p. iii).
47. See Bernheim (2002, p. 219).
48. See Bernheim (2002, p. iii).
49. See Bernheim (2002, p. 220).

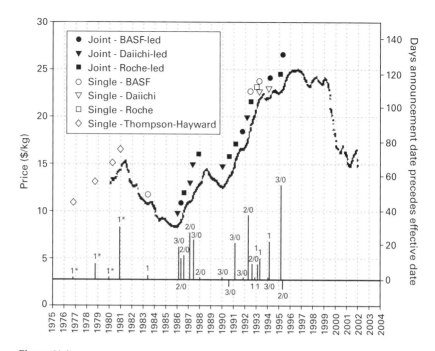

Figure 11.4
Prices and price announcements for Calpan (B5) SD feed grade

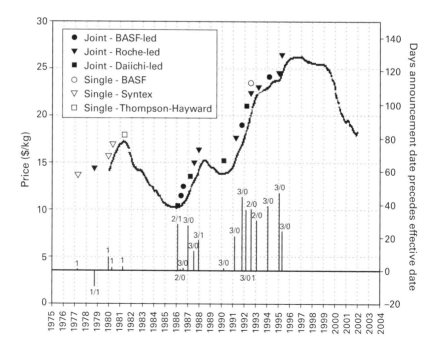

Figure 11.5
Prices and price announcements for Calpan (B5) USP

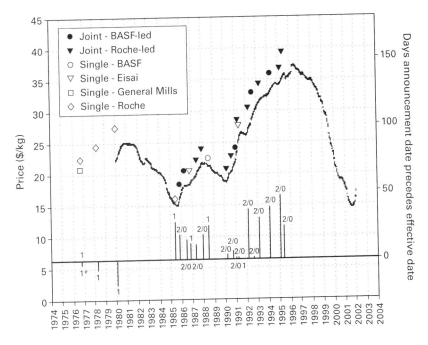

Figure 11.6
Prices and price announcements for E acetate oil USP

11.9.3   E Acetate Oil USP

Figure 11.6 shows the prices and price announcements for E acetate oil USP. The plea period for this vitamin was January 1990 to February 1999, with Bernheim (2002) dating the start of the conspiracy at January 1985.[50] The cartel firms were Roche, BASF, and Eisai.[51]

50. See Bernheim (2002, p. iii).
51. See Bernheim (2002, p. 204).

12 Plus Factors for Rings

As described in chapter 11, the term "plus" in "plus factors" refers to factors, above and beyond a parallel movement in prices, that lead to the inference of collusion. However, if an item being sold at an auction or purchased through a procurement is sufficiently unique in its characteristics, then the notion of a parallel movement in prices, akin to what we might observe among oligopolists who make similar products, is not meaningful. Thus, in some auction contexts, factors that would indicate explicit collusion are not truly "plus" factors. Nevertheless, we continue to use the terminology "plus factors," but for the case of rings we use the longer term "plus factors for rings."

12.1 Two Cautions

Two cautions must be raised regarding plus factors for rings at both auctions and procurements. First, if the auctioneer or procurer is acting as an agent (in a principal-agent relationship), and if that agency relationship can be compromised to the financial benefit of the auctioneer/procurer, then auction/procurement outcomes that may look like collusion could instead be the compromise of the agency relationship. For example, if the auctioneer/procurer is bribed to treat one bidder in a favorable way, then we may see depressed auction prices or elevated procurement prices when in fact there is no collusion among the bidders.[1] The favoritism may take many forms such as, but not limited to (1) excluding other qualified bidders from the auction/procurement, (2) scoring the bids so as to favor the bribing bidder, and (3) providing

---

1. Bribery is not needed. The auctioneer/procurer may just choose to exert low levels of effort and slant all aspects of the allocation mechanism toward one bidder with whom they are more familiar.

the bribing bidder with information before and/or during the auction/procurement so as to increase the expected payoff to that bidder. If other bidders are aware of the favoritism, or suspect it, then their interest in participating in the auction/procurement will be diminished, the bidding will be depressed, and awards will go disproportionately to the favored bidder. The outcomes and conduct will look much like collusion among a subset of bidders with the favored bidder as the ring leader. However, in this example there is no collusion among the bidders, although the activity is clearly anti-competitive.[2]

As a natural extension, suppose that it is not just one bidder who is bribing the auctioneer/procurer but, instead, a ring. One could argue this is more likely because a ring can spread the costs of bribing an auctioneer/procurer among all members, whereas an individual bidder must bear all those costs alone.

In what follows, we assume that the auctioneer/procurer is acting as a good agent of the principal, but it should be kept in mind that plus factors for rings may be picking up breakdowns in the agency relationship when in fact there is no collusion among bidders. Some plus factors will allow us to separate the two.

Second, usually the term "bidder collusion" implies that two or more serious bidders are suppressing their interbidder rivalry. However, auction/procurement rules often specify that a minimum number of bidders must be present in order for the auction/procurement to occur. In such cases, when there is only one real bidder, that bidder may manufacture shill bidders to fulfill the auction/procurement rules.[3] Technically, there is collusion between the real bidder and the shill bidders, and a competitive process has been subverted. We will not address this issue further other than to note an example. In Russian oil and gas lease auctions of the past few years, at least two registered bidders were required for the auction to proceed. The data from these

---

2. Although one can characterize the auctioneer/procurer's relationship with the favored bidder as collusion, it can also be characterized as a breakdown of the principal-agent relationship.

3. When there are several real bidders, but only one of them has been informed of an auction, where the auction has a requirement that some number of bids be received before the auction is declared valid and an award is made, it can be the case that this one bidder, on its own and with no ex ante consultation with its conspirators, submits accommodating bids that are seemingly genuine.

For cases where collusive bidding, including the submission of identical, sham, fictitious, complementary, fraudulent, dummy, and unreasonable bids, was prohibited in consent decrees, see the cases listed in Commerce Clearing House, Inc. (1988) *Trade Regulation Reports,* Bidding Practices, ¶4680.381, pp. 8931–32.

auctions suggest that in cases where there was only one actual bidder, that bidder would arrange for an agent to register in order to satisfy the requirement that there be at least two registered bidders. We discuss our findings from the Russian oil and gas lease auctions in the appendix to this chapter.

12.2 Common Issues

In the remainder of this chapter, to simplify language, we discuss plus factors for rings in terms of auctions rather than procurements. The discussion for simple procurements is analogous.[4]

As in part III, we focus on two well-known auction formats, the ascending-bid auction and the sealed-bid auction. The plus factors for rings that are relevant for the two auction formats have some overlap, but there are plus factors for rings that are distinct for each as well. Also, there are plus factors for rings for each kind of auction that could not be avoided by the ring without causing a substantive change to the fundamentals of the ring mechanism, while there are other plus factors for rings that could be avoided without requiring a substantive change to the ring mechanism.

For example, if there are n bidders and k of those are in a ring (where $k \leq n$), then the ring has $k - 1$ free bids to use to its benefit. Suggestions that one can detect bid rigging by looking for patterns in the bidding, such as identical bids submitted by ring members,[5] presumes that the ring is careless with its $k - 1$ free bids, or is somehow blocked from undertaking interfirm transfers and must rely on bid-taker randomization to divide the collusive gain.[6] A well-functioning bidding ring

---

4. If bids among qualified bidders are evaluated solely in terms of price, then we call the procurement "simple."
5. See the U.S. Department of Justice primers listed in chapter 8, footnote 1. In addition, Executive Order 10936, which was signed by President John F. Kennedy on April 24, 1961, places great emphasis on the inference of anti-competitive conduct from the submission of identical bids: "REPORTS OF IDENTICAL BIDS. WHEREAS it is in the interest of the United States to obtain truly competitive bids in connection with its procurement, and sale of property and services pursuant to public invitations for bids and, the prevalence of identical bidding is harmful to the effective functioning of a system of competitive bids; WHEREAS identical bidding may constitute evidence of the existence of conspiracies to monopolize or restrain trade or commerce; and . . . ." (Website of the American Presidency Project, http://www.presidency.ucsb.edu/ws/index.php?pid =58874#axzz1JndmkCgU, accessed April 24, 2011)
6. See McAfee and McMillan (1992). See also Comanor and Schankerman (1976), who argue that emphasis on identical bids is misplaced.

would use its free bids in ways that support the goals of the ring and do not trivially reveal the presence of the ring. However, there are certain bid patterns and auction outcomes that can arise from the presence of a ring that would be difficult for a ring to avoid without disrupting the functioning of the ring.

We focus on "super-plus factors for rings," where the probability of observing the factor given the absence of a ring is close to zero. There are two super-plus factors for rings that are common for ascending-bid and sealed-bid auctions. First, the presence of interbidder transfers is a super-plus factor for a ring. These transfers are associated with the side payments emerging from knockouts that are used to allocate the collusive gain among members of the ring. These transfers can take a number of different forms. There can be direct cash transfers associated with settling the ring accounts from a recent auction knockout. Or there can be subcontracting relationships and/or joint ownership arrangements that were not declared prior to the auction. The absence of predeclaration is key because if two or more firms are going to bid as a single entity, and they have a legitimate reason for doing so, they can notify the auctioneer as part of the registration process and seek preapproval for doing so.

Second, a super-plus factor for a ring is a divergence between observed prices and those generated by a predictive model. Analogous to the cartel case, if a predictive model that is estimated for a benchmark where a ring is presumed not to be operating provides a prediction of auction prices during an alleged conspiracy period that is substantially higher than the prices that were realized at the auction, and the difference is statistically significant, then there is a strong inference of a ring. Both of these super-plus factors for rings—interbidder transfers and predicted prices diverging from observed prices—are substantive in the sense that if the ring wanted to abandon transfers or elevate prices so as to avoid detection, the ring mechanism would need to be changed and ring surplus would be reduced.

12.3 Plus Factors for Rings for an Ascending-Bid Auction

The bidding rule for a ring at an ascending-bid auction can be quite simple—ring members simply do not bid if another ring member is actively bidding. This rule implies that the winning bidder and the last underbidder, as well as any two bidders who are directly competing with one another at the auction as the price ascends, would never both be ring members. This bidding rule also implies that if a ring member wins the item, the ultimate owner of the item may end up being any member of the ring. Each of these implies a super-plus factor for a ring.

Because most ascending-bid auctions allow for reentry by bidders (bidders can stop actively bidding for a while and then start bidding again), it is commonly thought that only two bids are meaningful in terms of economic content—those of the winner and the last underbidder. However, this is not true when collusion is a possibility.

Suppose that the entire bidding history of each auction is recorded—the amount of each bid and the identity of the bidder. If similar items are sold at the auction and there exists a subset of bidders who never bid against one another at any meaningful level of the bidding,[7] then it may be reasonable to infer that these bidders are in a ring. However, the ring can take actions that mitigate that inference. Specifically, if the ring occasionally has members bid against one another for one or two increments, then the inference is more difficult.[8] But it is much simpler logistically for a ring to instruct members never to bid when another ring member is active than to instruct members to do so only sparingly to impair inference about the existence of the ring. The added difficulty this latter action creates for implementation of the ring's bidding at the main auction makes the absence of competitive bidding within a subset of bidders a substantive super-plus factor, albeit one that may require a large number of auctions to infer collusion.

If it is observed that the auction winner does not own the item shortly after the conclusion of the auction, but another bidder who was present at the auction owns the item, then this observation is also a super-plus factor for rings. An almost immediate change of ownership is likely the result of a post-auction knockout. Because the ascending-bid auction produces an efficient allocation of items, one would not expect there to be a noncollusive reason for an immediate post-auction resale to a bidder who was present at the auction.[9] This is a substantive

---

7. Ring members may bid against one another when the price is quite low, perhaps below any reserve price that the auctioneer might have. This competition is not meaningful. The interbidder competition becomes meaningful when it reaches a price where the auctioneer may reasonably award the item to the highest bidder if the bidding were to stop. (See Graham and Marshall 1987.)

8. For the cost of one bid increment, the ring can have the last two bidders be ring members when the ring wins an item.

9. See Garratt, Tröger, and Zheng (2009) on the susceptibility of the English auction to collusion when resale is allowed.

super-plus factor for a ring because a ring would be forced to change its mechanism if post-auction reallocations were not possible.

Another way that competition might be suppressed by colluding bidders is to have ring bidders, other than the one with the highest value, not register for the bidding or just not show up at the auction. In practice, rings may require that their members attend the main auction in order to be eligible for divisions of the collusive gain.[10] Thus, light attendance at an ascending bid auction is not a super-plus factor.

12.4 Plus Factors for Rings for a Sealed-Bid Auction

A ring at a sealed-bid auction confronts some different issues than a ring at an ascending-bid auction. At a sealed-bid auction, ring members reveal their values prior to the auction so that the ring can determine the best bid to submit at the main auction in light of the highest value among its members. Because the ring can send the bidder with the highest value to the main auction to submit the ring's high bid, it is unlikely that we would observe the immediate resale of the item after the auction among ring members. However, unlike the ascending-bid auction, an inefficient outcome is possible at the sealed-bid auction if bidders are asymmetric, which can result in resale after the auction. Thus, the occurrence of resale at a sealed-bid auction is not a super-plus factor for rings, as it is at an ascending-bid auction. In fact, collusion would potentially cause us to expect a diminished volume of post-auction resale at a sealed-bid auction relative to noncollusive conduct because the ring can coordinate bidding in such a way that the highest-valuing ring member submits the highest bid among all ring members. Overall, a pair of bidders involved in post-auction resale at a sealed-bid auction may not be members of a ring, which again is in contrast to the ascending-bid auction, where bidders involved in post-auction resale are likely to be ring members.

If the ring does not restrict its members from bidding at the auction, but simply instructs them to bid less than the ring's high bid, then an inference of a ring is possible from observing that a number of nonwinning bids do not have anything to do with potential underlying values. This methodology has been advocated in the past,[11] but it is not sub-

10. An exception is the New York City stamp ring described in chapter 9.6.2.
11. See Porter and Zona (1993).

stantive in the sense that the ring is free to alter losing bids by its members in any way it desires, as long as they remain losing. Specifically, the ring could ask all ring bidders other then the one with highest value to submit a rescaled version of the bid that they would have submitted acting noncollusively, where the rescaling ensures all bids are below the bid of the ring's highest-valuing member.

In some sealed-bid environments, the ring bidder with highest value may have an incentive to submit a bid that is too low in the sense that other ring members would have a strong incentive to attempt a secret deviation and win the item through a shill bidder. To deter secret deviations of this nature, the ring may want its highest-valuing member to submit a higher bid, but one that is still less than its noncollusive bid. For example, the highest-valuing ring member may have a value of $100,000, and would have bid $90,000 acting noncollusively, but given the size of the ring and the bidders outside the ring, the highest-valuing ring member wants to submit a bid of $50,000 at the main auction. The bid of $50,000 may create a substantial incentive for other ring members to engage in secret deviations through the use of a shill bidder. For example, if another ring member has a value of $60,000, and expects to receive a split of the collusive gain that is less than $10,000, that member will have an incentive to bid $50,001, or thereabouts, through a shill bidder. Thus, the ring may instruct its highest-valuing member to bid more than $50,000, say $65,000. But the highest-valuing ring bidder must be given an incentive to bid $65,000 rather than $50,000. In order to have the highest-valuing ring bidder follow instructions and submit a bid of $65,000, the ring may instruct another ring bidder to submit a bid just below $65,000.[12] This second bid will always lose to the highest-valuing ring member's bid, but it serves the purpose of ensuring the highest-valuing ring member bids high enough to deter cheating by lower-valuing ring members. Thus, a ring may need to submit two bids that are close to one another. The frequent closeness of two bids allows the inference of collusion. This plus factor for rings is substantive because if the ring abandons submitting close bids, it creates an incentive for secret deviations by members.[13]

12. See proposition 3 in Marshall and Marx (2007).
13. After ranking all bids, if it is frequently the case that a sequential pair are close, especially if they are not the highest pair, then there is an inference of collusion. The identity of the bids in the pair can be used to infer ring membership.

12.5   Changing from Ascending Bid to Sealed Bid

A sudden change in the auction format from ascending bid to sealed bid can provide substantial information regarding collusion by bidders because the former is less robust against collusion than the latter. If the auction prices greatly increase after the change, it would be reasonable to infer that a ring was present at the ascending-bid auction. Of course, if the ring is able to remain coherent and stable after the change, then there will be little effect on price. The absence of a change is not evidence of the absence of collusion, but a substantial increase in the price would lead to the inference of collusion at the ascending-bid auctions.

Other factors can be at play that increase the price from the change that have nothing to do with collusion. For example, risk aversion by bidders is likely to increase prices paid at sealed-bid auctions relative to ascending-bid auctions. However, those kinds of increases in price will be small relative to the size of the price changes that will be observed if a large effective cartel reverts to noncollusive bidding as a result of the change to a sealed-bid auction.

12.6   Conclusion

Many of the plus factors for cartels are not relevant for rings given the narrower focus of a ring and the occasional nature of a ring's conspiracy. Plus factors for rings largely concern the implementation of the suppression of bidding rivalry among ring members, the outcomes of that suppression in terms of reduced prices paid to auctioneers, and the allocation of the collusive gain. The contrast between ascending-bid and first-price auctions in terms of plus factors for rings further highlights the robustness of first-price auctions to collusion relative to ascending-bid auctions.

12.7   Appendix: Shill Bidding at Russian Oil and Gas Auction

For the past few years, the Russian government has held ascending-bid auctions for oil and gas leases.[14] The auction rules require that there be at least two bidders at the auction for it to proceed. The Russian gov-

---

14. Data on these auctions are available on the website for the Center for the Study of Auctions, Procurements and Competition Policy at Penn State: http://econ.la.psu.edu/CAPCP/. This appendix draws from the online appendix associated with Marshall and Marx (2009).

ernment sets a reserve price for each lease and determines the bid increments. The lowest feasible bid is one bid increment above the reserve price.

Three empirical regularities are worth noting about the Russian oil and gas lease auctions. First, of the auctions with more than two bidders, there often appears to be vigorous competition. Second, in the large plurality of auctions that have only two bidders, many end after submission of only one bid, which is the smallest increment needed to award the lease. Third, many, but not all, of the bidders that participate in the two-bidder auctions never win any oil or gas leases in our data. Thus, for many of these two-bidder auctions it appears that the second bidder is a shill bidder that is acting as the agent of the winning bidder. Their presence appears to be motivated solely by the auction rule requiring that at least two bidders be present. The process is such that it may not be clear whether one of the bidders is a shill of the other.

With regard to the design of these auctions, the bidder registration process,[15] which occurs in advance of the main auction, reveals some but not all information about the bidders. The results below illuminate the importance of the information revealed through the bidder registration process for inhibiting or facilitating collusion.

We have data for 620 auctions from 2004 to 2007. For 121 auctions the data are complete, but for 499 auctions there is only partial information available currently. On average, the 121 auctions for which the data are complete are slightly larger than the others in the sense that their average reserve price is 71,503,769 rubles and the average reserve price for the remaining 499 is 49,484,900 rubles. Of the 121 auctions where the data are complete, five were canceled. In addition, in one of the auctions, criteria other than just the bid were used in making the award. Most of our focus is on the remaining 115 auctions for which the data are complete. In what follows, we refer to these auctions as the "subsample of 115 auctions."

Table 12.1 focuses on the subsample of 115 auctions and shows the distribution of auctions by number of participants and winning bids (in terms of the number of bid increments above the reserve price). As the table shows, 20 percent of the auctions involved two bidders where only one bidder bid and won the object at the lowest feasible price of one bid increment above the reserve price. Also shown in the table, for auctions with six or more participants the winning bid is always 20 or

---

15. What we refer to as registration corresponds to the application and approval process of the Russian oil and gas lease auctions.

Table 12.1
Winning bids and number of participants for the subsample of 115 auctions

Participants	Winning bids—fraction within Z bid increments of reserve					
	$Z = 1$	$Z = 2$	$Z = \{3, \ldots, 19\}$	$Z = \{20, \ldots, 99\}$	$Z \geq 100$	Total
2	0.20	0.10	0.03	0.03	0.02	0.37
3	0.01	0.03	0.08	0.12	0.06	0.30
4	0.01	0.00	0.02	0.02	0.07	0.11
5	0.01	0.01	0.02	0.01	0.04	0.09
6	0.00	0.00	0.00	0.01	0.03	0.03
7	0.00	0.00	0.00	0.01	0.01	0.02
8	0.00	0.00	0.00	0.01	0.00	0.01
9	0.00	0.00	0.00	0.01	0.03	0.03
10	0.00	0.00	0.00	0.01	0.01	0.02
11	0.00	0.00	0.00	0.00	0.02	0.02
Total	0.23	0.13	0.15	0.22	0.28	1.00

more increments above the reserve price, but for auctions with five or fewer participants there is at least one auction for which the winning bid was only one increment above the reserve price, which is the lowest feasible bid.

Table 12.2 shows the data in slightly different form by conditioning the distributions on the number the participants in the auctions. The table clearly shows differences in the distribution of winning bids between auctions with two bidders, auctions with three to five bidders, and auctions with six or more bidders.

Examining further the data for the subsample of 115 auctions, there are 43 two-bidder auctions. In 34 of these 43 two-bidder auctions (79 percent), the winning bid is only one or two bid increments above the reserve price. One possible explanation for the apparently low interest in these auctions is that they may be small licenses of interest only to regional bidders. The average reserve price for this sample of 34 two-bidder auctions with winning bids that are one or two bid increments above the reserve price is 27,515,294 rubles, which is less than half the average reserve price for the full set of 620 auctions.

If only a single bidder registers for an auction, then the auction is not held. So, if a license is only of interest to a single bidder, then that bidder may have an incentive to arrange for a second bidder to register but not compete at the auction. Our data are suggestive of this type of behavior. To see this, focus on the 34 two-bidder auctions with winning

Table 12.2
Proportion of auctions with winning bids of varying numbers of bid increments above the reserve price conditional on number of participants for the subsample of 115 auctions

Number of participants	Number of bid increments that the winning bid is above the reserve price					Sum	Number of auctions
	1	2	3–19	20–99	100 or more		
2	53%	26%	9%	7%	5%	100%	43
3	3%	9%	26%	41%	21%	100%	34
4	8%	0%	15%	15%	62%	100%	13
5	10%	10%	20%	10%	50%	100%	10
6 or more	0%	0%	0%	33%	67%	100%	15
Combined	23%	13%	15%	22%	28%	100%	115

bids that are one or two bid increments above the reserve price. For these auctions we assign identifying letters to each of the participants (bidder names are often long and are in Russian). See the table 12.4 at the end of this appendix for the details of these assignments.

As shown in table 12.3, there are 24 distinct winning bidders and 26 distinct losing bidders. There are 26 distinct ordered pairs of winning and losing bidders. Also shown in the table, it is often the case that the losing bidder never wins any auctions in our sample of 620 auctions. For example, bidder Y won 6 two-bidder auctions with a winning bid of one or two bid increments above the reserve price, and in all six of these auctions, bidder Y's opponent was bidder $1Y$. Bidder $1Y$ never won any of the auctions for which we have data. Also shown in the table, bidders $1L$ and $1N$ show up as both winning and losing bidders—bidder $1L$ won an auction with $1N$ as the losing bidder, and bidder $1N$ won an auction with bidder $1L$ as the losing bidder (bidder $1L$ also won an auction with bidder $1M$ as the losing bidder).

These data suggest that some of the losing bidders might not have been competitive bidders. We use the data to classify the 26 distinct losing bidders in the 34 two-bidder auctions with a winning bid of one or two bid increments above the reserve price as "pure shills," "occasional shills," or "rotating bidders" as follows:

We classify 13 of the losing bidders, B, D, H, L, P, X, $1Y$, $1A$, $1C$, $1I$, $1K$, $1R$, and $1T$, as "pure shills" because:

1. the losing bidder either did not bid or bid only once (the object was sold at one or two bid increments above the reserve price),

Table 12.3
Bidder identities for the sample of 34 two-bidder auctions for which data are complete and the winning bid is one or two bid increments above the reserve price

Auctions with two bidders and a winning bid that is one or two bid increments above the reserve price

Winner	Loser	Number of auctions	Other auctions in our sample of 620 auctions won by the second-place bidder
1B	1C	1	
1D	1E	1	1
1F	1G	1	1
1H	1I	1	
1J	1K	1	
1L	1M	1	2
1L	1N	1	1
1N	1L	1	2
1O	1P	1	1
1Q	1R	1	
1S	1T	1	
1U	1V	1	3
A	B	1	
C	D	1	
E	F	1	2
G	H	2	
I	J	1	1
K	L	1	
M	N	2	1
M	Q	2	1
O	P	1	
R	S	1	1
T	U	1	
V	X	1	
Y	1Y	6	
Z	1A	1	
Total		34	17

2. the losing bidder never won a lease at any of the 620 auctions for which we have data, and

3. the losing bidder did not participate in any auction in the absence of the winning bidder.

We classify 2 of the losing bidders, 1L and 1N, as "rotating bidders" because as a pair, the two bidders participated in multiple two-bidder auctions, with each bidder winning at least one auction at a price only one or two bid increments above the reserve price.

Finally, we classify the remaining 11 losing bidders, F, J, N, Q, S, U, 1E, 1G, 1M, 1P, and 1V, as "occasional shills." These bidders either did not bid or bid only one time, allowing the other bidder to win the item at a price one or two bid increments above the reserve price. But these bidders either won auctions in our sample of 620 auctions (bidder 1G), or participated in auctions without their partner (bidder U), or both (bidders F, J, N, Q, S, 1E, 1M, 1P, 1V).

Particularly in the cases of pure shills, one might suspect that these losing bidders were merely shills for the winning bidder, attending the auction to fulfill the requirement that there be at least two bidders at the auction.

Because the Russian oil and gas lease auctions would be classified as semitransparent in the terminology of Marshall and Marx (2009), the results of that paper (especially proposition 5) suggest that there is no role for shills in a well-functioning cartel. However, if we consider the 13 "pure shills" identified in the Russian oil and gas data, we find that two of these pure shills, L and X, participated with their partners (the winning bidders) in auctions with more than two bidders.[16] The model of Marshall and Marx (2009) is not dynamic, so perhaps dynamic considerations create a role for shill bidding. For example, the partners might use these other auctions to try to establish the credibility of their shills as bidders. The model of Marshall and Marx (2009) also assumes a nonstrategic auctioneer (except for setting a fixed reserve price), but perhaps with a strategic auctioneer there is a role for shills to disguise

---

16. Bidder L and its partner, bidder K, participated in a three-bidder auction, which K won (5 bid increments) and a four-bidder auction, which neither K nor L won (320 increments). Bidder X and its partner, bidder V, participated in a four-bidder auction, which V won (12 increments). Bidder B participated in another two-bidder auction with its partner, bidder A. The number of bid increments in this auction is not known. None of the other pure shills participated in any auctions outside the 34 auctions on which we have focused.

Table 12.4
Assignment of identifying letters to bidders in Russian oil and gas lease auctions with two participants and a winning bid of one or two bid increments above the reserve price

Participant	Company
A	ООО "РосНедра Астрахань"
B	ООО "ВолжСторНЭСТ"
C	ЗАО "Нефтегазовая компания АФБ"
D	ЗАО "Концерн "Нефтепродукт"
E	ООО "Интенсификация и повышение нефтеотдачи пласта"
F	ООО "ЗААБ Инвест"
G	ЗАО "Фроловское нефтегазодобывающее управление"
H	ЗАО "Вольновскнефть"
I	ЗАО "Транс Нафта"
J	ООО "Газнефтесервис"
K	ООО "Авангард"
L	ООО "Истенойл"
M	ОАО "Новосибирскнефтегаз"
N	ООО "Тагульское"
O	ООО "Северное сияние"
P	ООО "Гранит"
Q	ОАО "Тюменнефтегаз"
R	ООО ПКФ "Селена"
S	ООО "ДДМ"
T	ОАО "Пермоблнефть"
U	ООО ПФК "Центртехснаб"
V	ООО "Парма-Ресурс"
X	ООО "Проминвест"
Y	ОАО "АНК Башнефть"
1Y	ООО "Башминерал"
Z	ООО "ДНК"
1A	ООО "Жиллеттойл ЛТД"
1B	ОАО "Ингушнефтегазпром"
1C	ООО "НПЦ Ингушроссгео"
1D	ООО "Холмогорнефтегаз"
1E	ОАО "Самотлорнефтегаз"
1F	ОАО "Сахалин-Девелопмент"
1G	ООО "Томгазнефть"
1H	ОАО "Уралнефть"
1I	ООО "Уралтрансгаз"
1J	ОАО "Батайскнефтегаз"
1K	ОАО "Аксайнефтегаз"
1L	ООО "Славутич"
1M	ООО "Союзнефтестрой"
1N	ООО "ФУТЭК"
1O	ОАО "Негуснефть"
1P	ОАО "Ульяновскнефть"
1Q	ООО "Холдинговая компания Сигма-групп"
1R	ОАО "Инвестиционная группа "Алроса"
1S	ОАО "Эвенкийская топливно-энергетическая компания"
1T	ООО "Горно-промышленная компания "Самсон"
1U	ООО "НК "Мангазея"
1V	ОАО "Сибнефть-Ноябрьскнефтегаз"

the presence of a cartel or limit the auctioneer's ability to behave strategically (e.g., by using a "quick knock" to try to allocate the item to a noncartel bidder). Finally, the model assumes that the number and identities of the cartel bidders are common knowledge within the cartel. If this were not the case, a cartel member might have an incentive to develop a shill and enter that shill into the cartel in order to capture an additional share of the collusive gain.

13 Coordinated Effects in Horizontal Mergers

Whereas the two previous chapters deal with detection of existing collusion, this chapter concerns the anticipation of future collusion following a merger. Detection is about economic evidence that leads to the inference of collusion whereas anticipation is about the characteristics of the product/market/industry that lend themselves to collusion after two or more firms have combined.

13.1 Horizontal Merger Guidelines

In some cases, when firms reach a decision to merge into a single corporate entity, they must notify federal authorities of their intent to do so and undergo scrutiny regarding the potential negative consequences of the merger for consumer surplus.[1] Sometimes the federal authorities will actively contest the merger. The economic grounds for contesting a merger are identified in the Horizontal Merger Guidelines.[2] The guiding charge is offered in the second paragraph of the Guidelines:

The Agencies seek to identify and challenge competitively harmful mergers while avoiding unnecessary interference with mergers that are either competitively beneficial or neutral. Most merger analysis is necessarily predictive, requiring an assessment of what will likely happen if a merger proceeds as compared to what will likely happen if it does not. Given this inherent need for prediction, these Guidelines reflect the congressional intent that merger

---

1. The most relevant of statutes in this regard is section 7 of the Clayton Act, 15 USC §18, which notes the social concern regarding mergers as, "in any line of commerce or in any activity affecting commerce in any section of the country, the effect of such acquisition may be substantially to lessen competition, or to tend to create a monopoly."
2. U.S. Department of Justice and Federal Trade Commission Horizontal Merger Guidelines (hereafter "Guidelines"), August 19, 2010 (available at http://www.justice.gov/atr/public/guidelines/hmg-2010.html).

enforcement should interdict competitive problems in their incipiency and that certainty about anticompetitive effect is seldom possible and not required for a merger to be illegal. (Guidelines, p. 1)

Basically, the Guidelines identify two separate concerns regarding a merger: unilateral effects and coordinated effects. Unilateral effects refer to the elimination of competition between two firms that alone constitutes a substantial lessening of competition and thus a substantial reduction in consumer surplus.[3] From the viewpoint of economic analysis, unilateral effects concern the consequences of the merger, assuming no increased coordination in the industry, in terms of price and nonprice attributes of products affected by the merger. Coordinated effects refer to the future effects of the merger with regard to potential increased coordination among firms in the industry, whether this be tacit or explicit collusion.[4]

13.2   Unilateral and Coordinated Effects Analyses

A typical unilateral effects economic analysis would involve the estimation of product demands, coupled with a relevant model of rivalry, to determine the static impact of the merger on prices (and perhaps nonprice attributes as well). As a simple example, and one that is specifically called out in section 6.1 of the Guidelines, one can think of the differentiated product price competition model of chapter 5, where the demand system would be estimated from available data. Alternatively, a procurement model might better describe the product/market/industry, as identified in section 6.2 of the Guidelines. With regard to the merger of just two firms,[5] these models would be used to determine the impact on prices as a consequence of reducing the size of the industry by one firm, with the corresponding changes to the size of the merged firm.

The unilateral effects associated with a merger are of social interest, but the coordinated effects of a merger are perhaps a more substantial

---

3. Unilateral effects are described in section 6 of the Guidelines.
4. Coordinated effects are described in section 7 of the Guidelines. See Davidson and Deneckere (1984), Kovacic et al. (2007, 2009), and Gayle et al. (2011). The results of Bos and Harrington (2010) suggest that the most severe coordinated effects may come from mergers involving moderate-sized firms, rather than the largest or smallest firms. There is also a literature on the effects of vertical mergers on incentives for collusion, for example, Nocke (2007), Nocke and White (2007), and Normann (2009).
5. In the late 1800s and early 1900s, it was common for several firms to combine at once. Today it is more common for mergers to occur between a pair of firms.

concern because an adverse outcome with respect to coordinated conduct in the industry can potentially have a greater effect—eliminating competition among a subset of firms in the industry beyond just the firms involved in the merger. Nevertheless, the economic analysis of mergers remains largely focused on unilateral effects, while coordinated effects analysis consists largely of extrapolations from simple measurements, such as merger-induced changes in Herfindahl indices and economic intuitions by federal authorities regarding anticipated negative consequences of the merger in terms of future coordination in the industry.

There are numerous recent economic and econometric advances that can be applied to unilateral effects analyses. For example, in the past twenty-five years, there has been much progress in the estimation of demand systems, which now plays a prominent role in many unilateral effects analyses. A major impediment to the economic analysis of coordinated effects was the emphasis in the 1997 Guidelines on assessing the increased probability of coordinated conduct from a merger. Directly measuring the increase in probability of coordinated conduct can be a daunting task, especially because anticipated coordinated conduct with respect to the post-merger environment includes both tacit and explicit collusion.

The 2010 revisions to the Guidelines shift the focus away from the post-merger change in probability of coordinated effects to the post-merger change in payoffs associated with coordinated conduct: "The Agencies regard coordinated interaction as more likely, the more the participants stand to gain from successful coordination."[6]

This seemingly small change is a substantial one in that it provides immediate leverage for federal authorities to investigate coordinated effects. The reason is simple—a unilateral effects model that has already been developed can be used to understand the post-merger change in payoff of future coordinated effects. A unilateral effects model analyzes the consequences on price and consumer surplus from a combination of two firms in the industry—the number of competing firms decreases by one. A model that is designed to address such a question can typically also be employed to analyze a range of conjectures about changes in the industry, including further reductions in the number of actively competing firms as a result of collusion among a subset of the remaining firms.

6. Guidelines, sec. 7.2.

Such an analysis can be used to calculate the payoffs to each firm from post-merger collusion. Of course, the unilateral effects model can be used to provide the payoffs from such conjectured explicit collusion in the pre-merger world as well. The contrast between the pre-merger and post-merger incremental payoffs to a specific conjecture of explicit collusion provides information about the incremental incentives for explicit collusion in the post-merger, versus pre-merger, world. Once the unilateral effects analysis is in place, it is a valuable tool for examining the incremental incentives for coordinated effects that emerge from the merger. One can just "turn the crank" to obtain key insights regarding coordinated effects. This type of coordinated effects analysis based on the extension of the unilateral effects model need not replace other types of coordinated effects analysis.

This incremental analysis does not directly address the increased post-merger *probability* of coordinated interaction, but it does so indirectly because it is reasonable to assume that if the post-merger payoff to a given incremental coordination among firms has increased substantially compared to what it was pre-merger, that the likelihood of its occurring post-merger is higher than what it was pre-merger.

This incremental analysis does not address the kind of post-merger coordination that may occur and is focused on explicit collusion. In this sense, the analysis provides bounds for what might happen. However, by looking at the pre-merger world through the same lens as the post-merger world, the incremental payoffs for coordinated interaction that are contrasted are an apples-to-apples comparison.

Research by Kovacic et al. (2006, 2009) and Gayle et al. (2011) has explored this line of analysis. These authors have examined *Hospital Corp of America v. FTC*,[7] *FTC* v. *Arch Coal*,[8] and the recent BASF/Ciba merger.[9] The FTC objected to the first two mergers on the grounds of coordinated effects. In what follows, we discuss how one might approach the analysis of coordinated effects in *Hospital Corporation* within the context of the model of differentiated products price competition discussed in chapter 5.

---

7. 807 F.2d 1381 (7th Cir. 1986).
8. *Fed. Trade Comm'n* v. *Arch Coal, Inc.*, 329 F. Supp. 2d 109 (DDC 2004).
9. FTC Press Release, April 2, 2009, "FTC Intervenes in BASF's Proposed $5.1 Billion Acquisition of Ciba Holding Inc" (http://www.ftc.gov/opa/2009/04/basf.shtm, accessed December 18, 2010). Case No COMP/M.5355 - BASF/ CIBA, Notification of 22 January 2009 pursuant to Article 4 of Council Regulation No 139/20041 (available at http://ec.europa.eu/competition/mergers/cases/decisions/m5355_20090312_20212 _en.pdf, accessed December 17, 2010).

13.3   Coordinated Effects Analysis of *Hospital Corporation*

In the early 1980s, in the Chattanooga, Tennessee, area, prior to the proposed merger, Hospital Corporation of America (HCA) owned and operated one of the eleven hospitals in Chattanooga, giving it a 14 percent market share. The area hospitals offered different services. Some were larger and more comprehensive in their care options than others. HCA proposed to purchase two other hospital firms in the area and by doing so would own or have managerial control of five of the eleven hospitals, bringing its market share up to 26 percent. The four largest hospital firms in the area had 79 percent of the pre-merger market but would have 92 percent of the post-merger market. The FTC objected to the merger based on the concern of post-merger coordinated effects.

The Singh and Vives (1984) model of differentiated products price competition described in chapter 5 can be extended to allow eleven firms of different sizes. Such a model can be calibrated to match the characteristics of the pre-merger industry, including such things as the pre-merger market shares of the firms.[10] The calibration can capture the substitutability between hospitals and differences in hospital quality.

We can define various scenarios and evaluate firm and industry performance for these scenarios using the model. Four scenarios of interest are as follows:

1. *Pre-acquisition noncooperative:* All pre-merger firms act noncollusively.

2. *Post-acquisition noncooperative:* HCA and its acquisitions act as one firm, but all other firms and the post-merger HCA entity act noncollusively.

3. *Pre-acquisition cooperative:* HCA and a subset of firms not involved in the merger collude, acting as one firm, but that combined entity and all other firms, including the ones to be acquired by HCA compete with one another.

4. *Post-acquisition cooperative:* HCA and the firms acquired by it collude with a subset of firm not involved in the transaction, acting as one firm, but acting noncooperatively with respect to the remaining firms.

10. See Kovacic et al. (2009) for a calibration associated with HCA's market.

The contrast between the first two scenarios is a unilateral effects analysis. If an economic model is available to study that contrast, then that model is also available to examine the contrast between the other scenarios. In particular, the contrast between the first and third scenarios tells us about pre-merger coordinated effects, while the contrast between the second and fourth scenarios tells us about post-merger coordinated effects. The contrast between these two contrasts tells us about the change in coordinated effects from the pre-merger to the post-merger world.

The calibrations provided in Kovacic et al. (2009) for the examination of the *Hospital Corporation* transaction produce two key findings using the pre-merger noncooperative scenario as the benchmark. First, their model shows that prior to the merger, if HCA were to collude with the other three largest hospitals in the area, the combined profit of the four hospitals would increase by 9 percent, but if this collusion occurred after the merger, the combined profits of the four would increase by 65 percent. Second, with noncollusive interaction, the merger would cause the merged entity's prices to increase by under 50 percent, but if collusion occurred after the merger, then the prices of the merged entity would increase by over 100 percent.

This kind of incremental quantification of the effects of the merger informs the discussion as to whether coordinated effects are a concern. For example, in the example above, the combined profits of the four largest firms in the market increased by 65 percent with collusion in the post-merger world, but if those combined profits instead increased by a substantially smaller amount, that would indicate that the post-merger incentives for collusion are lower and that coordinated effects are probably less of a concern. Similarly, in the example above the post-merger collusive price increased by over 100, but if that number were substantially lower, then there would be less concern about coordinated effects.

13.4 Conclusion

Without the ability to quantify post-merger coordinated effects, there is no way to inform the debate regarding the possible coordinated effects associated with a merger. Once the opposing parties have agreed to a unilateral effects model, they each have the tool in hand to have a quantifiable and informed discussion regarding coordinated effects.

This type of analysis can be extended to accommodate a range of economically meaningful issues such as efficiencies from the merger. For example, the cost parameters used in the calibrated model could be adjusted to reflect post-merger efficiencies. Alternatively, the model could be used to identify a threshold level for the efficiency gains required to balance concerns associated with coordinated effects. This threshold could then be compared to estimates of actual efficiencies.

Divestitures can be investigated within the context of the model to evaluate the implications for coordinated effects associated with various possible divestitures. Potential entry, capacity expansions, and quality improvements can also be quantifiably accommodated. Such quantification may allow debate to focus on model calibration, estimation, and rivalry conditions in the industry, topics that can find grounds in scientific discourse.

References for EC Decisions

Amino acids: Case COMP/36.545/F3—Amino acids, Comm'n Decision (Jun 7, 2000).

Carbonless paper: Case COMP/E-1/36.212—Carbonless paper, Comm'n Decision (Dec 20, 2001).

Cartonboard: IV/C/33.83—Cartonboard, Comm'n Decision (Jul 13, 1994).

Choline chloride: Case COMP/E-2/37.533—Choline chloride, Comm'n Decision (Sep 12, 2004).

Citric acid: Case COMP/E-1/36.604—Citric acid, Comm'n Decision (Dec 5, 2001).

Copper plumbing tubes: Case COMP/E-1/38.069—Copper plumbing tubes, Comm'n Decision (Sep 3, 2004).

Electrical and mechanical carbon and graphite products: Case C38.359—Electrical and mechanical carbon and graphite products, Comm'n Decision (Dec 3, 2003).

Food flavor enhancers: Case COMP/C37.671—Flood flavour enhancers, Comm'n Decision (Dec 17, 2002).

Graphite electrodes: Case COMP/E-1/36.490—Graphite electrodes, Comm'n Decision (Jul 18, 2001).

Hydrogen peroxide: Case COMP/F/38.620—Hydrogen peroxide, Comm'n Decision (May 3, 3006).

Industrial and medical gases: Case COMP/E-3/36.700—Industrial and medical gases, Comm'n Decision (Jul 24, 2002).

Industrial bags: Case COMP/38354—Industrial bags, Comm'n Decision (Nov 30, 2005).

Industrial tubes: Case COMP/E-1/38.240—Industrial tubes, Comm'n Decision (Dec 16, 2003).

Methionine: Case C.37.519—Methionine, Comm'n Decision (Jul 2, 2002).

Methylglucamine: Case COMP/E-2/37.978—Methylglucamine, Comm'n Decision (Nov 27, 2002).

Monochloroacetic acid: Case COMP/E-1/.37.773—MCAA, Comm'n Decision (Jan 19, 2005).

Needles: Case F-1/38.338—PO/Needles, Comm'n Decision (Oct 26, 2004).

Organic peroxides: Case COMP/E-2/37.857—Organic peroxides, Comm'n Decision (Dec 10, 2003).

Plasterboard: Case COMP/E-1/37.152—Plasterboard, Comm'n Decision (Nov 27, 2002).

Pre-insulated pipe: Case No IV/35.691/E-4—Pre-insulated pipe cartel, Comm'n Decision (Oct 21, 1998).

Rubber chemicals: Case COMP/F/38.443—Rubber chemicals, Comm'n Decision (Dec 21, 2005).

Soda-ash—Solvay: COMP/33.133-B: Soda-ash—Solvay, CFK, Comm'n Decision (Dec 13, 2000).

Sorbates: Case COMP/E-1/37.370—Sorbates, Comm'n Decision (Oct 1, 2003).

Specialty graphite (isostatic and extruded): Case COMP/E-2/37.667—Specialty graphite, Comm'n Decision (Dec 17, 2002).

Vitamins: Case COMP/E-1/37.512—Vitamins, Comm'n Decision (Nov 21, 2001).

Wood pulp: IV/29.725—Wood pulp, Comm'n Decision (Dec 19, 1984).

Zinc phosphate: Case COMP/E-1/37.027—Zinc phosphate, Comm'n Decision (Dec 11, 2001).

References

ABA Section of Antitrust Law. 2007. *Antitrust Law Developments,* 6th edition. Chicago: American Bar Association.

Abreu, D. 1986. Extremal equilibria of oligopolistic supergames. *Journal of Economic Theory* 39: 191–225.

Abreu, D., Pearce, D., and Stacchetti, E. 1986. Optimal cartel equilibria with imperfect monitoring. *Journal of Economic Theory* 39 (1): 251–69.

Abreu, D., Pearce, D., and Stacchetti, E. 1990. Toward a theory of discounted repeated games with imperfect monitoring. *Econometrica* 58 (5): 1041–63.

Albano, G. L., Germano, F., and Lovo, S. 2006. Ascending auctions for multiple objects: The case for the Japanese design. *Economic Theory* 28 (2): 331–55.

Aoyagi, M. 2003. Bid rotation and collusion in repeated auctions. *Journal of Economic Theory* 112 (1): 79–105.

Aoyagi, M. 2007. Efficient collusion in repeated auctions with communication. *Journal of Economic Theory* 134 (1): 61–92.

Argenton, C. 2011. Joint predation. Working paper. CentER & TILEC, Tilburg University.

Asker, J. 2010. A study of the internal organization of a bidding cartel. *American Economic Review* 100: 724–62.

Athey, S. 2001. Single crossing properties and the existence of pure strategy equilibria in games of incomplete information. *Econometrica* 69: 861–90.

Athey, S., and Bagwell, K. 2001. Optimal collusion with private information. *RAND Journal of Economics* 32 (3): 428–65.

Athey, S., and Bagwell, K. 2008. Collusion with persistent cost shocks. *Econometrica* 76: 493–540.

Athey, S., Bagwell, K., and Sanchirico, C. 2004. Collusion and price rigidity. *Review of Economic Studies* 71: 317–49.

Aubert, C., Kovacic, W., and Rey, P. 2006. The impact of leniency and whistleblowing programs on cartels. *International Journal of Industrial Organization* 24: 1241–66.

Ausubel, L. M., and Cramton, P. 2004. Auctioning many divisible goods. Papers and Proceedings of the Eighteenth Annual Congress of the European Economic Association. *Journal of the European Economic Association* 2 (2/3): 480–93.

Ausubel, L., and Milgrom, P. 2002). Ascending auctions with package bidding. *Frontiers of Theoretical Economics* 1 (1): article 1.

Avery, C. 1998. Strategic jump bidding in English auctions. *Review of Economic Studies* 65 (2): 185–210.

Ayres, I. 1987. How cartels punish: A structural theory of self-enforcing collusion. *Columbia Law Review* 87: 295.

Bagwell, K., and Staiger, R. W. 1997. Collusion over the business cycle. *RAND Journal of Economics* 28: 82–106.

Bagwell, K., and Wolinsky, A. 2002. Game theory and industrial organization. In R. J. Aumann and S. Hart, eds., *Handbook of Game Theory*, vol. 3. Amsterdam: North-Holland, 1851–95.

Bain, J. S. 1951. Relation of profit rates to industry concentration. *Quarterly Journal of Economics* 55: 293–324.

Bain, J. S. 1960. Price leaders, barometers, and kinks. *Journal of Business* 33: 193–203.

Bajari, P. 2001. Comparing competition and collusion: A numerical approach. *Economic Theory* 18: 187–205.

Bajari, P., and Fox, J. T. 2007. Measuring the efficiency of an FCC spectrum auction. Working paper. University of Minnesota.

Bajari, P., and Summers, G. 2002. Detecting collusion in procurement auctions. *Antitrust Law Journal* 70 (1): 143–70.

Bajari, P., and Ye, L. 2003. Deciding between competition and collusion. *Review of Economics and Statistics* 85 (4): 971–89.

Baker, J. B. 2002. Mavericks, mergers, and exclusion: Proving coordinated competitive effects under the antitrust laws. *New York University Law Review* 77: 135–73.

Baldwin, L. H., Marshall, R. C., and Richard, J.-F. 1997. Bidder collusion at Forest Service timber auctions. *Journal of Political Economy* 105 (4): 657–99.

Banerji, A., and Meenakshi, J. V. 2004. Buyer collusion and efficiency of government intervention in wheat markets in northern India: An asymmetric structural auctions analysis. *American Journal of Agricultural Economics* 86 (1): 236–53.

Barnett, T. O., and Wellford, H. B. 2008. The DOJ's single-firm conduct report: Promoting consumer welfare through clearer standards for section 2 of the Sherman Act. http:// www.justice. gov/atr/public/speeches/238599.pdf (accessed January 12, 2011).

Belleflamme, P., and Bloch, F. 2004. Market sharing agreements and collusive networks. *International Economic Review* 45: 387–411.

Benoit, J.-P., and Krishna, V. 1987. Dynamic duopoly: Prices and Quantities. *Review of Economic Studies* 54: 23–35.

Bernheim, B. D. 2002. Expert report of B. Douglas Bernheim. MDL 1285. *In Re: Vitamins Antitrust Litigation*, Misc. 99–0197 (TFH), May 24, 2002.

Bernheim, B. D., and Whinston, M. D. 1990. Multimarket contact and collusive behavior. *RAND Journal of Economics* 21: 1–26.

Bittlingmayer, G. 1985. Did antitrust policy cause the great merger wave? *Journal of Law and Economics* 28: 77–118.

Blume, A., and Heidhues, P. 2008. Modeling tacit collusion in auctions. *Journal of Institutional and Theoretical Economics* 164: 163–84.

Bolotova, Y., Connor, J. M., and Miller, D. J. 2008. The impact of collusion on price behavior: Empirical results from two recent cases. *International Journal of Industrial Organization* 26: 1290–1307.

Booth, D. L., Kanetkar, V., Vertinsky, I., and Whistler, D. 1991. An empirical model of capacity expansion and pricing in an oligopoly with barometric price leadership: A case study of the newsprint industry in North America. *Journal of Industrial Economics* 39: 255–76.

Borenstein, S., and Shepard, A. 1996. Dynamic pricing in retail gasoline markets. *RAND Journal of Economics* 27: 429–51.

Bos, I., and Harrington, J. E. 2010. Endogenous cartel formation with heterogeneous firms. *RAND Journal of Economics* 41: 92–117.

Bresnahan, T. F., and Reiss, P. C. 1991. Entry and competition in concentrated markets. *Journal of Political Economy* 99: 977–1009.

Brock, W. A., and Scheinkman, J. A. 1985. Price setting supergames with capacity constraints. *Review of Economic Studies* 52: 371–82.

Brusco, S., and Lopomo, G. 2002. Collusion via signalling in simultaneous ascending bid auctions with heterogeneous objects, with and without complementarities. *Review of Economic Studies* 69 (2): 407–36.

Burns, A. R. 1936. *The Decline of Competition: A Study of the Evolution of American Industry.* New York: McGraw-Hill.

Caillaud, B., and Jéhiel, P. 1998. Collusion in auctions with externalities. *RAND Journal of Economics* 29 (4): 680–702.

Carlton, D. W., Gertner, R. H., and Rosenfield, A. M. 1997. Communications among competitors: Game theory and antitrust. *George Mason Law Review* 5: 423–40.

Cassady, R. 1967. *Auctions and Auctioneering.* Berkeley: UC Press.

Chakrabarti, S. K. 2010. Collusive equilibrium in Cournot oligopolies with unknown costs. *International Economic Review* 51: 1209–38.

Chamberlin, E. H. 1933. *The Theory of Monopolistic Competition.* Cambridge: Harvard University Press.

Chang, M.-H. 1991. The effects of product differentiation on collusive pricing. *International Journal of Industrial Organization* 9 (3): 453–69.

Che, Y.-K., and Kim, J. 2006. Robustly collusion-proof implementation. *Econometrica* 74 (4): 1063–1107.

Che, Y.-K., and Kim, J. 2009. Optimal collusion-proof auctions. *Journal of Economic Theory* 144: 565–603.

Chen, C.-L., and Tauman, Y. 2006. Collusion in one-shot second-price auctions. *Economic Theory* 28 (1): 145–72.

Clark, D. S. 1983. Price-fixing without collusion: An antitrust analysis of facilitating practices after Ethyl Corp. *Wisconsin Law Review* 1983: 887–952.

Coase, R. 1937. The nature of the firm. *Economica* 4: 386–405.

Comanor, W. S., and Schankerman, M. A. 1976. Identical bids and cartel behavior. *Bell Journal of Economics* 7 (1): 281–86.

Compte, O. 2002. On failing to cooperate when monitoring is private. *Journal of Economic Theory* 102: 151–88.

Compte, O., Jenny, F., and Rey, P. 2002. Capacity constraints, mergers and collusion. *European Economic Review* 46: 1–29.

Compte, O., Lambert-Mogiliansky, A., and Verdier, T. 2005. Corruption and competition in procurement auctions. *RAND Journal of Economics* 36 (1): 1–15.

Connor, J. 2008. *Global Price Fixing*, 2nd ed. Berlin: Springer.

Cooper, T. E. 1986. Most-favored-customer pricing and tacit collusion. *RAND Journal of Economics* 17: 377–88.

Cramton, P. C., and Palfrey, T. R. 1990. Cartel enforcement with uncertainty about costs. *International Economic Review* 31: 17–47.

Cramton, P., and Schwartz, J. A. 2000. Collusive bidding: Lessons from the FCC spectrum auctions. *Journal of Regulatory Economics* 17 (3): 229.

Cramton, P., and Schwartz, J. A. 2002. Collusive bidding in the FCC spectrum auctions. *Contributions to Economic Analysis and Policy* 1 (1):1–18.

Cyrenne, P. 1999. On antitrust enforcement and the deterrence of collusive behavior. *Review of International Economics* 14: 257–72.

D'Aspremont, C., Jacquemin, A., Gabszewicz, J. J., and Weymark, J. A. 1983. On the stability of collusive price leadership. *Canadian Journal of Economics, Revue Canadienne d'Economique* 16: 17–25.

Davidson, C. 1984. Cartel stability and tariff policy. *Journal of International Economics* 17: 219–37.

Davidson, C., and Deneckere, R. J. 1984. Horizontal mergers and collusive behavior. *International Journal of Industrial Organization* 2: 117–32.

Davidson, C., and Deneckere, R. J. 1990. Excess capacity and collusion. *International Economic Review* 31: 521–41.

Dechenaux, E., and Kovenock, D. 2007. Tacit collusion and capacity withholding in repeated uniform price auctions. *RAND Journal of Economics* 38 (4): 1044–69.

Deltas, G. 2002. Determining damages from the operation of bidding rings: An analysis of the post-auction "knockout" sale. *Economic Theory* 19 (2): 243–69.

Demougin, D., and Fishman, A. 1991. Efficient budget balancing cartel equilibria with imperfect monitoring. *Economic Theory* 1: 373–83.

Deneckere, R. J. 1983. Duopoly supergames with product differentiation. *Economics Letters* 11: 37–42.

Deneckere, R. J., and Kovenock, D. 1992. Price leadership. *Review of Economic Studies* 59: 143–62.

Deneckere, R., Kovenock, D., and Lee, R. 1992. A model of price leadership based on consumer loyalty. *Journal of Industrial Economics* 40: 147–56.

Dequiedt, V. 2007. Efficient collusion in optimal auctions. *Journal of Economic Theory* 136 (1): 302–23.

Diamantoudi, E. 2005. Stable cartels revisited. *Economic Theory* 26: 907–21.

Dolbear, F. T., Lave, L. B., Bowman, G., Lieberman, A., Prescott, E., Rueter, F., et al. 1968. Collusion in oligopoly: An experiment on the effect of numbers and information. *Quarterly Journal of Economics* 82: 240–59.

Donsimoni, M.-P. 1985. Stable heterogeneous cartels. *International Journal of Industrial Organization* 3: 451–67.

Donsimoni, M.-P., Economides, N., and Polemarchakis, H. 1986. Stable Cartels. *International Economic Review* 27 (2): 317–27.

Ellison, G. 1994. Theories of cartel stability and the joint executive committee. *RAND Journal of Economics* 25: 37–57.

Evans, W. N., and Kessides, I. N. 1994. Living by the "golden rule": Multimarket contact in the U.S. airline industry. *Quarterly Journal of Economics* 109: 341–66.

Fabra, N. 2003. Tacit collusion in repeated auctions: Uniform versus discriminatory. *Journal of Industrial Economics* 51 (3): 271–93.

Fehl, U., and Güth, W. 1978. Internal and external stability of bidder cartels in auctions and public tenders: A comparison of pricing rules. *International Journal of Industrial Organization* 5 (3): 303–13.

Feinstein, J. S., Block, M. K., and Nold, F. C. 1985. Asymmetric information and collusive behavior in auction markets. *American Economic Review* 75 (3): 441–60.

Fershtman, C., and Gandal, N. 1994. Disadvantageous semicollusion. *International Journal of Industrial Organization* 12: 141–54.

Fershtman, C., and Pakes, A. 2000. A dynamic game with collusion and price wars. *RAND Journal of Economics* 31 (2), 207–36.

Feuerstein, S., and Gersbach, H. 2003. Is capital a collusion device? *Economic Theory* 21: 133–54.

Friedman, J. W. 1971. A non-cooperative equilibrium for supergames. *Review of Economic Studies*, 28: 1–12.

Friedman, J. W., and Thisse, J.-F. 1994. Sustainable collusion in oligopoly with free entry. *European Economic Review* 38: 271–83.

Fudenberg, D., and Maskin, E. 1986. The folk theorem in repeated games with discounting or incomplete information. *Econometrica* 54: 533–54.

Fudenberg, D., Levine, D., and Maskin, E. 1994. The folk theorem with imperfect public information. *Econometrica* 62: 997–1039.

Garratt, R. J., Tröger, T., and Zheng, C. Z. 2009. Collusion via resale. *Econometrica* 77 (4): 1095–1136.

Gayle, W.-R., Marshall, R. C., Marx, L. M., and Richard, J.-F. 2011. Coordinated effects in the 2010 horizontal merger guidelines. Working paper. Penn State University.

Gellhorn, E., and Kovacic, W. E. 1994. *Antitrust Law and Economics in a Nutshell*. St. Paul, MN: West.

Gerlach, H. 2009. Stochastic market sharing, partial communication and collusion. *International Journal of Industrial Organization* 27: 655–67.

Giacomini, R., and White, H. 2006. Tests of conditional predictive ability. *Econometrica* 74 (6): 1545–78.

Graham, D. A., and Marshall, R. C. 1987. Collusive bidder behavior at single-object second price and English auctions. *Journal of Political Economy* 95: 1217–39.

Graham, D. A., Marshall, R. C., and Richard, J.-F. 1990. Differential payments within a bidder coalition and the Shapley value. *American Economic Review* 80: 493–510.

Graham, D. A., Marshall, R. C., and Richard, J.-F. 1996. Lift-lining. *Advances in Applied Micro-Economics* 6: 15–40.

Green, E. J., and Porter, R. H. 1984. Noncooperative collusion under imperfect price information. *Econometrica* 52 (1): 87–100.

Haltiwanger, J., and Harrington, J. E. 1991. The impact of cyclical demand movements on collusive behavior. *RAND Journal of Economics* 22: 89–106.

Hammond, S. D. 2005. Cracking cartels with leniency programs. http://www.justice.gov/atr/public/speeches/212269.pdf.

Harrington, J. E. Jr. 1989. Collusion among asymmetric firms: The case of different discount factors. *International Journal of Industrial Organization* 7: 289–307.

Harrington, J. E. Jr. 2003. Some implications of antitrust laws for cartel pricing. *Economics Letters* 79: 377–83.

Harrington, J. E. Jr. 2004a. Cartel pricing dynamics in the presence of an antitrust authority. *RAND Journal of Economics* 35: 651–67.

Harrington, J. E. Jr. 2004b. Post-cartel pricing during litigation. *Journal of Industrial Economics* 52 (4): 517–33.

Harrington, J. E. Jr. 2006. How do cartels operate? *Foundations and Trends in Microeconomics* 2 (1): 1–105.

Harrington, J. E. Jr. 2008. Detecting cartels. In P. Buccirossi, ed., *Handbook of Antitrust Economics*. Cambridge: MIT Press, 213–58.

Harrington, J. E. Jr., and Skrzypacz, A. 2007. Collusion with monitoring of sales. *RAND Journal of Economics* 38: 314–31.

Harrington, J. E. Jr., and Skrzypacz, A. 2010. Private monitoring and communication in cartels: Explaining recent collusive practices. *American Economic Review,* forthcoming.

Hay, G. A. 1982. Oligopoly, shared monopoly, and antitrust law. *Cornell Law Review* 67: 439–53.

Heeb, R. D., Kovacic, W. E., Marshall, R. C., and Marx, L. M. 2009. Cartels as two-stage mechanisms: Implications for the analysis of dominant-firm conduct. *Chicago Journal of International Law* 10: 213–31.

Hendricks, K., and Porter, R. H. 1989. Collusion in auctions. *Annals of Economics and Statistics/Annales d'Économie et de Statistique* 15/16: 217–30.

Hendricks, K., Porter, R., and Tan, G. 2008. Bidding rings and the winner's curse. *RAND Journal of Economics* 39 (4): 1018–41.

Henry, B. R. 1994. Benchmarking and antitrust. *Antitrust Law Journal* 62: 483–512.

Hexner, E. 1943. *The International Steel Cartel.* Chapel Hill: University of North Carolina Press.

Horner, J., and Jamison, J. 2007. Collusion with (almost) no information. *RAND Journal of Economics* 38: 804–22.

Hortaçsu, A., Martinez-Jerez, A., and Douglas, J. 2006. The geography of trade on eBay and MercadoLibre. Working paper 06–09. NET Institute

Huck, S., Normann, H.-T., and Oechssler, J. 2004. Through trial and error to collusion. *International Economic Review* 45: 205–24.

Inoue, A., and Kilian, L. 2006. On the selection of forecasting models. *Journal of Econometrics* 130 (2): 273–306.

Ishii, R. 2009. Favor exchange in collusion: Empirical study of repeated procurement auctions in Japan. *International Journal of Industrial Organization* 27 (2): 137–44.

Jones, F. D. 1922. *Trade Association Activities and the Law: A Discussion of the Legal and Economic Aspects of Collective Action through Trade Organizations.* New York: McGraw-Hill.

Kandori, M. 1991. Correlated demand shocks and price wars during booms. *Review of Economic Studies* 58: 171–80.

Kandori, M., and Matsushima, H. 1998. Private observation, communication and collusion. *Econometrica* 66: 627–52.

Kaysen, C. 1951. Collusion under the Sherman Act. *Quarterly Journal of Economics* 65 (2): 263–70.

Kihlstrom, R., and Vives, X. 1992. Collusion by asymmetrically informed firms. *Journal of Economics & Management Strategy* 1 (2): 371–96.

Kihlstrom, R. E., and Vives, X. 1989. Collusion by asymmetrically informed duopolists. *European Journal of Political Economy* 5: 371–402.

Klemperer, P. 1998. Auctions with almost common values. *European Economic Review* 42: 757–69.

Klemperer, P. 2000. Why every economist should learn some auction theory. In M. Dewatripont, L. Hansen, and S. Turnovsky, eds., *Advances in Economics and Econometrics Invited Lectures to Eighth World Congress of the Econometric Society.* Cambridge, UK: Cambridge University Press, 25–55.

Klemperer, P. 2002. What really matters in auction design. *Journal of Economic Perspectives* 16 (1): 169–89.

Knittel, C. R., and Stango, V. 2003. Price ceilings as focal points for tacit collusion: Evidence from credit cards. *American Economic Review* 93: 1703–29.

Knittel, C. R., and Lepore, J. J. 2010. Tacit collusion in the presence of cyclical demand and endogenous capacity levels. *International Journal of Industrial Organization* 28: 131–44.

Kovacic, W. E., Marshall, R. C., Marx, L. M., and Raiff, M. E. 2007. Lessons for competition policy from the vitamins cartel. In V. Ghosal and J. Stennek, eds., *The Political Economy of Antitrust*. Amsterdam: Elsevier, 149–76.

Kovacic, W. E., Marshall, R. C., Marx, L. M., and Raiff, M. E. 2006. Bidding rings and the design of anti-collusion measures for auctions and procurements. In N. Dimitri, G. Piga, and G. Spagnolo, eds., *Handbook of Procurement*. Cambridge University Press, 149–76.

Kovacic, W. E., Marshall, R. C., Marx, L. M., and Schulenberg, S. P. 2009. Quantitative analysis of coordinated effects. *Antitrust Law Journal* 76 (2): 397–430.

Kovacic, W. E., Marshall, R. C., Marx, L. M., and White, H. L. 2010. *Plus factors and agreement in antitrust law*. Michigan Law Review, forthcoming.

Kovacic, W. E., Marshall, R. C., Marx, L. M., and White, H. L. 2011. Plus factors and agreement in antitrust law. *Michigan Law Review* 110 (3): 393–436.

Krishna, V. 2009. *Auction Theory*. New York: Academic Press.

Kuhn, K.-U. 2001. Fighting collusion by regulating communication between firms. *Economic Policy* 16: 167–204.

Kuipers, J., and Olaizola, N. 2008. A dynamic approach to cartel formation. *International Journal of Game Theory* 37: 397–408.

Kumar, V., Marshall, R. C., Marx, L. M., and Samkharadze, L. 2011. Cartel versus merger. Working paper. Penn State University.

Kwasnica, A. M., and Sherstyuk, K. 2001. Collusion via signaling in multiple object auctions with complementarities: An experimental test. Working paper. Penn State University.

Kwoka, J. E. 1979. The effect of market share distribution on industry performance. *Review of Economics and Statistics* 61: 101–109.

LaCasse, C. 1995. Bid rigging and the threat of government prosecution. *RAND Journal of Economics* 26 (3): 398–417.

Laffont, J.-J., and Martimort, D. 1997. Collusion under asymmetric information. *Econometrica* 65: 875–91.

Laffont, J.-J., and Martimort, D. 2000. Mechanism design with collusion and correlation. *Econometrica* 68: 309–34.

Lambson, V. E. 1987. Optimal penal codes in price-setting supergames with capacity constraints. *Review of Economic Studies* 54: 385–97.

Lambson, V. E. 1994. Some results on optimal penal codes in asymmetric Bertrand supergames. *Journal of Economic Theory* 62: 444–68.

Lebrun, B. 1996. Existence of an equilibrium in first price auctions. *Economic Theory* 7: 421–43.

Lebrun, B. 1999. First price auctions in the asymmetric N bidder case. *International Economic Review* 40: 125–42.

Lebrun, B. 2006. Uniqueness of the equilibrium in first-price auctions. *Games and Economic Behavior* 55 (1): 131–51.

Lee, G. M. 2010. Optimal collusion with internal contracting. *Games and Economic Behavior* 68: 646–69.

Levenstein, M. C. 1997. Price wars and the stability of collusion: A study of the pre–World War I bromine industry. *Journal of Industrial Economics* 45: 117–37.

Levenstein, M., and Suslow, V. Y. 2006. What determines cartel success? *Journal of Economic Literature* 44: 43–95.

Levenstein, M., and Suslow, V. Y. 2010. Breaking up is hard to do: Determinants of cartel duration. *Journal of Law and Economic,* forthcoming.

Levin, D. 2004. The competitiveness of joint bidding in multi-unit uniform-price auctions. *RAND Journal of Economics* 35 (2): 373–85.

Liski, M., and Montero, J.-P. 2006. Forward trading and collusion in oligopoly. *Journal of Economic Theory* 131: 212–30.

Lommerud, K. E., and Sorgard, L. 2001. Trade liberalization and cartel stability. *Review of International Economics* 9: 343–55.

Lopomo, G., Marshall, R. C., and Marx, L. M. 2005. Inefficiency of collusion at English auctions. *Contributions in Theoretical Economics* 5: (1): article 4.

Lyk-Jensen, P. 1996. Some suggestions on how to cheat the auctioneer: Collusion in auctions when signals are affiliated. Working paper. University of Copenhagen.

Lyk-Jensen, P. 1997a. Post-auction knock-outs. Working paper. University of Copenhagen.

Lyk-Jensen, P. 1997b. Collusion at auctions with affiliated signals. Working paper. Université de Toulouse.

Maasland, E., and Onderstal, S. 2007. Auctions with financial externalities. *Economic Theory* 32 (3): 551–74.

Madhavan, A., Masson, R., and Lesser, W. 1988. Cooperation or retaliation: An empirical analysis of cartelization. Unpublished working paper. Cornell University.

Mailath, G., and Zemsky, P. 1991. Collusion in second price auctions with heterogeneous bidders. *Games and Economic Behavior* 3: 467–86.

Markham, J. W. 1951. The nature and significance of price leadership. *American Economic Review* 41: 891–905.

Marshall, R. C., and Marx, L. M. 2007. Bidder collusion. *Journal of Economic Theory* 133: 374–402.

Marshall, R. C., and Marx, L. M. 2009. The vulnerability of auctions to bidder collusion. *Quarterly Journal of Economics* 124 (2): 883–910.

Marshall, R. C., Marx, L. M., and Raiff, M. E. 2008. Cartel price announcements: The vitamins industry. *International Journal of Industrial Organization* 26: 762–802.

Marshall, R. C., Marx, L. M., and Samkharadze, L. 2011. Dominant-firm conduct by cartels. Working paper. Penn State University.

Marshall, R. C., and Meurer, M. J. 2001. The economics of bidder collusion. In K. Chatterjee and W. Samuelson, eds., *Game Theory and Business Applications*. Dordrecht: Kluwer Press, 339–70.

Marshall, R. C., and Meurer, M. J. 2004. Bidder collusion and antitrust law: Refining the analysis of price fixing to account for the special features of auction markets. *Antitrust Law Journal* 72 (1): 83–118.

Marshall, R. C., Meurer, M. J., and Richard, J.-F. 1994. Litigation settlement and collusion. *Quarterly Journal of Economics* 109 (1): 211–40.

Marshall, R. C., Meurer, M. J., Richard, J.-F., and Stromquist, W. 1994. Numerical analysis of asymmetric first price auctions. *Games and Economic Behavior* 7: 193–220.

Maskin, E. S., and Riley, J. G. 1996a. Uniqueness in sealed high bid auctions. Working paper. Harvard and UCLA.

Maskin, E. S., and Riley, J. G. 1996b. Existence in sealed high bid auctions. Working paper. Harvard and UCLA.

Maskin, E. S., and Riley, J. G. 2000a. Asymmetric auctions. *Review of Economic Studies* 67: 413–38.

Maskin, E. S., and Riley, J. G. 2000b. Equilibrium in sealed high bid auctions. *Review of Economic Studies* 67: 439–54.

Matsushima, H. 2001. Multimarket contact, imperfect monitoring, and implicit collusion. *Journal of Economic Theory* 98: 158–78.

McAfee, P. R., and McMillan, J. 1992. Bidding rings. *American Economic Review* 82: 579–99.

McAfee, P. R., and McMillan, J. 1996. Analyzing the airwaves auction. *Journal of Economic Perspectives* 10: 159–76.

McMillan, J. 1994. Selling spectrum rights. *Journal of Economic Perspectives* 8 (3): 145–62.

Miklós-Thal, J. 2011. Optimal collusion under cost asymmetry. *Economic Theory* 46: 99–125.

Milgrom, P. 2004. *Putting Auction Theory to Work*. Cambridge: Cambridge University Press.

Milgrom, P. R., and Weber, R. J. 1982. A theory of auctions and competitive bidding. *Econometrica* 50: 1089–1122.

Miller, N. H. 2009. Strategic leniency and cartel enforcement. *American Economic Review* 99 (3): 750–68.

Motta, M., and Polo, M. 2003. Leniency programs and cartel prosecution. *International Journal of Industrial Organization* 21: 347–79.

Mouraviev, I., and Rey, P. 2010. Collusion and leadership. Working paper. Toulouse School of Economics.

Myerson, R. B. 1981. Optimal auction design. *Mathematics of Operations Research* 6: 58–73.

Nocke, V. 2007. Collusion and dynamic (under-) investment in quality. *RAND Journal of Economics* 38: 227–49.

Nocke, V., and White, L. 2007. Do vertical mergers facilitate upstream collusion? *American Economic Review* 97 (4): 1321–39.

Normann, H.-T. 2009. Vertical integration, raising rivals' costs and upstream collusion. *European Economic Review* 53: 461–80.

Pavlov, G. 2008. Auction design in the presence of collusion. *Theoretical Economics* 3: 383–429.

Pesendorfer, M. 2000. A study of collusion in first-price auctions. *Review of Economic Studies* 67 (3): 381–411.

Porter, M. E. 1980. *Competitive Strategy: Techniques for Analyzing Industries and Competitors.* New York: Free Press.

Porter, R. H. 1983. Optimal cartel trigger price strategies. *Journal of Economic Theory* 29 (2): 313–38.

Porter, R. H. 1983b. A study of cartel stability: The joint executive committee, 1880–1886. *Bell Journal of Economics* 14: 301–14.

Porter, R. H., and Douglas Zona, J. 1993. Detection of bid rigging in procurement auctions. *Journal of Political Economy* 101 (3): 518–38.

Porter, R. H., and Douglas Zona, J. 1999. Ohio school milk markets: An analysis of bidding. *RAND Journal of Economics* 30 (2): 263–88.

Posner, R. A. 1976. *Antitrust Law: An Economic Perspective.* Chicago: University of Chicago Press.

Posner, R. A. 2001. *Antitrust Law,* 2nd ed. Chicago: University of Chicago Press.

Priest, G. L. 1977. Cartels and patent license arrangements. *Journal of Law and Economics* 20 (2): 309–77.

Prokop, J. 1999. Process of dominant-cartel formation. *International Journal of Industrial Organization* 17: 241–57.

Racine, J. 2000. A consistent cross-validatory method for dependent data: *hv*-block cross validation. *Journal of Econometrics* 99 (1): 39–61.

Raith, M. 1996. A general model of information sharing in oligopoly. *Journal of Economic Theory* 71: 260–88.

Rey, P., and Stiglitz, J. 1995. The role of exclusive territories in producers' competition. *RAND Journal of Economics* 26: 431–51.

Riley, J. G., and Samuelson, W. 1981. Optimal auctions. *American Economic Review* 71: 381–92.

Robinson, M. S. 1985. Collusion and the choice of auction. *RAND Journal of Economics* 16: 141–45.

Ross, T. W. 1992. Cartel stability and product differentiation. *International Journal of Industrial Organization* 10: 1–13.

Rotemberg, J. J., and Saloner, G. 1986. A supergame-theoretic model of price wars during booms. *American Economic Review* 76 (3): 390–407.

Rotemberg, J. J., and Saloner, G. 1989. Tariffs vs quotas with implicit collusion. *Canadian Journal of Economics. Revue Canadienne d'Economique* 22: 237–44.

Rotemberg, J. J., and Saloner, G. 1990. Price leadership. *Journal of Industrial Economics* 39: 93–111.

Samkharadze, L. 2011. Buyer resistance to cartel conduct. Working paper. Penn State University.

Sannikov, Y., and Skrzypacz, A. 2007. Impossibility of collusion under imperfect monitoring with flexible production. *American Economic Review* 97 (5): 1794–1823.

Scherer, F. M. 1980. *Industrial Market Structure and Economic Performance*. Chicago: Rand MacNally.

Schmalensee, R. 1985. Standards for dominant firm conduct: What can economics contribute? Working paper 1723–85. Sloan School of Management. http://dspace.mit.edu/bitstream/handle/1721.1/2128/SWP-1723–12868188.pdf?sequence=1 (accessed January 12, 2011).

Schultz, C. 2005. Transparency on the consumer side and tacit collusion. *European Economic Review* 49: 279–97.

Scott Morton, F. 1997. Entry and predation: British shipping cartels 1897–1929. *Journal of Economics and Management Strategy* 6: 679–724.

Selten, R. 1973. A simple model of imperfect competition, Where 4 are few and 6 are many. *International Journal of Game Theory* 2: 141–201.

Senate Committee on Patents. 1942. Hearings before the Committee on Patents on S. 2303 and S. 2491, Part 5, 77th Cong. 2nd Sess. (May 13 & 16, 1942).

Shao, J. 1993. Linear model selection by cross-validation. *Journal of the American Statistical Association* 88 (422): 486–94.

Singh, N., and Vives, X. 1984. Price and quantity competition in a differentiated duopoly. *RAND Journal of Economics* 15 (4): 546–54.

Skrzypacz, A., and Hopenhayn, H. 2004. Tacit Ccollusion in repeated auctions. *Journal of Economic Theory* 114 (1): 153–69.

Slade, M. E. 1992. Vancouvers gasoline-price wars: An empirical exercise in uncovering supergame strategies. *Review of Economic Studies* 59: 257–76.

Smith, A. 1981. *An Inquiry into the Nature and Causes of the Wealth of Nations*, vol. 1, edited by R. H. Campbell and A. S. Skinner. Indianpolis: Liberty Classics.

Spagnolo, G. 2004. Divide et impera: Optimal leniency programmes. Discussion paper 4840. CEPR.

Spagnolo, G. 2005. Managerial incentives and collusive behavior. *European Economic Review* 49: 1501–23.

Staiger, R. W., and Wolak, F. A. 1992. Collusive pricing with capacity constraints in the presence of demand uncertainty. *RAND Journal of Economics* 23: 203–20.

Stenbacka, R. 1994. Financial structure and tacit collusion with repeated oligopoly competition. *Journal of Economic Behavior and Organization* 25: 281–92.

Stigler, G. J. 1947. The kinky oligopoly demand curve and rigid prices. *Journal of Political Economy* 55: 432–49.

Stigler, G. J. 1964. A theory of oligopoly. *Journal of Political Economy* 72: 44–61.

Stocking, G. W., and Watkins, M. W. 1991. *Cartels in Action: Case Studies in International Business Diplomacy*. Buffalo, NY: Hein.

Sullivan, E. T., and Harrison, J. L. 1988. *Understanding Antitrust and Its Economic Implications*. New York: Bender.

Tan, G., and Yilankaya, O. 2007. Ratifiability of efficient collusive mechanisms in second-price auctions with participation costs. *Games and Economic Behavior* 59 (2): 383–96.

Temporary National Economic Committee. 1940. Hearings before the Temporary National Economic Committee, Part 5, Cartels, 75th Cong. 3rd Sess. (January 15–19, 1940).

Thomas, C. J. 2005. Using reserve prices to deter collusion in procurement competition. *Journal of Industrial Economics* 53 (3): 301–26.

Thoron, S. 1998. Formation of a coalition-proof stable cartel. *Canadian Journal of Economics* 31: 63–76.

Tirole, J. 1988. *The Theory of Industrial Organization*. Cambridge: MIT Press.

Turner, D. F. 1962. The definition of agreement under the Sherman Act: Conscious parallelism and refusals to deal. *Harvard Law Review* 75 (4): 655–706.

Vasconcelos, H. 2005. Tacit collusion, cost asymmetries, and mergers. *RAND Journal of Economics* 36 (1): 39–62.

Vickrey, W. 1961. Counterspeculation, auctions and competitive sealed tenders. *Journal of Finance* 16: 8–37.

Vickrey, W. 1962. Auctions and bidding games. In *Recent Advances in Game Theory*. Princeton Conference Series 29. Princeton: Princeton University Press, 15–27.

Waehrer, K. 1999. Asymmetric private values auctions with application to joint bidding and mergers. *International Journal of Industrial Organization* 17 (3): 437–52.

Weber, R. 1997. Making more from less: Strategic demand reduction in the FCC spectrum auctions. *Journal of Economics and Management Strategy* 6 (3): 529–48.

Werden, G. J., and Baumann, M. G. 1986. A simple model of imperfect competition in which four are few but three are not. *Journal of Industrial Economics* 34: 331–35.

Wernerfelt, B. 1989. Tacit collusion in differentiated Cournot games. *Economics Letters* 29: 303–306.

White, H., Marshall, R. C., and Kennedy, P. 2006. The measurement of economic damages in antitrust civil litigation. *Economics Committee Newsletter* 6 (1): 17–22.

Wilcox, C. 1940. *Competition and Monopoly in American Industry, Monograph No. 21, Senate Committee Print (76th Congress, 3d Session), Investigation of Concentration of Economic Power, Temporary National Economic Committee*. Washington, DC: Government Printing Office.

Williamson, O. E. 1985. *The Economic Institutions of Capitalism*. New York: Free Press.

Index of Authors

Index of Subjects and Cases

Capper–Volstead Act (1922), 156, 220
Carbon brush cartel, 117. *See also*
  Electrical and mechanical carbon and
  graphite products decision (EC)
Carbone Lorraine, 36n.30
Carbonless paper decision (EC), 265
  and allocation, 126
    market shares, 34n.22, 122n.40
  and cartel initiation, 32n.14, 33n.15,
    45n.54
  and information exchange, 46n.56
  and price increases, 38n.34, 39n.37,
    40n.44, 115n.19
  and third-party facilitation, 126
Cartel(s), x, 2–3
  and bidding rings, 55–56, 188
  collusive structures of, 106–109, 137–38
    (*see also specific structures*)
    allocation structures, 106, 107–108,
      120–30
    enforcement structures, 104, 106, 107,
      109, 130
    interdependence of, 108
    pricing structures, 105, 106–107, 110–20
    and third-party facilitation, 138–42 (*see
      also* Third-party facilitation)
  and competition on price vs. value, 86
  detection of, 22–23, 211 (*see also*
    Detection of cartels, narrative of; Plus
    factors)
    vs. anticipation, 257
    as infrequent, 47
    lack of resources for (cartel narrative),
      51
  in dominant-firm role, 155–56, 214
    and bargaining power of buyers and
      suppliers, 151–53
    direct actions against noncartel firms,
      147–49
    and government intervention, 153–55
    and threat of new entrants, 150–51
    and threat of substitute products,
      149–50
    vs. true dominant firm, 145–47, 155,
      155n.30
  as industrial, x, 71, 81, 112
  instances of
    alkali, 150nn.17,18
    Alkali (World), 156n.33
    amino acids, 30–31n.8
    bath gel, 86n.1
    carbon brush, 117

cast-iron pipe, 189, 190, 191–92, 196
citric acid, 31n.8, 33n.16
European steel manufacturers, 8, 8n.19
Explosives, 132, 144n.3
Graphite Electrodes, 151n.19
Incandescent Lamp, 86n.2, 132, 137,
  147n.5, 148n.9, 151n.21
International Steel, 132, 148nn.7,8,
  156n.33
International Steel (Second), 149n.11
laundry detergent, 86n.1
Magnesium, 119n.32, 151n.21
Nitrogen, 117n.27, 148n.7, 150n.16
OPEC, 118, 220
Second International Steel, 149n.11
Steel, 137, 137n.66, 144n.3
vitamin industry, 18, 33nn.17,19,
  47n.59, 93, 101, 114, 122n.41, 149n.10,
  221–22, 223, 223n.24
membership in
  commitments of, 50
  corporate divisions as participating in,
    71
  desirability or undesirability of,
    101–103, 104
  and market-share controversies, 147
  outcomes for various levels of, 101–103
  outcomes from number of firms and
    industry characteristics in, 99
  principles of conduct, 75
  and procurement bids, 163
  rationale for illegality of, 21–22
  and secret deviation, 7, 105–106 (*see also*
    Secret deviations)
  sharing mutually beneficial investments
    in, 143–45
  stealth desirable for, 23
  subcartels in, 62n.16
  Switzerland as meeting place of, 30n.6,
    47
  as outside EC jurisdiction, 139n.67
Cartel, narrative of, 29–30
  and basic commitments of members, 50
  cartel initiated, 30–33
  division of market share, 33–36
  questions on, 49–50
  price increases decided and announced,
    36–40
  questions and answers from member
    firms, 44–54
  redistributions, 42–44, 45
  sales force issues, 41–42